Department of Economic and Social Affairs

World Economic and Social Survey 2012

In Search of New Development Finance

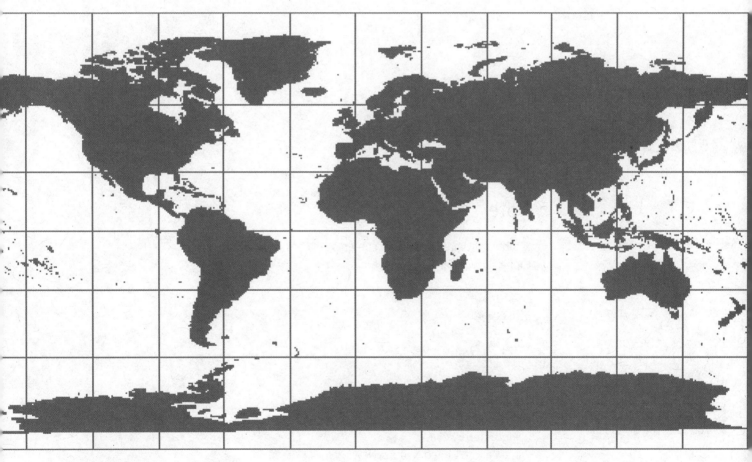

United Nations
New York, 2012

DESA

The Department of Economic and Social Affairs of the United Nations Secretariat is a vital interface between global policies in the economic, social and environmental spheres and national action. The Department works in three main interlinked areas: (i) it compiles, generates and analyses a wide range of economic, social and environmental data and information on which States Members of the United Nations draw to review common problems and to take stock of policy options; (ii) it facilitates the negotiations of Member States in many intergovernmental bodies on joint courses of action to address ongoing or emerging global challenges; and (iii) it advises interested Governments on the ways and means of translating policy frameworks developed in United Nations conferences and summits into programmes at the country level and, through technical assistance, helps build national capacities.

Note

Symbols of United Nations documents are composed of capital letters combined with figures.

E/2012/50/Rev. 1
ST/ESA/341
ISBN 978-92-1-109165-6
eISBN 978-92-1-055511-1

United Nations publication
Sales No. E.12.II.C.1

Preface

Achieving the Millennium Development Goals and addressing global challenges such as climate change require considerable financing. Finding the necessary resources will be challenging, especially for least developed countries. Official development assistance (ODA) is falling well short of what countries need, and commitments to provide more aid remain unfulfilled. In the midst of difficult financial times, many donor countries have cut back on development assistance. In 2011, aid flows declined in real terms for the first time in many years.

The need for additional and more predictable development financing has led to a search for alternative, innovative sources. A number of initiatives have been launched during the past decade, most of which have been used to fund global health programmes that have helped to provide immunizations and AIDS and tuberculosis treatments to millions of people in the developing world.

While these initiatives have successfully used novel methods to channel development financing, they have not yielded much additional funding, thus leaving available finance well short of what is needed. This is one reason why proposals to mobilize resources for development through sources beyond ODA, including innovative finance mechanisms, have generated renewed interest from both Governments and civil society.

This year's *World Economic and Social Survey* shows that such proposals could raise hundreds of billions of dollars in additional finance. If they are to become viable, however, strong international agreement is needed, along with adequate governance mechanisms, to manage the allocation of additional resources for development and global public goods.

World Economic and Social Survey 2012 is a valuable resource for implementing the decisions reached at the United Nations Conference on Sustainable Development (Rio+20). I commend it to all those seeking a solid financial underpinning for the post-2015 development agenda.

BAN KI-MOON
Secretary-General

Acknowledgements

The *World Economic and Social Survey* is the annual flagship publication on major development issues prepared by the Department of Economic and Social Affairs of the United Nations Secretariat (UN/DESA).

The *Survey* was prepared under the general supervision and direction of Rob Vos, Director of the Development Policy and Analysis Division (DPAD) of UN/DESA. Until his retirement in December 2011, Manuel F. Montes led the team that prepared the report. The core team at DPAD included Diana Alarcón, Christina Bodouroglou, Bilge Erten, Lydia Gatan, Barry Herman, Nicole Hunt, S. Nazrul Islam, Alex Julca, Oliver Schwank, Shari Spiegel, David Stubbs and David Woodward. Israel Machado of DPAD and Ramona Kohrs of the Department of Public Information provided bibliographical support.

The report further benefited from inputs from and comments by Vladimir Popov of DPAD, Tserenpuntsag Batbold, Michael Lennard, Mariangela Parra-Lancourt, Benu Schneider, and Krishnan Sharma of the Financing for Development (FfD) Office of UN/DESA, Wei Liu and David O'Connor of the Division for Sustainable Development (DSD) of UN/DESA, Daniel Titelman of the Economic Commission for Latin America and the Caribbean and Frank Schroeder of the secretariat of the Secretary-General's High-level Advisory Group on Climate Change Financing.

We gratefully acknowledge the background research contributions of Valpy FitzGerald, Ricardo Gottschalk, Gail Hurley, Suhas Ketkar, Akbar Noman, José Antonio Ocampo and Rehman Sobhan. Helpful feedback was also received from Mike Rowson of University College London and Peter Poore. Thanks are further due to the participants of the two workshops organized to facilitate the preparation of this Survey, for the insights they provided. They included, apart from those already mentioned, Nilufer Cagatay, Amanda Glassman, Stephany Griffith-Jones, Inge Kaul, Yukimi Konno, John Langmore, Pedro Martins, Julien Meimon, Bertrand Murguet, Léonce Ndikumana, Gorik Ooms, Sanjay G. Reddy, Rodney Schmidt and Bradford K. Smith.

Critical overall guidance was provided by Jomo Kwame Sundaram, Assistant Secretary-General for Economic Development at UN/DESA.

Overview

In search of new development finance

Innovative financing sources to meet global challenges

In 2001, a United Nations High-level Panel on Financing for Development, chaired by the former President of Mexico, Ernesto Zedillo, recommended a number of strategies for the mobilization of resources to fulfil the commitments made in the United Nations Millennium Declaration[1] to sustained development and poverty eradication[2]. The Panel concluded that substantial amounts of financial resources would be needed to achieve the international development goals. In addition, it made a strong case for tapping international sources of financing for the provisioning of global public goods, including for the prevention of contagious diseases, research for the development of vaccines and agricultural crops, combating climate change, and preservation of biodiversity. While there are no generally accepted estimates of the financing needs for meeting international development goals and global public goods, and while all such estimates are a matter of judgement, by any measure, needs tend to exceed, by far, the funds available for such purposes.

For many low-income countries, official development assistance (ODA) remains an important vehicle for financing development, given low levels of domestic savings and limited access to private capital flows. ODA has increased since the adoption of the Millennium Declaration, reaching $133 billion in 2011. Yet, flows would need to more than double in order to meet the long-standing United Nations target of 0.7 per cent of donor-country gross national income (GNI). Immediate prospects for meeting that target any time soon are grim, given fiscal pressures in donor countries. There are additional concerns that ODA has not been a very stable and reliable source of financing. The perceived need for additional and more assured funding has led to a search for innovative sources of development financing to complement traditional ODA.

Recently, a number of innovative financing initiatives have been launched. Many of these have been used to help finance new global health programmes and some to finance programmes for climate change mitigation and adaptation. The global health funds have immunized millions of children and distributed treatments for AIDS and tuberculosis to millions of people in the developing world. While international taxes (including a levy on air travel) have added to public funds for international cooperation, so far, these innovative mechanisms have not proved to be major fundraisers. In all, an estimated $5.8 billion in health financing and $2.6 billion in financing for climate and other environmental protection programmes have been managed through such mechanisms since 2002. The funds have been mobilized in part through "securitization" of existing ODA commitments which are not additional to traditional ODA. However, most of these intermediated resources are not additional to traditional ODA. In fact, while difficult to estimate, probably only a few hundred million dollars have been added annually.

---

[1]   See General Assembly resolution 55/2.

[2]   See A/55/1000.

An array of other options with large fundraising potential have been proposed (see figure O.1 and table O.1), but have not been agreed upon internationally thus far. These include taxes on financial and currency transactions and on greenhouse gas emissions, as well as the creation of new international liquidity through issuance of special drawing rights (SDRs) by the International Monetary Fund IMF), to be allocated with a bias favouring developing countries or leveraged as development financing. Though their potential may be high, these proposals are subject to political controversy. For instance, many countries are not willing to support international forms of taxation, as these are said to undermine national sovereignty.

There are also challenges in the use and allocation of funds mobilized internationally. Most existing innovative financing mechanisms earmark resources upfront for specific purposes, as is the case for the global health funds. There are perceived benefits in doing so. Advocates argue that the earmarking helps build political support and attract funds by establishing a clear link between fundraising and popular causes. This may come at a cost, however, since earmarking funds can limit domestic policy space for channelling resources to nationally defined priorities.

The international community will need to come to grips with such issues if it wishes to go beyond traditional modalities of development assistance and meet the financing needs for addressing global challenges. *World Economic and Social Survey 2012* analyses the nature of the challenges associated with generating new sources of development finance. It confirms the potential of a number of mechanisms, but concludes that realizing that potential will require international agreement and corresponding political will to tap sources, as well as the design of appropriate governance of uses and allocation mechanisms.

Figure O.1
The wide-ranging potential of (proposed and some existing) innovative sources of development finance

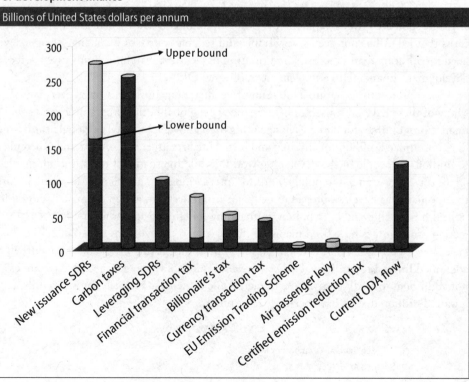

Source: UN/DESA.

Table O.1
Innovative sources of development finance and intermediation

	Description	Current level of resources (billions of US dollars per year)	Approximate potential revenue (billions of US dollars per year)	Comment
New sources of finance				
Public sector revenue				
European Union Emission Trading Scheme (proceeds from initial allocations)	EU Governments auction: sell or allocate permits for emission allowances	0.2	1-5	Germany has agreed to allocate 15 per cent to international climate finance. The proportion for other countries is not specified Financing is additional to existing ODA
Proceeds from certified emission reduction (CER) trading (2 per cent tax on new issuance)	2 per cent tax on CERs under the Clean Development Mechanism	0.06	0.06-0.75	Additional financing for climate adaptation in developing countries
Solidarity levy on airline taxes	Small tax levied on airline tickets, proceeds earmarked for UNITAID	0.2	1-10	$1.0 billion was raised between 2006 and 2010. Although financing is additional to existing ODA it is still accounted for as ODA by Development Assistance Committee members
Norway's tax on CO_2 emissions from aviation fuel	Tax on CO_2 emissions from aviation fuel in Norway	0.02	0.02	Norway contributes a portion of the proceeds of a tax on CO_2 emissions from aviation fuels to UNITAID
Carbon tax (proposal)	Tax on use of fossil fuels and other products contributing to CO_2 emissions	-	250	A tax of $25 per ton of CO_2 emissions by developed countries. Allocation of revenue for international climate financing would likely require an international agreement. Financing is additional to existing ODA
Currency transaction tax (CTT) (proposal)	Tiny tax on major currency foreign-exchange transactions	-	40	Assumes 0.005 per cent tax. Revenue would be additional to existing ODA
Financial transaction tax (FTT) (proposal)	Tax on financial transactions, such as equity trades, bonds and derivatives. Includes CTTs	-	15-75 (excluding taxes on currencies)	A European Union FTT could raise €55 billion per year (excluding taxes on currencies), although it is unclear how much will go to development. Revenue would be additional to existing ODA
International billionaire's tax (proposal)	Tax of 1 per cent on individual wealth holdings of $1 billion or more	-	40-50	Proposal is not yet in any international agenda. Revenue would be additional to existing ODA
Capturing global resources				
New SDR issuance (proposal)	Regular annual allocations in favour of developing countries	-	160-270	Additional international liquidity would increase reserve availability and, while not a form of development financing, would free up domestic resources for development
Leveraging SDRs (proposal)	Idle SDR holdings of reserve-rich countries are leveraged for investment in development	-	100	Assumes $100 billion of annual allocation to developed countries would be made available to international financial institutions in a way that preserves their status as reserve asset

(cont'd)

Table O.1 (cont'd)

	Description	Current level of resources (billions of US dollars per year)	Approximate potential revenue (billions of US dollars per year)	Comment
Intermediate financing mechanisms				
Capturing global resources				
Ownership of global resources (proposal)	Charge royalties for natural resource extraction beyond 100-mile exclusive economic zones	-	Unclear	Requires agreement on regimes for managing global commons, such as the International Seabed Authority. Revenue would be additional to existing ODA
Mechanisms that restructure cash flows				
International Finance Facility for Immunisation (IFFIm)	Future aid flows securitized to front-load resources to finance GAVI Alliance	0.6	0.6	Between 2006 and 2011, IFFIm raised $3.6 billion on the basis of donor commitments of $6.3 billion. IFFIm restructures existing ODA and as a result is not additional
Debt2Health	Donors grant debt relief in exchange for a commitment by the debtor to invest half of the debt relief in Global Fund local programmes	0.02	Limited scalability	Between 2007 and 2011, Debt2Health deals worth €170.2 million were concluded, one half of which countries contributed to the Global Fund. This is additional to existing ODA for countries that are current on their debt payments
Debt-for-nature swaps	Debt relief in exchange for local investments in the environment	0.05	Limited scalability	Has raised an estimated $1.1 billion-$1.5 billion since the late 1980s. This is additional to existing ODA for countries that are current on their debt payments
Mechanisms to manage risk				
Pilot advance market commitment for vaccines	Guaranteed future donor co-payments for vaccines	0.5	1.5 (committed)	Financing comes out of ODA budgets with small amount of additional financing provided by the Gates Foundation
Affordable Medicines Facility - malaria (AMFm)	A subsidy to drug manufacturers of malaria therapies (artemisinin-based combination therapies (ACTs))	0.2	Limited scalability	About half the financing comes from UNITAID. Based on the composition of UNITAID financing, in total, half of AMFm financing is from traditional ODA, 40 per cent from innovative financing and 10 per cent from philanthropy
Caribbean Catastrophe Risk Insurance Facility (CCRIF)	A regional catastrophe insurance pool	0	0.068	Donor countries and the World Bank capitalized the insurance fund. Initial payments came out of ODA budgets
Mechanisms that leverage citizen or private sector resources				
Product Red	A brand licensed to private firms	0.04	Limited scalability	Raises funds for the Global Fund. Financing comes from participating companies and is additional to ODA

Source: UN/DESA.

What is innovative development financing?

A broad range of mechanisms may be regarded as constituting innovative development finance

There is no one set definition of innovative development finance. The Leading Group on Innovative Financing for Development describes it as comprising all mechanisms for raising funds for development that are complementary to official development assistance, predictable and stable, and closely linked to the idea of global public goods. According to the Leading Group, innovative development finance should be linked to the process of globalization, either through taxing sectors considered to have gained most from globalization, such as the financial sector, or by taxing global public "bads", such as carbon emissions.

The lack of a precise definition has caused many studies to offer a broad interpretation and consider all types of non-conventional forms of finance under the rubric of innovative development financing, ranging from the mechanisms mentioned earlier, such as securitization of ODA commitments, international taxes and new SDR allocations, to all kinds of "other innovations", such as local currency bonds and currency hedges, gross domestic product (GDP)-linked bonds, incentives to channel worker remittances to developmental investments and publicly guaranteed weather insurance mechanisms.

The present *World Economic and Social Survey* focuses on mechanisms that are relevant as international public finance

The present *Survey* discusses a more limited set of mechanisms falling within the realm of international public finance, that is, forms of financing directly supporting achievement of international development goals and provisioning of global public goods. Specifically, the *Survey* includes those mechanisms that share all the following characteristics: (a) official sector involvement, including the use of public sector resources, as well as arrangements in which official financing plays a catalytic role in leveraging private sector and/or philanthropic resources; (b) international cooperation and cross-border transfer of resources to developing countries; and (c) innovation, in the sense that mechanisms are used in a new context or incorporate innovative features with respect to the type of resources or the way they are collected, or their governance structures. An additional desirable characteristic of the mechanisms considered is the capacity to generate additional development financing over and above existing ODA.

By this definition, most "other innovations" are not covered in this assessment. The definition does imply, however, that the assessment cannot be restricted exclusively to funding considerations. Funding, allocation and spending cannot be fully separated. As is the case in some existing mechanisms, the effective use of funds may influence availability. Several innovative financing mechanisms that channel resources to global health programmes, for instance, leverage future ODA commitments for more immediate disbursements tied to preventing specific communicable diseases.

The feasibility of new financing depends not only on sources, but also on how funds are channelled to end uses

Two main sources are considered: taxes levied on international transactions and/or taxes that are internationally concerted, such as the air-ticket solidarity levy, financial or currency transaction taxes and carbon taxes; and revenues from global resources, such as SDR allocations and proceeds derived from the extraction of resources from the global commons, through, for example, seabed mining in international waters. Proposals on potential sources of finance for international development cooperation in both categories have been discussed for decades, although most of these, with the exception of the proposal on an airline levy, have not yet been adopted.

Some innovations focus on intermediation mechanisms designed to better match funding and needs by facilitating front-loading of resources (which include several mechanisms channelling resources to global health funds and some debt-for-development swap mechanisms), by mobilizing public means to guarantee or insure natural disaster risks or technology development for public causes, or by securing specific-purpose voluntary contributions from the private sector for official development cooperation. Various mechanisms of these types do exist, but they are not large in size.

Several global funds that act as allocation mechanisms are generally also considered to come under the rubric of innovative development financing. Disbursement mechanisms in the health sector include the Global Fund to Fight AIDS, Tuberculosis and Malaria, UNITAID and the GAVI Alliance. These mechanisms collect financing directly from sources or through intermediary financing mechanisms. UNITAID is the only disbursement mechanism that obtains the bulk of its financing from an innovative source, the air-ticket solidarity levy. Other funds rely mainly on traditional sources of financing.

To fully understand the potential of innovative development financing, it is important to examine its effectiveness in terms of the full flow of funds from their sources to the point of their actual disbursements for development.

Proposed sources of innovative development finance

The appeal of potential mechanisms for more automatic and assured flows of funds for international cooperation, especially if they can mobilize substantial amounts of resources, has led to multiple proposals on how to establish those mechanisms. While recognizing that these proposals have been long-standing, this *Survey* argues that certain forms of international taxation and leveraging of international reserve assets have great potential to significantly enhance resources for international development cooperation, warranting greater efforts to overcome the obstacles that have prevented tapping such potential in the past.

International reserve asset creation could boost finance for development and global public goods…

In one such proposal, the IMF would issue more international liquidity in the form of special drawing rights. Proposed annual allocations of SDR 150 billion–250 billion would be received mainly by developed countries, as the SDRs are distributed according to country quotas in IMF. However, if instead, two thirds were allocated to developing countries, they would receive $160 billion–$270 billion annually. The "seigniorage" from such issuance, which now accrues to the international reserve currency countries, could be allocated for use in part by the international community in favour of developing countries. Admittedly, changing the SDR allocation formula would constitute a significant political undertaking, as it will require an amendment to the IMF Articles of Agreement. Amending the Articles, like decisions for a general SDR allocation under existing rules, requires an 85 per cent approval of member votes, giving the United States of America an effective veto. Indeed, United States support for regular SDR allocations would imply a measure of global solidarity, as the seigniorage embodied in the new SDRs would be largely at the expense of seigniorage no longer accruing to the United States. Nevertheless, such a change could result in a significant strengthening of the international monetary system, which should be supported by all IMF member countries.

Such regular issuance of SDRs has no direct link to development finance, however. SDRs remain a reserve asset, but their additional availability, arranged through international coordination, could reduce the need for individual developing countries to set aside foreign-exchange earnings in reserve holdings of their own as a form of self-insurance against global market shocks.

…potentially yielding approximately $100 billion per year for international cooperation

An SDR allocation serves to create real purchasing power for the holder receiving the allocation. The question then is how to deploy that purchasing power for development or global public goods. It is estimated that over $100 billion per year of "idle" SDRs of reserve-rich countries could be converted into longer-term development finance. What is proposed is not to directly spend SDRs, but rather to float bonds backed by SDRs. In one proposal, a "Green Climate Fund" would issue $1 trillion in bonds, backed by $100 billion in SDR equity in a leverage ratio of 10 to 1. In another proposal, idle SDRs would be used to purchase bonds directly from multilateral development banks. Clearly, such leveraging is the main attraction of such proposals, given the large investment resources needed to address climate change. The Green Climate Fund (or global fund to fight climate change) could collect market-based interest payments from at least some borrowers, which it would then use to pay its bondholders. As low-income countries may not be able to afford such loans, the fund would also receive additional annual contributions from donors to enable it to underwrite its concessional activities.

The main concept underlying the proposal entails using SDRs to purchase long-term assets. The attraction resides in the ability to tap the large pool of "unused" SDRs, in order to invest them either for development purposes or, as in the above proposal, in equity shares in a Green Climate Fund. Through regular substantial SDR allocations, over $100 billion in development financing per year could be raised. An argument against this is that it would breach the very purpose of SDRs, which were created solely for transactions of a purely monetary nature. Leveraging them in such a way as to expose their holders to risks of illiquidity would distort the purpose for which they were created. The viability of the proposal may thus be seen to depend on how much risk would be involved and on designing the financial instrument for leveraging SDRs carefully enough to maintain its function as a reserve mechanism. The risks may be limited as long as the proposal is restricted to leveraging "idle" SDRs, which is similar to the existing practice of a fair number of countries of moving excess foreign currency reserves into sovereign wealth funds, where the liquidity and risk characteristics of specific assets in the fund determine whether or not those assets still qualify as reserve holdings.

An internationally concerted carbon tax could raise $250 billion per year...

Discussion continues on the issue of appropriate policies for reducing greenhouse gas emissions and for mobilizing more automatic, assured and substantial additional flows to finance climate change mitigation and adaptation. The most straightforward approach to reducing emissions through financial incentives would be to impose a tax on carbon dioxide (CO_2) emissions so as to encourage economic actors to reduce the emissions under their control, through shifting, for example, to less carbon-emitting activities and energy sources. The price incentive should also stimulate increased output of more carbon-efficient products and services. However, there is little agreement on how much to tax, what to tax (fuels, for example, are not the only source of greenhouse gases), or whom to tax (should it be, for example, the final consumer or the producer of the greenhouse gases) and how to use the tax revenue that would be collected.

If global policy could be designed as if for a single economy, then a single global tax could be set (and adjusted over time) to steer overall emissions in the direction of a particular target to be achieved by a particular date. However, the world is made up of many countries which would experience different impacts on overall consumption and production from a single tax. The differential impact of a uniform carbon tax would cause objections to be raised by Governments and could frustrate agreement on the tax, especially since it is unlikely that those making the smallest sacrifices under a uniform tax would fully compensate those making the largest. Indeed, the 1997 Kyoto Protocol[3] to the 1992 United Nations Framework Convention on Climate Change[4] mandates only that higher-income countries make specific targeted reductions, as those countries are responsible for most of the man-made concentrations of CO_2 in the atmosphere and are best able to bear the economic burden. In this vein, a tax of $25 per ton of CO_2 emitted by developed countries is expected to raise $250 billion per year in global tax revenues. Such a tax would be in addition to taxes already imposed at the national level, as many Governments (of developing as well as developed countries) already tax carbon emissions, in some cases explicitly, and in other cases, indirectly through taxes on specific fuels.

Channelling the funds for international cooperation would require a separate political agreement, such as the 2009 Copenhagen Accord[5] through which developed countries promised to provide $30 billion over the period 2010-2012 (with pledges made so far coming close to that amount) and $100 billion per year by 2020 in new and additional resources to support climate mitigation and adaptation programmes in developing countries.[6]

3　United Nations, *Treaty Series*, vol. 2303, No. 30822.
4　Ibid., vol. 1771, No. 30822.
5　See FCCC/CP/2009/11/Add.1,decision 2/CP.15.
6　Ibid., decision 2/CP.15, para. 8.

…and a small currency transaction tax could add an estimated $40 billion…

A tax on international currency transactions is deemed attractive principally because of the huge volume of daily transactions. While proponents assert that a very tiny tax would mobilize very substantial funds without materially affecting the market, opponents have argued that those that trade currencies work on very fine margins and that even a tiny tax would have a significant impact, as banks continually adjust their currency exposures. Proponents reply that technological advances and investments in the infrastructure of international payments over recent years have significantly reduced the cost of making financial transactions and that the proposed tax would reverse that reduction only minimally. Hence, while the currency transaction tax is broadly considered feasible, it might possibly reduce the earnings from such transactions.

A small tax of half a "basis point" (0.005 per cent) on all trading in the four major currencies (the dollar, euro, yen and pound sterling) might yield an estimated $40 billion per year. While the revenue may not be scalable by raising the tax rate because higher rates would affect trading volumes, even a low tax rate would limit high-frequency trading to some extent. It would thus result in the earning of a "double dividend" by helping reduce currency volatility and raising revenue for development. While a higher rate would limit trading to a greater extent, this might be at the expense of revenue.

…but in all cases, separate agreements would be needed on the use of the tax for international development cooperation

In all cases, the allocation of revenues for development would require a separate political agreement. One objection to a currency transaction tax arises from a fear that the financial institutions of a participating country would be at a disadvantage in global competition for financial business. Even though existing evidence from cases of implementation of such forms of taxation suggests that the fear may be unwarranted, the concern would be best overcome through adoption of the tax by international agreement. There should also be little reason for concern if the tax, as proposed, was imposed at a very low rate. The deeper problem, however, seems to lie in securing enough political support to earmark at least an agreed share of the proceeds for international development cooperation. Yet, the Group of Twenty has put the idea of an internationally concerted financial transaction tax in its agenda and agreed, at the Cannes Summit in November 2011, that new sources of funding need to be found over time to address development needs, which could include taxing the financial sector.

Existing sources of innovative financing for development

Recently developed mechanisms of "innovative development finance" are very different in nature. While limited in scale and tied to specific purposes, they have provided few resources additional to traditional ODA.

With the exception of two forms of international taxation (levies on air travel and a 2 per cent tax on transactions under the Clean Development Mechanism), existing mechanisms considered in the present analysis may be divided into three types: (a) mechanisms for transforming the time profile of development finance; (b) mechanisms for mitigating risk; and (c) mechanisms for harnessing voluntary private contributions.

Official development assistance can be effectively front-loaded

The principal aim of the first type is to secure financial resources for immediate use for development purposes. The International Finance Facility for Immunisation (IFFIm) is one such mechanism. It binds ODA commitments over a long period (6-23 years in practice) and securitizes those commitments to provide funds for immediate use by the GAVI Alliance. Debt conversion mechanisms, such as the Debt2Health scheme and debt-for-nature swaps, also fall within this category. Resources are freed up through cancellation of debts owed to bilateral creditors or by purchasing commercial bank debt at a discount on the secondary market. Part or all of the associated debt-service payments are redirected to a specific public use or non-governmental project, most commonly in the field of health or the environment.

These mechanisms have not mobilized additional funding; further, the amount of redirected resources has been modest by any measure. IFFIm has received donor commitments totalling $6.3 billion over a five-year period, generating a front-loaded fund of $3.6 billion, of which $1.9 billion has been disbursed since its establishment in 2006. Disbursements have been limited in part by the need for a very high level of liquidity to maintain creditworthiness. IFFIm disbursements will be offset in the long term by the diversion of ODA to service IFFIm bonds. The main benefit of these mechanisms clearly lies not in the raising of new resources, but rather in a more effective use of resources (see below).

Debt-forgiveness to debt-distressed countries is not considered innovative development financing in this report, as it does not directly generate any new stream of financial resources. No systematic data on "debt-for-development" swaps is available. In the aggregate, the amount of resources generated through such mechanisms has been modest thus far. For instance, between 2007 and 2011, $107 million in resources was freed up through debt conversions for use by the Global Fund under the Debt2Health scheme.

Aid effectiveness can also be improved by guaranteeing and insuring risks

The second type of mechanism tries to secure funds to cover certain public-health and natural disaster risks through internationally arranged guarantees or insurance schemes. Under advance market commitments, which constitute one such scheme and are used mostly for disease prevention, ODA or funding from private philanthropic sources or both are utilized to guarantee a predetermined level of demand and prices for a particular technology-intensive good (such as pneumococcal vaccines) with a view to providing an assured market for producers so as to incentivize product development. Under the Affordable Medicines Facility - malaria (AMFm), a pilot scheme managed by the Global Fund to Fight AIDS, Tuberculosis and Malaria, lower prices are negotiated with producers of artemisinin-based combination therapies for malaria, in return for an assured market and a temporary subsidy, as a means of displacing older and less effective (but cheaper) alternatives from the market.

By the end of 2011, the pilot advance market commitment for pneumococcal vaccines had secured $1.5 billion in funding from bilateral and philanthropic sources, while the amount raised by the Affordable Medicines Facility - malaria was somewhat smaller, $312 million (including $180 million of financing, provided by UNITAID and sourced from the innovative air-ticket levy).

The Caribbean Catastrophe Risk Insurance Facility pools public finance risks arising from natural disasters, such as hurricanes and earthquakes. The Facility is capitalized by donors and allows members of the Caribbean Community (CARICOM) to collectively insure potential damages above a certain threshold level.

Innovative financing can be tapped by harnessing voluntary private contributions

Additional mechanisms seek voluntary contributions from private agents for defined purposes. Under one well-known scheme, Product Red, companies are licensed to use the brand for specific products in return for donating a share of the profits from these goods and services to the Global Fund to Fight AIDS, Tuberculosis and Malaria. MassiveGood (2010-2011), another—but short-lived—scheme, sought to raise funds for UNITAID, by securing small contributions from the purchase of tickets for air travel.

While it is only mechanisms in this category that provide resources additional to traditional (bilateral and private philanthropic) development finance, the amounts generated have been very limited. Product Red raised a total of $190 million in its first five years of existence, while MassiveGood was cancelled after less than two years owing to disappointing results.

Existing mechanisms generate limited additional resources, but enhance aid effectiveness

While meaningful assessment is limited by their recent establishment, these mechanisms have generally served their respective purposes well. The International Finance Facility for Immunisation has front-loaded ODA resources effectively, keeping borrowing and administrative costs low. The pilot advance market commitment has accelerated the introduction of vaccines to fight pneumococcal disease (although still on a substantially more limited scale than originally envisaged). The preliminary results for the Affordable Medicines Facility - malaria appear broadly positive; and the Caribbean Catastrophe Risk Insurance Facility appears to be functioning effectively, having made several payouts, including to Haiti following the 2010 earthquake.

The potential for scaling up and replication needs to be tested

These mechanisms also have some potential for scaling up and/or replication for other uses. There are few technical limits to scaling up the International Finance Facility for

Immunisation, although such scaling up is currently constrained by financial market conditions and fiscal pressure on aid budgets. Its application is also limited to contexts in which front-loading is appropriate, like vaccination programmes requiring quick expansion of coverage to be effective in containing the spread of diseases, or in cases where large indivisible investments are needed upfront to facilitate the diffusion of a new technology, such as renewable energy. Likewise, the advance market commitment for pneumococcal vaccines has some potential for use in other, similar contexts, although this is less clear in cases other than that of vaccines—cases, for example, where product specification is more complex, or cases involving the development of new technologies (as opposed to the commercialization of technologies already at an advanced stage of development). There may also be potential to replicate the Caribbean Catastrophe Risk Insurance Facility in some geographical contexts, which could be enhanced by risk-pooling through regional arrangements or multiregional arrangements so as to maximize the spread of risks.

In sum, these mechanisms may be able to meet specific needs, which is their principal aim. However, given their limited size and limited capacity to raise new funds, they do not contribute much, if anything, to closing the gap between current and projected levels of ODA and financial needs for development and global public goods.

Uses and global management of innovative development finance

Most of the resources raised to date under the rubric of innovative financing for development have been devoted to health. However, the expectation is that, in the near future, substantial amounts of additional finance will become available for climate change mitigation and adaptation, which would be channelled through dedicated funds managing allocation for specific end uses.

In the area of global public health, most innovative financing resources have been used for control of communicable diseases, particularly diseases with global or wide geographical scope (HIV/AIDS, tuberculosis and malaria). In the area of climate finance, most initiatives focus on mobilizing resources for programmes for climate change mitigation, which have a clear global public-good nature, but few on addressing developing-country adaptation needs. Mitigation programmes account for about two thirds of the resources channelled through innovative financing mechanisms.

Overall, existing mechanisms tend to prioritize financing global public goods rather than supporting broader national-level development processes.

Global health funds are purpose-effective...

Financing needs for health are considerable, and despite much greater priority attached to those needs by donors in recent years, a considerable gap remains between estimated needs and any realistic estimate of future ODA for health. The World Health Organization (WHO) estimates additional annual spending needed to achieve the Millennium Development Goals for health at $29 per person, implying a total increase in health spending in developing countries by $251 billion between 2009 and 2015. Financing the entire increase with domestic resources will be challenging for many low-income countries.

Innovative financing for health has largely passed through or funded programmes of the GAVI Alliance (the International Finance Facility for Immunisation and the advance market commitment for pneumococcal vaccines), the Global Fund to Fight AIDS, Tuberculosis and Malaria (the Affordable Medicines Facility-malaria, Debt2Health and Product Red) and UNITAID (figure O.2). While the International Finance Facility for Immunisation has provided a substantial proportion (64 per cent) of GAVI funds since its inception in 2006, innovative financing mechanisms account for a much smaller proportion of Global Fund resources (2 per cent since 2002). Moreover, while both the GAVI Alliance and the Global Fund have been very successful in generating resources for carrying out their respective mandates, this success has lain primarily in attracting ODA, either directly or through innovative mechanisms: only the $190 million raised for the Global Fund by Product Red is additional to ODA. Only UNITAID is funded mainly by innovative sources, as 75 per cent of its resources come from air travel levies.

Figure O.2
Only a small share of the financing of global health funds comes from additional innovative sources

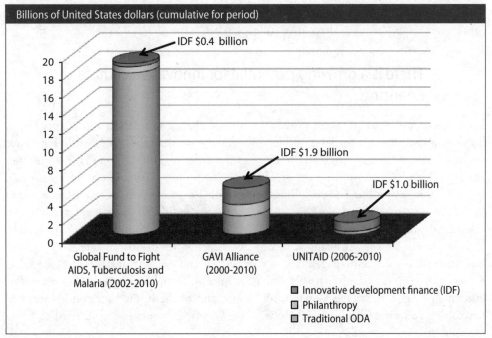

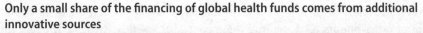

Source: UN/DESA.

The GAVI Alliance and the Global Fund have generally performed well in respect of meeting their respective goals and have maintained reasonably stable and predictable levels of overall funding. The resource situation is potentially vulnerable, however, because of the heavy reliance of the Global Fund on bilateral funding and of the GAVI Alliance on the International Finance Facility for Immunisation.

...but a case can be made for consolidating them under the Global Fund

More controversial is the set-up of global-health funds as vertical (disease- or intervention-specific) funds. First, they do not directly help reduce health financing gaps as such, because the shortages primarily are in covering the cost of overall health services (medical personnel in particular) and do not mainly pertain to the cost of controlling specific diseases. Second, they may have adverse impacts on national health systems in recipient countries (see below). Third, they further fragment the aid architecture by adding new players and mechanisms.

While the issue of fragmentation arises primarily with respect to other bilateral and multilateral programmes, fragmentation in this case could be eased if most—if not all—vertical programmes were consolidated under the Global Fund. This would require that a broader health mandate be given to the Global Fund, for which it is suited in view of the Fund's fairly inclusive and transparent governance structure. To deal with the second concern, greater efforts should be made to ensure that global funding for control of communicable diseases is adequately aligned with national policy priorities and that it strengthens—rather than weakens—national health systems. As conceived, the Health System Strengthening Platform—established by the GAVI Alliance, the Global Fund and the World Bank—was to make an important step in this direction. Unfortunately, thus far, use of this Platform has been limited, partly owing to the reluctance of some GAVI and Global Fund donors to go beyond current restrictive mandates, as well as the limited engagement of other donors. Overcoming these constraints will be critical. The fact that the existing mechanisms are not designed to address the first concern (continued financing gap) would require seeking alternative funding mechanisms.

There is a growing potential for innovative climate financing…

Estimates of additional financing needs for climate change mitigation and adaptation in developing countries are great—considerably greater even than those for health. Estimates of additional investment needs in 2030 are in the order of $140 billion–$175 billion per annum (plus additional upfront investments of $265 billion–$565 billion) for mitigation, and a further $30 billion–$100 billion per annum for adaptation. *World Economic and Social Survey 2011* (United Nations, 2011a) estimated additional investment needs of developing countries for sustainable development, including for climate change mitigation and adaptation, and for ensuring access to clean energy for all, sustainable food production and forest resource management, at about $1 trillion per year in the coming decades. As recognized, inter alia, by the Copenhagen Accord, from the perspective both of fair burden-sharing in financing global public goods and of the limited economic means of developing countries, a substantial share of the required financing would need to come from international transfers.

Innovative financing for climate change is still incipient, but it does have the potential to grow considerably in the coming years and could contribute significantly to fulfilling commitments made under the Copenhagen Accord. Total resources raised over the past decade through innovative financing mechanisms (excluding an unquantifiable amount of debt-for nature swaps over the last 25 years) amount to a mere $1 billion, however: $168 million was raised by the Adaptation Fund, from a 2 per cent tax on transactions under the Clean Development Mechanism, and $841 million from Germany's auctions of permits under the EU Emission Trading Scheme, channelled through its International Climate Initiative. However, in the case of the Adaptation Fund, only a fraction ($30 million) has been disbursed so far, half of which was used to cover administrative costs.

Two mechanisms in particular are expected to generate substantial resources for climate change programmes in the next few years. First, from 2013, the European Union is to auction carbon emissions allowances, which will generate an estimated

$20 billion–$35 billion in annual revenues; some countries have indicated their intention to allocate half for climate change programmes (although inasmuch as this includes domestic programmes, much less is likely to be devoted to programmes in developing countries). Germany is expected to channel 15 per cent of its revenue (or an estimated $500 million per year) to international climate-related programmes from 2013. If all European Union members do the same, over $5 billion per year would become available for international climate financing from auctioning European Union emission allowances.

Second, it is envisaged that the Reducing Emissions from Deforestation and Forest Degradation plus Conservation (REDD+) initiative, which has hitherto operated essentially as a coordinating mechanism for conventional multilateral and bilateral aid projects, should evolve into an innovative mechanism based on carbon trading.

…but existing climate financing mechanisms are highly fragmented

The minimal level of disbursements from the Adaptation Fund and the unknown level from the International Climate Initiative makes assessment of these mechanisms impossible. This is itself a source of concern. Climate funds more generally have been closely aligned with their goals and, in some cases, have been strongly results-oriented, while generally maintaining a commitment to country ownership. They also have the potential to provide stable and predictable levels of funding. An important caveat relates to uncertainty about the durability of many of these funds. As in the case of global health funds, the proliferation of climate funds in recent years has contributed to the fragmented nature of the international aid architecture.

Scaling up innovative financing will require governance changes to be effective

In order for innovative financing to contribute significantly to meeting the financing requirements for development and global public goods (including health and climate change mitigation and adaptation), it will need to be scaled up considerably in both areas and to shift towards mechanisms that generate additional resources, instead of merely frontloading or redirecting already committed official development finance. Replicating of existing mechanisms, while maintaining the close link between the raising and the use of funds, would risk considerably compounding the proliferation of financing channels and the fragmentation of the aid architecture, particularly for climate financing.

This problem could be greatly eased by consolidating disbursement mechanisms for (traditional and innovative) development finance into fewer institutions characterized by broader but clearly defined mandates, close coordination among such mechanisms, and the pooling of resources from multiple (traditional and innovative) sources in each institution. It is also essential that governance structures for such programmes have a balanced representation of funding Governments and agencies, and recipients, and also ensure adequate accountability mechanisms.

In practice, it is unlikely that small-scale mechanisms, such as those developed to date, can fulfil more than a small fraction of financing needs. Together with the need to avoid further fragmentation of the aid architecture, this factor presents a strong case for larger-scale mechanisms that generate more substantial resources with greater flexibility in their use—for example, internationally coordinated taxes and SDR allocations. Such mechanisms, however, raise a number of issues for global economic governance. For instance, many countries are not willing to support international forms of taxation, as these are seen to compromise national sovereignty. It has, in the past, proved difficult to secure the necessary support for SDR allocations. As indicated, in the absence of an amendment to the IMF Articles of Agreement, a very small share of such allocations accrue to low-income and least developed countries (3.2 per cent and 2.3 per cent, respectively). Orienting the resources raised for development would therefore require establishing additional financial mechanisms, for example, through creating trust funds or using SDRs to purchase bonds from multilateral development banks.

For the actual disbursement of funds, it would be best to avoid creating additional disbursement channels and to use existing ones instead (including the global fund for public health programmes and the Green Climate Fund which are being created), provided disbursements can be consolidated and channelled through fewer mechanisms with broader (for example, sector-wide) remits—again, with appropriate governance mechanisms to ensure full representation of recipients' interests.

Even if scaled up, the types of innovative development financing discussed here are unlikely to generate additional resources in the amounts needed to meet all financing needs for development and the provisioning of global public goods. Strengthening domestic resources will thus be crucial as well. International cooperation might also support such domestic efforts through international tax cooperation that would reduce tax avoidance and evasion.

Managing innovative development finance at the national level

Assessment of the role of innovative financing in supporting development processes in recipient countries is difficult, in part because such financing tends to come with conventional financing. In any case, at the individual-country level, such financing thus far has been rather insignificant in macroeconomic terms and relative to sources of external financing, even in the poorest countries. Even in the health sector, where it is most developed, innovative development financing has not, as yet, reached a significant level relative to health expenditure (figure O.3). In only 12 very low income countries (mostly in sub-Saharan Africa) do innovative financing mechanisms account for 2 per cent or more of public-health spending, and in no case does the figure exceed 4.4 per cent. In countries with income per capita of more than $1,200, the figure rarely exceeds 0.2 per cent.

Aligning innovative development financing with national development strategies is essential

Global health funds are considered to have made significant contributions to disease control in recipient countries. Nonetheless, as indicated, these vertical funds have raised a number of aid-effectiveness concerns, particularly with regard to consistency with national ownership of development assistance as a result of insufficient alignment of externally funded programmes with national health strategies and inadequate embedding in national health systems during programme implementation. In some countries, especially those

Figure O.3

Innovative mechanisms finance a visible share of public-health expenditures only in a number of low-income countries

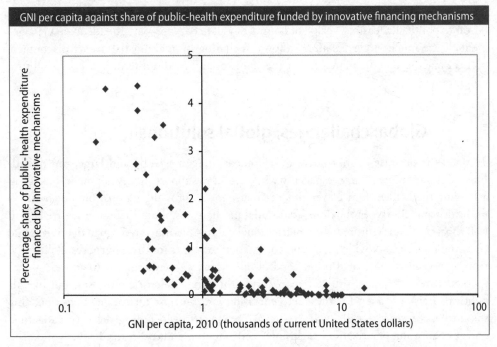

GNI per capita against share of public-health expenditure funded by innovative financing mechanisms

Sources: GAVI Alliance (http://www.gavialliance.org/results/disbursements/); Global Fund to Fight AIDS, Tuberculosis and Malaria (http://portfolio.theglobalfund.org/en/DataDownloads/Index); and World Development Indicators online database (available from http://databank.worldbank.org/ddp/home.do).

with limited institutional capacity and human resources, global health funds have drained human resources out of national health services and increased administrative burdens. At the same time, the fact that application for resources from the global funds is considered to be burdensome by a range of countries limits their access.

The challenges posed by vertical health funds have been recognized for decades. The funds have generally been justified as temporary means for achieving short-term results pending the development of effective health systems. However, health programme silos have become more widespread and tensions between silo programmes and national health systems remain. The limitations of the aforementioned Health System Strengthening Platform, as implemented, point to a missed opportunity to deal with this long-standing issue.

Country experiences in sub-Saharan Africa, Asia and Latin America and the Caribbean show that the relatively stable and predictable nature of resource availability from the global health funds does not necessarily translate into stable and predictable flows for individual recipients. Measurement issues aside, available evidence suggests that disbursements by both the Global Fund and the GAVI Alliance tend to be more volatile than traditional ODA flows. In a large number of countries, Global Fund and the GAVI disbursements show sharp fluctuations from one year to the next.

The nature of the impact of innovative financing, channelled through global climate and environmental funds, as a more recent phenomenon, has not yet become particularly discernible given the low disbursement rates to date. Embedding such financing in broader national sustainable development strategies is critical, given the cross-sectoral and economy-wide transformative changes that the investments are meant to engender.

Such concerns have raised doubts among recipient countries about the desirability of innovative development financing mechanisms. The fact that such mechanisms do not provide much additional finance but impose administrative burdens is a major concern. However, when a substantial scaling up of innovative development financing becomes politically feasible, recipient countries will need to prepare for adequate management of the much larger resource inflows, including by making them part of counter-cyclical macroeconomic management mechanisms and medium-term public expenditure programmes.

Global challenges, global solutions

To date, the promise of innovative development financing is, by and large, unfulfilled. Financing gaps remain large, especially with respect to supporting development, including achieving the Millennium Development Goals, and in providing global public goods, as for health and climate protection. Traditional mechanisms of official assistance are falling well short of what is required. The international community must recognize that it is in the common interest to provide stable and contractual resources for these purposes. Politically, tapping revenue from global resources and raising taxes internationally to address global problems are much more difficult than taxing for purely domestic purposes. But like all political decisions taken for the next generation and not just for the next election, this should be assessed carefully against alternative scenarios, including the very dangerous one of continuing polarization, exclusion, confrontation and insecurity in the world. The time has come to confront the challenge.

Sha Zukang
Under-Secretary-General
for Economic and Social Affairs
May 2012

Contents

Boxes

Figures

Tables

Explanatory Notes

The following symbols have been used in the tables throughout the report:

..   **Two dots** indicate that data are not available or are not separately reported.

–   **A dash** indicates that the amount is nil or negligible.

-      **A hyphen** indicates that the item is not applicable.

−   **A minus sign** indicates deficit or decrease, except as indicated.

.   **A full stop** is used to indicate decimals.

/   **A slash** between years indicates a crop year or financial year, for example, 2011/12.

-      **Use of a hyphen** between years, for example, 2012-2012, signifies the full period involved, including the beginning and end years.

     Reference to "dollars" ($) indicates United States dollars, unless otherwise stated.

     Reference to "billions" indicates one thousand million.

     Reference to "tons" indicates metric tons, unless otherwise stated.

     Annual rates of growth or change, unless otherwise stated, refer to annual compound rates.

     Details and percentages in tables do not necessarily add to totals, because of rounding.

The following abbreviations have been used:

ACTs	artemisinin-based combination (malaria) therapies
AGPM	Agricultural Pull Mechanism
AMCs	advance market commitments
AMFm	Affordable Medicines Facility - malaria
ART	antiretroviral therapy
CARICOM	Caribbean Community
CCRIF	Caribbean Catastrophe Risk Insurance Facility
CDM	Clean Development Mechanism
CER	certified emission reduction
CO_2	carbon dioxide
CTT	currency transaction tax
DAC	Development Assistance Committee of the Organization for Economic Cooperation and Development
DALY	disability-adjusted life year
DFID	Department for International Development of the United Kingdom of Great Britain and Northern Ireland
DPT3	diphtheria, pertussis and tetanus
ECLAC	Economic Commission for Latin America and the Caribbean
EU	European Union
EU ETS	European Union Emission Trading Scheme
FDI	foreign direct investment
FTT	financial transaction tax
G8	Group of Eight
G20	Group of Twenty
GCF	Green Climate Fund
GDP	gross domestic product
GEF	Global Environment Facility
GHG	greenhouse gas
Global Fund	Global Fund to Fight AIDS, Tuberculosis and Malaria
GNI	gross national income
Hib	*Haemophilus influenzae type B*
HIPC	Heavily-Indebted Poor Countries Initiative
IBRD	International Bank for Reconstruction and Development

IDA	International Development Association
IDF	innovative development finance
IFF	international finance facility
IFFIm	International Finance Facility for Immunisation
IMF	International Monetary Fund
MIF	Multilateral Investment Fund (Inter-American Development Bank)
N_2O	nitrous oxide
ODA	official development assistance
ODI	Overseas Development Institute (London)
OECD	Organization for Economic Cooperation and Development
OPEC	Organization of the Petroleum Exporting Countries
PRGF	Poverty Reduction and Growth Facility programme (IMF)
R&D	research and development
REDD+	Reducing Emissions from Deforestation and Forest Degradation plus Conservation initiative
SARS	severe acute respiratory syndrome
SDRs	special drawing rights
SWFs	sovereign wealth funds
SWIFT	Society for Worldwide Interbank Financial Telecommunication
UN/DESA	Department of Economic and Social Affairs of the United Nations Secretariat
UNDP	United Nations Development Programme
UNICEF	United Nations Children's Fund
UNU	United Nations University
VAT	value-added tax
WGP	world gross product
WHO	World Health Organization
WIDER	World Institute for Development Economics Research of the United Nations University
WWF	World Wildlife Fund

The designations employed and the presentation of the material in this publication do not imply the expression of any opinion whatsoever on the part of the United Nations Secretariat concerning the legal status of any country, territory, city or area or of its authorities, or concerning the delimitation of its frontiers or boundaries.

The term "country" as used in the text of this report also refers, as appropriate, to territories or areas.

For analytical purposes, unless otherwise specified, the following country groupings and subgroupings have been used:

Developed economies (developed market economies):

Australia, Canada, European Union, Iceland, Japan, New Zealand, Norway, Switzerland, United States of America.

Group of Eight (G8):

Canada, France, Germany, Italy, Japan, Russian Federation, United Kingdom of Great Britain and Northern Ireland, United States of America.

Group of Twenty (G20):

Argentina, Australia, Brazil, Canada, China, France, Germany, India, Indonesia, Italy, Japan, Mexico, Republic of Korea, Russian Federation, Saudi Arabia, South Africa, Turkey, United Kingdom of Great Britain and Northern Ireland, United States of America, European Union.

European Union (EU):

Austria, Belgium, Bulgaria, Cyprus, Czech Republic, Denmark, Estonia, Finland, France, Germany, Greece, Hungary, Ireland, Italy, Latvia, Lithuania, Luxembourg, Malta, Netherlands, Poland, Portugal, Romania, Slovakia, Slovenia, Spain, Sweden, United Kingdom of Great Britain and Northern Ireland.

EU-15:

Austria, Belgium, Denmark, Finland, France, Germany, Greece, Ireland, Italy, Luxembourg, Netherlands, Portugal, Spain, Sweden, United Kingdom of Great Britain and Northern Ireland.

New EU member States:

Bulgaria, Cyprus, Czech Republic, Estonia, Hungary, Latvia, Lithuania, Malta, Poland, Romania, Slovakia, Slovenia.

Economies in transition:

South-Eastern Europe:

Albania, Bosnia and Herzegovina, Croatia, Montenegro, Serbia, the former Yugoslav Republic of Macedonia.

Commonwealth of Independent States (CIS):

Armenia, Azerbaijan, Belarus, Georgia,[a] Kazakhstan, Kyrgyzstan, Republic of Moldova, Russian Federation, Tajikistan, Turkmenistan, Ukraine, Uzbekistan.

Developing economies:

Africa, Asia and the Pacific (excluding Australia, Japan, New Zealand and the member States of CIS in Asia), Latin America and the Caribbean.

Subgroupings of Africa:

Northern Africa:

Algeria, Egypt, Libya, Morocco, Tunisia.

Sub-Saharan Africa:

All other African countries, except Nigeria and South Africa, where indicated.

Subgroupings of Asia and the Pacific:

Western Asia:

Bahrain, Iraq, Israel, Jordan, Kuwait, Lebanon, Occupied Palestinian Territory, Oman, Qatar, Saudi Arabia, Syrian Arab Republic, Turkey, United Arab Emirates, Yemen.

South Asia:

Bangladesh, Bhutan, India, Iran (Islamic Republic of), Maldives, Nepal, Pakistan, Sri Lanka.

East Asia:

All other developing economies in Asia and the Pacific.

Subgroupings of Latin America and the Caribbean:

South America:

Argentina, Bolivia (Plurinational State of), Brazil, Chile, Colombia, Ecuador, Paraguay, Peru, Uruguay, Venezuela (Bolivarian Republic of).

Mexico and Central America:

Costa Rica, El Salvador, Guatemala, Honduras, Mexico, Nicaragua, Panama.

Caribbean:

Barbados, Cuba, Dominican Republic, Guyana, Haiti, Jamaica, Trinidad and Tobago.

---

a   As of 19 August 2009, Georgia officially left the Commonwealth of Independent States. However, its performance is discussed in the context of this group of countries for reasons of geographical proximity and similarities in economic structure.

Least developed countries:

Afghanistan, Angola, Bangladesh, Benin, Bhutan, Burkina Faso, Burundi, Cambodia, Central African Republic, Chad, Comoros, Democratic Republic of the Congo, Djibouti, Equatorial Guinea, Eritrea, Ethiopia, Gambia, Guinea, Guinea-Bissau, Haiti, Kiribati, Lao People's Democratic Republic, Lesotho, Liberia, Madagascar, Malawi, Mali, Mauritania, Mozambique, Myanmar, Nepal, Niger, Rwanda, Samoa, Sao Tome and Principe, Senegal, Sierra Leone, Solomon Islands, Somalia, Sudan, Timor-Leste, Togo, Tuvalu, Uganda, United Republic of Tanzania, Vanuatu, Yemen, Zambia.

Small island developing States and areas:

American Samoa, Anguilla, Antigua and Barbuda, Aruba, Bahamas, Barbados, Belize, British Virgin Islands, Cape Verde, Commonwealth of the Northern Mariana Islands, Comoros, Cook Islands, Cuba, Dominica, Dominican Republic, Fiji, French Polynesia, Grenada, Guam, Guinea-Bissau, Guyana, Haiti, Jamaica, Kiribati, Maldives, Marshall Islands, Mauritius, Micronesia (Federated States of), Montserrat, Nauru, Netherlands Antilles, New Caledonia, Niue, Palau, Papua New Guinea, Puerto Rico, Saint Kitts and Nevis, Saint Lucia, Saint Vincent and the Grenadines, Samoa, Sao Tome and Principe, Seychelles, Singapore, Solomon Islands, Suriname, Timor-Leste, Tonga, Trinidad and Tobago, Tuvalu, United States Virgin Islands, Vanuatu.

Parties to the United Nations Framework Convention on Climate Change:

Annex I parties:

Australia, Austria, Belarus, Belgium, Bulgaria, Canada, Croatia, Czech Republic, Denmark, Estonia, European Union, Finland, France, Germany, Greece, Hungary, Iceland, Ireland, Italy, Japan, Latvia, Liechtenstein, Lithuania, Luxembourg, Monaco, Netherlands, New Zealand, Norway, Poland, Portugal, Romania, Russian Federation, Slovakia, Slovenia, Spain, Sweden, Switzerland, Turkey, Ukraine, United Kingdom of Great Britain and Northern Ireland, United States of America.

Annex II parties:

Annex II parties are the parties included in Annex I that are members of the Organization for Economic Cooperation and Development but not the parties included in Annex I that are economies in transition.

Chapter I
Introduction

Summary

♦ Shortfalls in traditional official development assistance vis-à-vis commitments and perceived development financing needs have led to a search for innovative sources of development financing.

♦ The present *Survey* focuses on the use of innovative mechanisms which channel international financial support to development and health and climate-related global public goods.

♦ Existing innovative financing mechanisms, while successful in addressing specific global health needs, have mobilized little additional funding. The scope for scaling up these mechanisms also seems limited.

♦ More substantial resources could be raised through international taxes and capturing revenues from global resources. Long-standing proposals exist for tapping such funding sources, but have yet to be implemented.

♦ To assess the potential and effectiveness of innovative development financing, one needs to consider the full "flow of funds", comprising the mobilization of resources, the intermediation mechanisms, and the use of funds. A new framework is presented to make this assessment.

In search of new development finance

After falling in the 1990s, official development assistance (ODA) has increased considerably since the early 2000s, following the 9/11 terrorist attacks in 2001 and the Monterrey Consensus of the International Conference on Financing for Development (United Nations, 2002). Nonetheless, ODA levels are still significantly below internationally agreed targets. There is also concern that ODA has not been a stable and reliable source of financing. In addition, there is need for additional financing of international collective action to address global problems, such as mitigating the effects of climate change. The perceived need for additional and more assured funding has led to a search for innovative sources of development financing to complement traditional ODA.

The perceived need for additional and more assured financing for development has led to a search for innovative sources of financing

Over the past two decades, several innovative financing initiatives have been implemented by a number of countries. Many of these have been used to help finance new global health programmes, such as the Global Fund to Fight AIDS, Tuberculosis and Malaria, UNITAID and the GAVI Alliance. These programmes have been effective in

Existing initiatives have so far contributed only limited additional resources for development immunizing millions of children and in distributing AIDS and tuberculosis treatments to millions of people in the developing world. More recently, there has been a proliferation of funds dedicated to combating climate change. However, only limited resources for development, at about $5.8 billion for health and $2.6 billion for climate and other environmental protection programmes, have been managed through innovative mechanisms through 2011. Furthermore, the majority of these funds have been mobilized through innovative "intermediate financing mechanisms", such as the International Finance Facility for Immunisation (IFFIm), which restructure *existing* ODA commitments to better match funding and needs. In the broader context of development finance, the question is to what extent these mechanisms can or should be scaled up and/or replicated in other areas.

Proposals with larger fundraising potential have not yet been implemented

Other proposals with larger fundraising potential have generated enthusiasm among development practitioners, but have not yet been agreed on and implemented internationally, such as taxes on financial and currency transactions and on greenhouse gas emissions, as well as the creation of new international liquidity through issuance by the International Monetary Fund (IMF) of special drawing rights (SDRs) for development purposes. Though their potential may be high, these proposals are subject to political resistance. For instance, many countries are not willing to support international forms of taxation, as these are viewed as compromising national sovereignty. National taxation of financial transactions or fossil fuel consumption already exists in a number of countries, but the revenues are almost entirely used domestically, reflecting, in part, weak political will to dedicate more resources to global causes.

There are also challenges associated with the allocation of new international development financing. Most initiatives that have been implemented to date have earmarked resources to specific purposes, such as to the health funds discussed above. There are perceived benefits to doing so: such earmarking is believed to have helped build political support and attract funds by establishing a clear link between fundraising and popular causes.

However, earmarking funds can limit domestic policy space for channelling resources to nationally defined priorities. As a result, there is a tension between these programmes and the international commitment to development effectiveness, which emphasizes country responsibility for decision-making on national policies. In particular, most of the resources raised through existing innovative mechanisms have been channelled through funds that primarily target international or global public goods, such as combating particular communicable diseases or climate change. To be effective, such programmes often require internationally coordinated efforts. Thus, a related challenge is to reconcile the need for international coordination with the principle of country ownership of programmes. There are other challenges as well. For instance, it is hard to assess whether innovative sources of development finance raise additional resources or whether they serve as substitutes for traditional ODA, given the difficulty of establishing what the level of ODA from traditional sources would have been without the innovative funding.

Through an analysis of these and other challenges, the 2012 *World Economic and Social Survey* aims at appraising potential new forms of innovative development financing and gaining a better understanding of the potential and desirability of scaling up or replicating existing mechanisms.

Why innovative sources of development finance?

While proposals for some of what are now called "innovative" financing mechanisms can be traced back to the late nineteenth century, the initiatives proposed over the past 40 years were generally shaped in reaction to concerns about ODA trends. (See box I.1 for a discussion of the history of innovative development financing (IDF).) While ODA increased in absolute terms between the 1960s and early 2000s, it declined as a proportion of donor-country gross national income (GNI), thus moving away from, instead of towards, the 1970 internationally agreed target of 0.7 per cent of GNI, as shown in figure I.1.

Figure I.1

ODA from Development Assistance Committee (DAC) countries in United States dollars and as a proportion of donor-country gross national income, 1960-2010

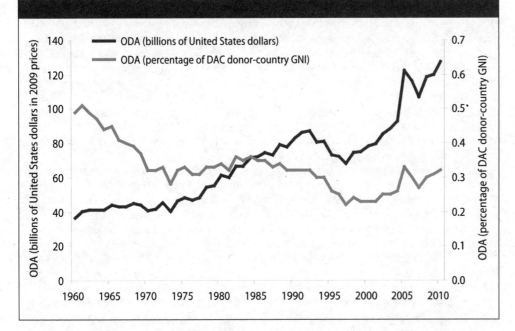

Source: OECD StatExtracts. Available from http://stats.oecd.org/index.aspx?datasetcode=ODA%5FDONOR (accessed 11 October 2011).

Traditional aid is seen to be rather volatile

In 2002, as part of their commitments under the Monterrey Consensus of the International Conference on Financing for Development (United Nations, 2002) donors agreed to significantly increase ODA in an effort to raise resources to finance the Millennium Development Goals. As can be seen in figure I.1, following these commitments, ODA flows increased in the early 2000s. However, ODA still remained substantially below the United Nations target of 0.7 per cent of donor GNI. In addition, ODA was not seen as a reliable source of financing. Indeed, in many low-income countries, aid has been more volatile than other capital flows (Markandya, Ponczek and Soonhwa, 2010; Bulíř and Hamann, 2003), two to four times more volatile than domestic tax revenue (Vargas Hill, 2005; United Nations Conference on Trade and Development, 2009), and about five times more volatile than the growth of gross domestic product (GDP) (Vargas Hill, 2005; Kharas, 2008).[1] Early advocates of IDF looked to new revenue sources, such as international taxes allocated directly to development, and issuance of special drawing rights (SDRs) for development

---

1   The coefficient of variation, or relative standard deviation, of net aid disbursements to sub-Saharan Africa is 0.21.

Box I.1

Origins of innovative financing for international cooperation

Proposals for using direct international taxation to finance an extensive international cooperation system date back to at least the late nineteenth century. Book V (entitled *The ultimate problem of international jurisprudence*) of *The Institutes of the Law of Nations: A Treatise of the Jural Relations of Separate Political Communities* published by James Lorimer in 1884, was a first contribution (see Frankman, 1996, p. 808). The idea of direct taxation by international institutions never took hold, however, although the idea continued to be discussed, especially in light of the "relative penury" of the League of Nations (ibid., p. 809).

The development cooperation system that evolved after the end of the Second World War was mainly financed by Government contributions and loans, directly and through multilateral institutions. Nevertheless, as discussed in chapter II, the basic idea of international taxation was kept alive in official and academic discourse, especially in light of the felt need to arrange more assured, predictable and larger flows of official development assistance (ODA). When international attention focused increasingly on global environmental issues and public-health imperatives in the 1990s, the need to mobilize even larger international public resources became manifest, and interest in adding to the standard financial modalities of cooperation intensified. During the special session of the General Assembly, held in Geneva from 26 June to 1 July 2000, to review the outcome of the 1995 World Summit for Social Development, the Government of Canada proposed that consideration be given to a currency transaction tax (CTT). This was a step too extreme for Japan, the member States European Union and the United States of America, however, and these countries adamantly fought the proposal. After reportedly tough negotiations, a compromise was forged by Norway and Canada which entailed conducting a "rigorous analysis" not of the CTT alone, but of a range of possible new and innovative sources of development financing.[a]

Some Governments continued to advocate for intergovernmental consideration of innovative financing mechanisms; and in 2002, in the more supportive "spirit of Monterrey", heads of State and Government gathered at the International Conference on Financing for Development recognize(d) (in paragraph 44 of the Monterrey Consensus of the International Conference on Financing for Development,[b] adopted by the Conference) "the value of exploring innovative sources of finance provided that those sources do not unduly burden developing countries".

In 2005, the World Institute for Development Economics Research (WIDER) of the United Nations University (UNU) published the analytical study that had been requested in 2000 at the twenty-fourth special session of the General Assembly (Atkinson, ed., 2005). While the study addressed innovative mechanisms of the sort discussed in this *Survey*, the focus had shifted from establishing assured and automatic mechanisms that could mobilize significant volumes of international funds over time to raising enough funds quickly in order to achieve the Millennium Development Goals (ibid., p. 3).

The new focus on finding cash fast for development cooperation brought a broad range of options into the discussion. Thus, in addition to examining proposals for a carbon-emission tax, the CTT and renewed International Monetary Fund (IMF) allocations of special drawing rights (SDRs), the WIDER study reported on a United Kingdom initiative for an international finance facility (IFF), which was later adopted, with the facility taking the form of the International Finance Facility for Immunization (IFFIm) (see main body of this chapter). It also noted calls for increased private donations, facilitating and encouraging workers' remittances and a global lottery.

Nevertheless, there was no global consensus on introducing any of the innovative mechanisms. Action depended on the commencement of work by a group of interested countries on developing selected proposals, introducing some of them, attracting new partners and, in that way, building an international constituency for action. The Presidents of Brazil, France and Chile met in Geneva in January 2004 (joined later by Spain) and with the support of the Secretary-General, launched an initiative to fight hunger and poverty. Just prior to that meeting, in November 2003, the President of France had commissioned an expert group to investigate innovative financing options. Its report considered options and orientations for an international tax system and related matters.[c]

Source: UN/DESA.

a See General Assembly resolution S-24/2, annex, para. 142 (g).

b *Report of the International Conference on Financing for Development, Monterrey, Mexico, 18-22 March 2002* (United Nations publication, Sales No. E.02.II.A.7), chap. I, resolution 1, annex.

c J. P. Landau, "Groupe de travail sur les nouvelles contributions financières internationales: rapport à Monseiur Jacques Chirac, le Président de la République" (Paris, Government of France, 2004).

Box I.1 (cont'd)

This report was complemented by the report of the Technical Group on Innovative Financing Mechanisms (A/59/398), issued on 1 October 2004 and circulated as a document of the General Assembly, which considered several of the proposals that were also being studied by the WIDER team, as well as additional modalities of cooperation.[d]

The Presidents of Brazil, Chile and France and the Prime Minister of Spain also convoked the first global intergovernmental dialogue on innovative means for financing development, at United Nations Headquarters on 20 September 2004. About 50 presidents and prime ministers attended, along with many other ministers and national representatives. The Secretary-General and the heads of IMF and the World Bank also participated. Some Governments were supportive, including that of the Netherlands (speaking on behalf of the European Union) which promised to review the proposals of the expert group report and those in the WIDER study. The New York Declaration on action against hunger and poverty,[e] the outcome of the dialogue, was widely endorsed. It "acknowledged that it is also appropriate and timely to give further attention to innovative mechanisms of financing—public or private, compulsory and voluntary, of universal or limited membership—in order to raise funds urgently needed to help meet the Millennium Development Goals and to complement and ensure long-term stability and predictability to foreign aid".

Reflected in this Declaration were both the earlier theme of mobilizing assured, predictable and large flows over time and a new concern which was to immediately mobilize resources to fund Millennium Development Goals-related programmes. As the Declaration stated in conclusion: "Hunger cannot wait." At the Millennium Summit, held at United Nations Headquarters from 14-16 September 2005, to take stock of the implementation of the United Nations Millennium Declaration,[f] 79 countries endorsed the New York Declaration, by then co-sponsored by Algeria, Brazil, Chile, France, Germany and Spain. The 2005 World Summit Outcome[g] itself "(took) note with interest of the international efforts, contributions and discussions, such as the Action against Hunger and Poverty, aimed at identifying innovative and additional sources of financing for development on a public, private, domestic or external basis to increase and supplement traditional sources of financing".[h]

Momentum was thus building. France propelled it further by convening the Paris Conference on Innovative Development Financing Mechanisms in Paris on 28 February and 1 March 2006 to launch the Leading Group on Solidarity Levies to Fund Development, out of which have emerged the air passenger ticket levy, the IFFIm and other initiatives. In February 2008, the Secretary-General added to the momentum when he appointed a senior French official, Philippe Douste-Blazy, as his Special Adviser on Innovative Financing for Development. Further momentum was provided when the international community reconvened in Doha from 29 November to 2 December 2008 at the Follow-up International Conference on Financing for Development to Review the Implementation of the Monterrey Consensus. This was reflected, inter alia, by the fact that The Doha Declaration on Financing for Development: an outcome document of the Follow-up International Conference on Financing for Development to Review the Implementation of the Monterrey Consensus,[i] mentioned numerous innovative financing initiatives.[j]

At the rhetorical level, at least, innovative financing had "arrived".

Mr. Douste-Blazy further broadened the scope of innovative financing for development in an effort that he coordinated in 2009 to bring together eight innovative financing mechanisms (the "I-8") and the international organizations and civil society actors associated with them. The I-8 included three mechanisms designed to engage the private sector in taking up the social challenge: the advance market commitments; Product RED; and an initiative proposed by the French Development Agency and a French bank to establish a socially responsible mutual fund that would invest in socially screened investments and in equities of investment funds selected by the Agency, while paying a yield only slightly higher than a money market fund.

A large number of innovations have thus been proposed and some have been implemented; but finding sufficient political support for international resource mobilization and tailoring the financing mechanism to international development needs remain ongoing challenges.

d The list included "mandatory mechanisms" (financial transaction tax, tax on arms trade, an international finance facility and SDRs for development), "political coordination" (addressing tax evasion and tax havens; increasing the benefits of remittances) and "voluntary mechanisms" (an affinity card identified with the implementation of the Millennium Development Goals and "ethical funds" for socially responsible investing).

e Available from http: http://www.diplomatie. gouv.fr/en/IMG/pdf/ Declaration_de_New_York_ sur_l_action_contre_la_ faim_et_la_pauvrete_20_ septembre_2004.pdf.

f See General Assembly, resolution 55/2.

g See General Assembly resolution 60/1.

h Ibid., para. 23(d).

i General Assembly resolution, 63/239, annex.

j Ibid., para. 51.

ODA falls well short
of needs for financing
development and global
public goods

purposes, to raise new financing, with the goal of averting instability by reducing dependence on annual budget approval processes in donor countries.

At the same time, additional financing needs were being identified in the environmental and public-health domains. As discussed in chapter IV, while estimates are imprecise and are matters of judgement, necessary financing of essential health in low-income countries is perceived to be considerable; by some accounts, approximately $250 billion additional public-health spending would be needed between 2009 and 2015 to enable low-income countries to achieve the health-related Millennium Development Goals. Financing needs associated with climate change are also significant, with some estimates of total (domestic and foreign) financing needs in the order of $1 trillion per year for climate change mitigation and adaptation, for ensuring access to clean energy for all, and for enhancing sustainable food production and forest resource management in developing countries. While not all of this will be financed with international public funds, there is a clear need for substantial additional resources (United Nations, 2011b).

Innovative financing
sources have recently
received renewed attention

In the aftermath of the financial crisis of 2008–2009, IDF has received renewed attention. The financial crisis led to mounting public indebtedness in many developed countries, in part owing to the recapitalization of domestic banking systems through Government programmes. This, in turn, put pressure on aid budgets of many donor countries and strengthened calls for innovative forms of fundraising to meet financing needs for development and provisioning of global public goods. In particular, there has been renewed interest in taxing financial transactions, which is seen by advocates as a means through which the financial sector can contribute to addressing global needs, as well as a means of raising funds that could be set aside to build stronger financial safety nets (Griffith-Jones and Persaud, 2012a). As discussed in chapter II, France, a member of the Leading Group on Innovative Financing for Development and 2011 Chair of the Group of Twenty (G20), put the option of an internationally agreed financial transaction tax in the agenda of the G20 Leaders Summit held in Cannes on 3 and 4 November.[2]

In addition, one of the responses to the crisis was the issuance of additional SDRs to strengthen the reserves of IMF member countries. This has led to renewed calls for more regular SDR allocations, not just for building reserves, but also for leveraging long-term financing for development and climate protection (United Nations, 2009a; Bredenkamp and Pattillo, 2010; and chap. II of this *Survey*).

Development and global public goods

IDF can be suitable for
funding both national
development programmes
and global public goods

IDF represents a potential form of global collective action for financing global social, economic and environmental goals. This role encompasses two primary aims of public finance. The first is a more efficient allocation of resources, either through public expenditures on goods not provided by the private sector (including public goods and public financing of private goods with major externalities), or through taxes and subsidies aimed at changing private sector behaviour. For example, taxation of carbon emissions aims to reduce demand for goods with high carbon content by charging emitters (producers or consumers) for their contribution to global warming. The second primary aim of public

---

2   The final communiqué of the Heads of State or Government included a statement on the need for new sources of funding to address development needs, including a reference to the financial transaction tax (FTT) (para. 28). As an indication of increased support for innovative sources of financing, the G20 asked Bill Gates to deliver a report at the Summit on innovation in financing for development, which included a recommendation for several international taxes, including a financial transaction tax (Gates, 2011).

finance is redistribution of income in a socially preferred direction. Revenues from the carbon tax, for instance, could be skewed towards developing countries to support their efforts to invest in climate protection or broader development efforts, which would be fair, considering their much lower (historical) contribution to global greenhouse gas emissions.

At the global level, ODA remains an important public finance vehicle for such "international distribution policies". Although there are many factors driving ODA, a key motivation is the desire to meet international solidarity goals, aimed at improving global equity, with taxpayers in wealthier countries contributing to poverty reduction and development in developing countries. There is, however, no independent mechanism for financing global or international public goods[3] that have substantial externalities across borders, such as controlling communicable diseases (for example, HIV/AIDS, severe acute respiratory syndrome (SARS) and poliomyelitis) and combating climate change (Kaul and Conceição, 2006). Although financing for development and financing global public goods are closely linked, there are differences between them, which have important implications for the distribution of resources.

Generally, there are substantial overlaps between development programmes and those for global public goods. ODA that finances social welfare programmes, infrastructure investments and other domestic needs is primarily designed to impact domestic development in poor countries. Such development programmes are also an essential complement to programmes that address global public goods-related concerns in both the health and environmental spheres. Projects that are designed primarily to impact development, such as those directed at climate change adaptation, can also have important global public-good components. For example, while weather monitoring stations reduce disease and poverty in developing countries, they also serve as a global public good in that they can be used to better monitor climate change globally (Dervis and Milsom, 2011). At the same time, global public goods can have potentially enormous developmental benefits. Mechanisms that control infectious diseases affecting developing countries (such as the HIV pandemic) can have substantial benefits for development. Similarly, investments in climate change mitigation in developing countries, such as public sector investment in clean transportation, electricity or other Green technologies, can reduce poverty and spur development, while also reducing greenhouse gas emissions (United Nations, 2011b).

There are cases, however, where the overlap between the spheres of development and global public goods is less pronounced. The international campaign to eradicate poliomyelitis provides a classic example of an expenditure directed at realizing a global public good. The global strategy is to seek universal immunization so that the polio virus will no longer exist in the world population, since today it can travel from infected to uninfected countries. For this reason, from a global perspective, universal immunization has a high priority. However, in a poor country that has no current incidence of polio, public officials may decide to spend their limited funds in other ways and suspend polio immunization until the disease reappears. In this context, there may be a misalignment between global and national priorities. While external support for polio vaccination in low-income countries is essential for eradication, this is more appropriately viewed as an investment in the production of a global good, than as support for those countries.

These examples highlight the overlaps between financing for global public goods and development assistance, as well as some important distinctions between them. First, financing of global public goods can lead to conflicts with principles of aid

Financing for development and financing global public goods are closely linked, but there are important differences between them

Vertical funds that finance global public goods conflict with principles of aid effectiveness

---

3   Binger (2003) presents several alternative definitions of global public goods. For the purpose of this publication, global public goods are goods that have cross-border externalities, and whose production, in sufficient supply, requires collective action by developed and developing countries.

effectiveness, which recognize that countries should be responsible for setting their own national priorities. Second, by their nature, global public goods benefit populations in both developed and developing countries, and in some cases may benefit the donor country more than the recipient. Thus, this kind of financing cannot appropriately be considered development financing. When global coordination is an important element in tackling the problem, a case can be made for asking countries to modify their national plans so as to accommodate the global public interest; but this also implies rethinking the relationship between developed and developing countries as partners in addressing global solidarity needs, rather than as "donors" and "beneficiaries".

Innovative financing
should be additional to
traditional ODA

Nonetheless, most financing of global public goods in developing countries, whether through IDF or traditional ODA mechanisms, is accounted for in donor-country aid budgets. The share of ODA used to finance global public goods appears to have been increasing substantially, from about 4 per cent in 1980 to 30–40 per cent in the early 2000s (Binger, 2003; United Nations Development Programme, 2003; Reisen, Soto and Weithöner, 2008). However, it is not clear that the increase in resources for global public goods has necessarily been at the expense of traditional ODA. Using data from 1997 through 2001, Reisen, Soto and Weithöner (2008) found that for every $1 increase in financing for global public goods, about 25 cents would have otherwise gone to other development assistance, with 75 cents coming from new or additional resources. They also found that development assistance to the poorest countries was largely unaffected by the increase in financing for global public goods. Furthermore, in most cases, investments in global public goods in developing countries have a developmental impact, so that the ultimate impact on development is difficult to quantify. Nonetheless, the concern that ODA that otherwise would be destined to support national development programmes might be diverted to finance global public goods has led several authors (for example, Binger, 2003; and Anand, 2002) to argue for separate accounting of financing for global public goods, as distinct from ODA, so as to ensure that financing for public goods is additional to existing development assistance. As discussed below, there are similar issues associated with IDF, particularly because it is being used to finance global public goods. However, in order to better understand these and other issues, it is first necessary to define IDF more precisely.

What do we mean by IDF?

There is no one agreed
definition of IDF

ODA comprises traditional donor-country and multilateral official outlays to developing-country Governments in the form of grants, concessional loans, and technical cooperation. Though some of these mechanisms have been categorized as "innovative", innovative development financing is here understood to be something else. "Innovative" sources of financing are not necessarily *new* mechanisms, but they are different ones. The question is what makes them different.

There is no one set definition of IDF. Indeed, there has been a proliferation of proposals labelled IDF by advocates and policymakers since IDF was introduced into the intergovernmental lexicon over a decade ago. In 2009, the Secretary-General, covering the spectrum of interpretations of IDF, concluded that "(t)he concept of innovations now extends to such diverse forms as thematic global trust funds, public guarantees and insurance mechanisms, cooperative international fiscal mechanisms, equity investments, growth-indexed bonds, counter-cyclical loans, distribution systems for global environmental services, microfinance and mesofinance, and so on" (United Nations, General Assembly, 2009, para. 13).

By this formulation, IDF encompasses practically any innovation in international financing available for developing countries. The breadth of such an all-inclusive approach, while of interest in terms of the number of mechanisms encompassed, extends beyond the role of IDF in international public finance. The Leading Group on Innovative Financing for Development (2011a)[4] has developed a set of guidelines for interpreting the role of IDF. The Leading Group describes IDF as "comprising mechanisms for raising funds for development that are complementary to official development assistance, predictable and stable, and closely linked to the idea of global public goods". By the Leading Group's interpretation, IDF should address solidarity imperatives, such as achievement of the Millennium Development Goals, as well as the emergence of new needs related to the preservation of global public goods, such as combating climate change; and should be closely linked to the idea of globalization, either by taxing sectors considered to have benefited most from globalization, such as the financial sector, or by taxing global public "bads", such as carbon emissions.

The Leading Group's guidelines are primarily qualitative, leaving open questions of whether or not certain mechanisms, such as those that essentially focus on private incomes or domestic policies, should be considered a form of IDF, such as remittances from international migrants and/or policies that attempt to provide incentives for the investment of these resources in developmental projects in migrants' home countries. The Organization for Economic Cooperation and Development (OECD) and the World Bank have put forth more precise, yet strikingly different, interpretations of IDF (as depicted in figure I.2). The OECD interpretation includes mechanisms beyond traditional measures that raise funds or stimulate actions in support of development (Sandor, Scott and Benn, 2009). On the other hand, the World Bank (2010a, p.1) includes mechanisms that generate additional funds and enhance efficiency of public and private financial flows and "make financial flows more results-oriented" and therefore regards all innovative uses of traditional development finance, including "results-based aid", private investment insurance, local currency bonds and currency hedges, and South-South development cooperation, as IDF. Using this broad definition, the World Bank estimates that a total of $57 billion of IDF was raised between 2000 and 2008, with $40 billion of the total raised through local currency bonds issued by multilateral development banks and $10.8 billion raised through South-South concessional development financing (Girishankar, 2009).

This *Survey* presents a more limited set of possible IDF mechanisms, focusing on the role of IDF in international public finance, with the aim of formulating policy goals for international cooperation. Specifically, the *Survey* includes those mechanisms that share all of the following characteristics:

This *Survey* focuses on innovative instruments of international public finance

- *Official sector involvement*, including the use of public sector resources, as well as structures in which official financing plays a catalytic role in leveraging private sector and/or philanthropic resources;
- *International cooperation and cross-border transfer of resources* to developing countries;
- *Innovation*, in that mechanisms are used in a new context or incorporate innovative features as to the nature of the resources, the way they are collected, or their governance structures.
- An important desirable characteristic of the mechanisms considered would also be, as indicated, their ability to raise *additional* resources over and above existing, traditional forms of ODA.

---

4 See box I.1 for a discussion of the history of the Leading Group.

Figure I.2
Various interpretations of innovative sources of development financing[a]

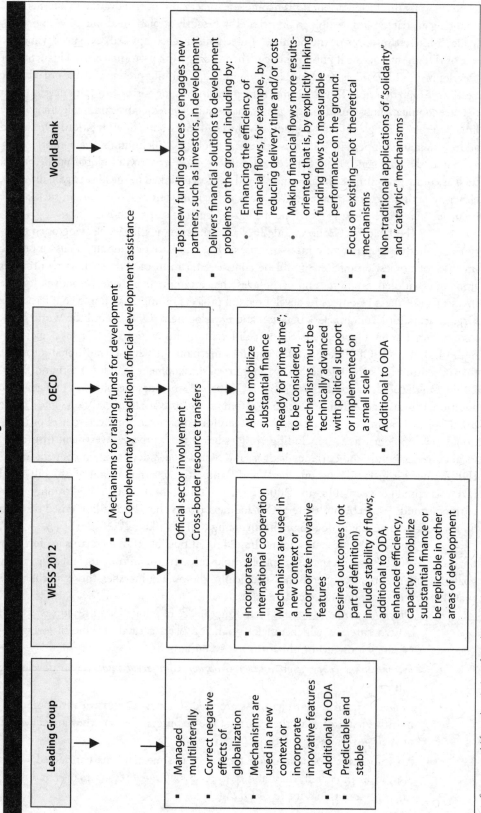

Leading Group

- Managed multilaterally
- Correct negative effects of globalization
- Mechanisms are used in a new context or incorporate innovative features
- Additional to ODA
- Predictable and stable

WESS 2012

- Official sector involvement
- Cross-border resource transfers

- Incorporates international cooperation
- Mechanisms are used in a new context or incorporate innovative features
- Desired outcomes (not part of definition) include stability of flows, additional to ODA, enhanced efficiency, capacity to mobilize substantial finance or be replicable in other areas of development

OECD

- Mechanisms for raising funds for development
- Complementary to traditional official development assistance

- Able to mobilize substantial finance
- "Ready for prime time"; to be considered, mechanisms must be technically advanced with political support or implemented on a small scale
- Additional to ODA

World Bank

- Taps new funding sources or engages new partners, such as investors, in development
- Delivers financial solutions to development problems on the ground, including by:
  - Enhancing the efficiency of financial flows, for example, by reducing delivery time and/or costs
  - Making financial flows more results-oriented, that is, by explicitly linking funding flows to measurable performance on the ground.
- Focus on existing—not theoretical mechanisms
- Non-traditional applications of "solidarity" and "catalytic" mechanisms

a See annex A.I for a description of mechanisms that qualify as IDF under the alternative interpretations.

Box I.2 lists the mechanisms discussed in this *Survey* based on the above criteria, with brief definitions of each. For example, a financial transaction tax (FTT) meets the requirement of official sector involvement. Although the concept of an FTT is not new, the innovation here is that the tax would be used in a new *context*, that is, for international cooperation. Given the lack of a global tax authority, a financial transaction tax is likely to be implemented and collected on a national basis, rather than at the global level. Nonetheless, the tax would still involve international cooperation if the revenue is dedicated to financing development or global public goods in developing countries. The concept of IDF deployed in the *Survey* would include an FTT, even if implemented by a single country, on condition that at least a portion of the revenues raised from the tax was dedicated to international development cooperation. However, if revenues raised from an FTT are spent on general budget financing in the country where the tax is levied (as is the case for the FTT being discussed in Europe), the FTT would be viewed as a domestic tax and would not fall under the definition of IDF as used in this publication.

By this definition of IDF, general debt relief is not considered IDF, though some debt swaps, such as Debt2Health, are included. Although debt swaps are not novel, the innovation of this and other programmes lies in the fact that the debt swaps are being offered to debtor countries current on their debt-service payments. As Debt2Health swaps are offered to countries that do not otherwise qualify for debt relief, the debt write-down frees up funds for development that would have otherwise been spent on debt financing, thus raising additional resources for development. The point is that in the case of debt relief for debt-distressed countries, the debtor country generally is expected to be unable to repay its debts in the first place. In the private sector, when a company defaults, the creditor is forced to write off the value of the debt; the creditor takes a loss, which is not considered a form of charity for the indebted firm. Similarly, debt write-offs to sovereigns unable to repay their debts should not be regarded as aid, and certainly not as IDF. There is no sovereign debt workout mechanism or bankruptcy court that addresses sovereign debt re-structuring, but a sovereign default should be viewed as just that—a bankruptcy where the creditor will take losses—and not as charity or aid (Herman, Ocampo and Spiegel, 2006).

> Debt conversion is considered IDF only if debt would not have been written off otherwise

Another mechanism included in box I.2 is the Caribbean Catastrophe Risk Insurance Facility (CCRIF). The Facility is a regional insurance fund capitalized by developed-country Governments and the World Bank. It therefore encompasses official sector international cooperation and cross-border financing. Its innovation lies in its being the first regional Government-run insurance fund. Membership fees paid by participating Governments are clearly an additional source of financing (although there is some question whether funding from developed countries represents new funds or are drawn from existing ODA budgets). However, weather insurance in Ethiopia, which is regarded as IDF by the World Bank, is considered an innovative form of domestic finance and thus not IDF in this *Survey*.

> Insurance mechanisms for reducing risks in developing countries may also be considered IDF

Overall, most of the mechanisms listed in box I.2 also conform to the other definitions. The *Survey* interpretation of IDF is consistent with the Leading Group's guidelines, and broadly similar to the OECD classification, but narrower than the World Bank's. There are, however, some exceptions. For example, the FTT discussed above would not currently be included in the OECD and World Bank formulations, since the OECD and World Bank focus only on mechanisms that have already been implemented, whereas the *Survey* is interested in the potential of proposals. One difference between the *Survey* framework and that of the Leading Group centres around how to apply the

Box I.2

Glossary of terms associated with innovative development financing mechanisms

Sources of financing

New issuance of special drawing rights (SDRs): SDRs are a reserve asset issued by the IMF which under certain conditions may be turned into a source of development. New SDRs could be issued annually on a regular basis and allocated in favour of developing countries. Doing so does not change their status as a reserve asset, but could reduce the need for developing countries to accumulate reserves on their own and free foreign-exchange earnings for development financing at home. Alternatively, idle SDRs held by reserve-rich countries could be used as guaranteed capital to leverage issuance of bonds by, for instance, multilateral development banks which in turn would be used to finance development programmes and/or the provisioning of global public goods.

Revenues from the ownership of global resources: "royalties" obtained from natural resource extraction beyond territorial limits, such as from the oceans beyond territorial limits, Antarctica or outer space, could be tapped for international development cooperation. As global resources lie outside national jurisdictions, any licensing and payment of royalties would have to involve an international authority that was recognized as the responsible agent for managing the specific commons. While fishing in international waters and other activities in the "commons" might be licensed in this way, only revenues from mining the seabed has thus far been seen as a source of international public revenue.

Solidarity levy on airline tickets: a tax levied on airline tickets which is coordinated internationally but implemented nationally. Currently, the levy is collected by a number of donor countries and funds are channelled to programmes like UNITAID and IFFIm. The tax is typically levied as a small, fixed contribution charged to airline passengers and considered small enough to avert negative incentives to air travel.

Carbon taxes: taxes on the use of fossil fuels. This type of tax would aim to contribute to reductions in CO_2 emissions, while revenues might be used for climate and other environmental protection programmes, nationally or internationally. The latter is not automatic, however, and would require international agreement.

Currency transaction tax (CTT): a tax on foreign currency transactions on major currency markets. A CTT is a type of financial transaction tax. To count as innovative development financing, at least a part of the revenue would be dedicated for international development coordination or programmes in developing countries in support of the provisioning of global public goods.

Financial transaction tax (FTT): a tax on financial transactions, such as equity trades, bonds, currencies or derivatives, which can be implemented nationally or internationally. To count as innovative development financing, at least a part of the revenue would be dedicated for international development coordination or programmes in developing countries in support of the provisioning of global public goods.

Share of proceeds from issuing new certified emission reduction units (CERs): under the Clean Development Mechanism (CDM), emission-reduction projects in developing countries earn certified emission reduction credits (CERs), which can be traded and used by industrialized countries to meet their emission reduction targets under the Kyoto Protocol to the United Nations Framework Convention on Climate Change. The present share of the CER proceeds is 2 per cent and this generates funds for the Adaptation Fund.

European Union Emission Trading Scheme (EU ETS): European Union Governments auction, sell or allocate permits to emit CO_2 (emission allowances) to large emitters. Allowances are traded and proceeds of the initial auction of permits accrue to member States. To count as innovative development financing, at least a part of the revenue would be dedicated for international development coordination or programmes in developing countries in support of the provisioning of global public goods.

The international "billionaire's" tax: a 1 per cent tax on individual wealth holdings of $1 billion or more. To count as innovative development financing, at least a part of the revenue would be dedicated for international development coordination or programmes in developing countries in support of the provisioning of global public goods.

Box I.2 (cont'd)

Intermediate financing mechanisms

Affordable Medicines Facility - malaria (AMFm): a subsidy to drug manufacturers of artemisinin-based combination (malaria) therapies (ACTs). The AMFm is managed by the Global Fund (see below), which negotiates the price of ACTs and subsidizes the prices to end-users.

Advance market commitments (AMCs): guaranteed future donor co-payments for vaccines against diseases that primarily affect low-income countries. The guaranteed demand provides an incentive for drug companies to engage in research, production and distribution of relevant vaccines.

International Finance Facility for Immunization (IFFIm): future aid flows are securitized in order to raise and front-load resources to finance GAVI immunization campaigns. The IFFIm issues bonds that are backed by donor commitments to pay specified amounts over a 20-year period.

Debt2Health: donor countries agree to reduce part of the repayment of a loan owed to them (from debtor countries that do not otherwise qualify for debt relief) in exchange for a commitment by the debtor to invest half of the debt relief in Global Fund programmes.

Debt-for-nature swaps: a portion of a country's foreign debt is forgiven in exchange for local investments in environmental conservation programmes.

Caribbean Catastrophe Risk Insurance Facility (CCRIF): a multi-country catastrophe insurance pool, created by the World Bank and funded by 16 participating countries. The Facility pools risks of "natural" disasters and provides a mechanism for assisting affected members in coping with the adverse impacts.

Product Red: a brand licensed to private companies, and designed to raise funds for the Global Fund. Each partner company creates a product with the Product Red logo in exchange for the opportunity to increase its own revenue through selling Product Red products. The company gives a percentage of the profit to the Global Fund.

Distribution mechanisms

Health programmes

The Global Fund to Fight AIDS, Tuberculosis and Malaria (Global Fund): a global health partnership that finances country-level programmes for the prevention, treatment and care of the three diseases.

GAVI Alliance: a global partnership on immunization which funds vaccines for children in the 70 poorest countries. Countries receive support for the introduction of new vaccines.

UNITAID: a drug purchasing facility that seeks to supply affordable medicines for HIV/AIDS, malaria and tuberculosis to low-income countries. UNITAID uses its purchasing power to lower market prices of drugs and to create sufficient demand for niche products with large public health benefits.

Climate change mitigation and adaptation programmes

Adaptation Fund: finances adaptation programmes in developing countries. Its primary financing source is a 2 per cent share of proceeds of CERs issued by the CDM.

Green Climate Fund (GCF): the main multilateral financing mechanism for disbursement of the additional resources for climate change action in developing countries pledged at the United Nations Climate Change Conference) held in Copenhagen in December 2009.

International Climate Initiative: finances climate protection projects in developing and transition countries and is funded by the proceeds from Germany's sales of tradable emission allowances under the European Union Emission Trading Scheme.

Norway's tax on CO_2 emission from aviation fuel: Norway contributes a portion of the proceeds of a tax on CO_2 emissions from aviation fuels to UNITAID.

Reducing Emissions from Deforestation and Forest Degradation plus Conservation (REDD+) initiative: acts as a coordinating mechanism for conventional bilateral and multilateral funding for developing countries to enable them to reduce their carbon emissions by slowing deforestation.

Special Energy and Climate Fund: starting in 2012, the Government of Germany will allocate *all* of the proceeds from auctioning emission allowances under the EU ETS to the Special Energy and Climate Fund, which finances national and international climate-related activities.

Source: UN/DESA.

criterion that flows *ideally* should be stable and predictable. The Leading Group considers the predictability of flows a criterion for determining whether a mechanism qualifies as IDF. However, the variability of flows is dependent on many factors, including unexpected political events and volatility in markets. In the approach taken here, the predictability of resource flows is seen as an indicator of the effectiveness of an IDF mechanism, rather than as a criterion for its inclusion.

The World Bank interpretation includes a host of mechanisms that do not meet all of the above criteria and are not listed in box I.2, including local currency bonds issued by multilaterals, International Bank for Reconstruction and Development (IBRD) and International Development Association (IDA) debt buy-downs,[5] and private and public Credit and Risk Guarantees (Girishankar, 2009). These mechanisms can have important developmental benefits. For example, multilateral issuance of local currency bonds can help develop local bond markets in developing countries. However, these bonds are likely to be issued in lieu of other World Bank bonds. Including local currency bonds in World Bank calculations of innovative sources inflates the size of IDF flows. In the *Survey* framework, these constitute improvements to traditional public financing rather than forms of IDF.

From sources to disbursements

Many mechanisms labelled innovative are actually not new sources of financing

Even the narrow list of initiatives presented in box I.2 covers a wide range of mechanisms. However, very few mechanisms listed are actually innovative *sources*, despite being called "innovative sources of development financing". Yet, mechanisms as diverse as IFFIm and the solidarity levy on airline tickets, which finances the GAVI Alliance, are often lumped together in discussions on innovative financing. Some mechanisms are designed to raise additional financing, but others, such as the IFFIm, restructure *existing* financing, and still others included in the discussion, such as the GAVI Alliance, are designed to disburse financing. IFFIm, for example, brings forward future ODA for present expenditure, which can be valuable without providing a net increase in funds. Concern about whether the resources mobilized through IFFIm are "additional" to existing aid does not diminish its relevance. This issue is completely different from the question whether a currency transaction tax (CTT), which raises financing from a new source, provides additional financing or substitutes ODA.

Innovations occur in intermediation and distribution mechanisms

The original proponents of IDF were focused on mechanisms that raised additional and stable sources of financing. The Organization for Economic Cooperation and Development (2011a) and the United Nations Development Programme (2012) categorize IDF according to the nature of the source. Categorizing by sources is useful for analysing the total size of potential financing available through IDF, including funds not necessarily earmarked for a particular sector. Since many mechanisms earmark funds for specific purposes, such as for health or climate protection programmes, it is possible to classify IDF by its uses. The 2011 report of the Secretary-General on innovative development financing categorizes mechanisms by uses, such as for the health or climate sectors (United Nations, General Assembly, 2011, annex).

---

5   These mechanisms raise the concessionality of IDA and IBRD loans. The donor blends an IBRD loan with a grant and uses the grant resources to buy down a part or the full amount of the principal and interest on the loan for countries experiencing debt distress. These mechanisms are not included in the 2012 Survey, as eligible countries were considered to be unable to repay their debt. The debt write-off therefore cannot be considered new financing.

As the goal of the *Survey* is to analyse the potential magnitude of new financing, the quality of that financing, and the effectiveness of the ultimate disbursements of IDF, understanding the full extent of the financing flows process, from raising resources to disbursements, is important. Figure I.3 gives an example of the flow of IDF financing from sources to uses in the health sector. It shows that there are innovations at each stage in the flow of that financing, but that each of these requires a different kind of analysis. Based on this mapping, IDF is divided into three categories: sources of financing, intermediate financing mechanisms, and disbursement mechanisms.

Sources of financing

There are two main categories under sources of financing: public sector revenues and revenues from global resources. Each category is associated with long-standing proposals—proposals that have been discussed for decades—although, with the exception of the airline levy, most of the proposed sources of international development cooperation have not yet been utilized.

Sources of financing include international taxes and SDR emissions

1. *Public sector revenues.* The main mechanisms in this category are taxes, including the financial transaction tax, carbon taxes, and the air-ticket solidarity levy. The establishment of these mechanisms should be coordinated by a group of countries (although nothing precludes an individual country from initiating such a policy, especially when there is the intention to demonstrate how this might be carried out). This category also includes revenues from auctions and sales of emission allowances in countries operating "cap and trade" emission reduction systems, as well the 2 per cent levy imposed on the payments for emission offset allowances that investors from developed countries buy from operators of emission-reducing investments in developing countries.

2. *Capturing global resources.* This category includes special drawing rights issued by IMF with a view to applying them towards development, which would allow the international community to capture some of the seigniorage otherwise earned by countries with reserve currencies. Also included are revenues from other potential sources of public goods, for example, the oceans beyond territorial limits, outer space and Antarctica, all of which are considered part of the "global commons".

Sources of financing in the health sector are listed on the left-hand side of figure I.3 including two sources of IDF: the solidarity levy on airline taxes and Norway's tax on CO_2 emissions from airline flights, a part of which is allocated to UNITAID. These two sources have been placed in the ODA box to reflect the fact that the revenues, even if raised from "innovative" sources, are currently channelled through ODA budgets and accounted for as such. IDF sources contribute only a small portion of existing financing (and if the chart had been drawn to scale would have been represented by a mere dot). Most existing resources channelled through innovative mechanisms are from ODA and, to a lesser extent, philanthropies (in particular the Bill and Melinda Gates Foundation).

As indicated in box I.2, the sources of innovative development finance that currently exist are limited to four mechanisms: the solidarity levy on airline tickets, Norway's airline emissions tax, the 2 per cent tax on payments for carbon emission reductions by developing countries, and auctioning of emission allowances under the European Union Emission Trading Scheme (EU ETS), with the total size of resources raised reaching about $0.5 billion annually, as of 2011.

Existing sources of innovative development finance have raised about $0.5 billion per year

Figure I.3
Innovative financing mechanisms in the health sector

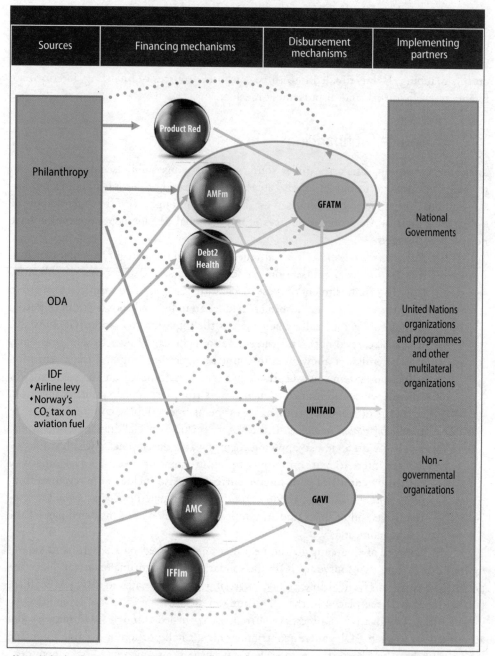

Note: Unbroken lines represent funding flows. Dotted lines trace funding flows directly from sources to disbursement mechanisms, bypassing financing mechanisms.
Abbreviations: AMFm: Affordable Medicines Facility - malaria (managed by the GFATM); AMC: Advance market commitment; IFFIm: International Finance Facility for Immunisation; GFATM: Global Fund to Fight AIDS, Tuberculosis and Malaria; GAVI: GAVI Alliance.

Intermediate financing mechanisms

Intermediate financing mechanisms restructure existing flows so as to better match financing with needs, reduce risk, or pool philanthropic funds or other private sector financing with official development cooperation. The mechanisms listed already exist, although they are not yet large in size (as discussed in chapter III). Most of these intermediate financing mechanisms do not raise "additional" public funds. Currently, all of them, except for Product Red, are primarily financed by traditional ODA (supplemented by voluntary contributions and philanthropy).

There are three types of intermediate mechanisms:

(a) *Mechanisms that front-load aid or convert debt.* In essence, these mechanisms convert future cash flow streams into upfront disbursements for developmental expenditures. Examples include Debt2Health and debt-for-nature swaps, as well as IFFIm;

(b) *Mechanisms for managing risk.* These can be guarantees or insurance. Advance market commitments (AMCs) are one example. Under advance market commitments, which are used mostly for disease prevention, ODA or funding from private philanthropic sources or both are utilized to guarantee a predetermined demand and price level for a technology-intensive good (such as vaccines) so as to provide an incentive for the product's development. International insurance pools, such as the Caribbean Catastrophe Risk Insurance Facility, also fit within this category;

(c) *Mechanisms that leverage citizen or private sector resources.* These are mechanisms that facilitate citizens' and corporate contributions to development or global public goods. Citizens' contributions are collected through these mechanisms and then channelled to disbursement funds. One well-known scheme is Product Red, under which companies are licensed to use the brand for specific products in return for donating a percentage of the profits from those products to the Global Fund to Fight AIDS, Tuberculosis and Malaria.

Intermediate financing mechanisms in the health sector are presented under "Financing mechanisms" in figure I.3. These include the Affordable Medicines Facility-malaria (AMFm), advance market commitments, IFFIm, Product Red and Debt2Health. As shown, these intermediate financing mechanisms are not designed to disburse financing directly to end-users. Instead, they channel financing to so-called vertical funds set up to allocate financing in the health sector. Those funds are presented under "Disbursement mechanisms" in figure I.3.

Distribution mechanisms

Distribution mechanisms are used to allocate resources and channel resources to end-users. Disbursement mechanisms in the health sector include the Global Fund to Fight AIDS, Tuberculosis and Malaria, UNITAID and the GAVI Alliance, as shown in figure I.3. These disbursement mechanisms finance activities in their priority areas by allocating resources to their implementing partners, ranging from national Governments and multilateral organizations to non-governmental organizations (see right-hand side of the figure).

> Most intermediate financing mechanisms do not raise additional funds

The disbursement mechanisms, as shown, collect financing either directly from ODA or through intermediary financing mechanisms. UNITAID is the only disbursement mechanism that obtains the bulk of its financing from innovative sources (IDF sources finance approximately 75 per cent of the budget of UNITAID, with traditional ODA and philanthropy financing the remainder). The other funds are financed primarily through traditional sources of financing, including ODA and philanthropic funds (as represented by the dashed lines in the figure I.3).

IDF effectiveness

Advocates of IDF have emphasized the need for stable and assured flows which are additional to existing financing (Griffith-Jones and Ocampo, 2011). In paragraph 5 of its resolution 65/146 of 20 December 2010, the General Assembly reiterated that such "mechanisms should be effective, should aim to mobilize resources that are stable and predictable, should supplement and not be a substitute for traditional sources of financing, should be disbursed in accordance with the priorities of developing countries and should not unduly burden such countries".

Stability and predictability, "additionality" and alignment with country priorities are three important characteristics of IDF. Each of these characteristics has a different relevance depending on the stages of the IDF flow, as depicted in figure I.3. For example, predictability needs to be measured both on an instrument-by-instrument basis and in terms of the overall flow of IDF from resource mobilization to disbursement. What matters most is the predictability of disbursements to the final recipient. This, in turn, is influenced by the predictability of the sources of financing in interaction with the intermediation mechanism. If sources of financing are not stable or predictable, it is still possible to design mechanisms to improve the stability of flows to the end-user. For instance, the intermediation mechanisms may help make flows of development financing more predictable by improving the time structure of disbursements. Alternatively, disbursement mechanisms can be structured to hold a portion of the funds in reserves, to be used in making disbursements during periods when new financing is limited.

"Additionality" is particularly relevant for new sources, but less so for intermediate financing or disbursement mechanisms. Most intermediate financing mechanisms, such as IFFIm which restructures existing ODA, by their very nature do not generate additional financing. However, as many of these mechanisms are earmarked for certain uses, such as global public goods in the health sector, they generally reallocate financing from other forms of ODA. The relevant question is not whether they raise new additional funds, but whether the new use of funds is more effective than the traditional uses would have been. The third requirement listed in the United Nations resolution, alignment with country priorities, is primarily relevant for disbursement mechanisms.

While, ultimately, an analysis of the effectiveness of individual mechanisms can be conducted only on a case-by-case basis, there are a number of additional assessment criteria that can be used to determine the potential and effectiveness of IDF flows at each stage of intermediation, as identified above. This section presents assessment indicators for the mechanisms at each of the stages: sources of financing, intermediate mechanisms of financing, and allocation of resources.

Sources of financing

There are several principles of effective taxation which can inform the analysis of most sources of financing.[6] One principle determines that taxation is effective if it raises substantial, assured and predictable flows of finance at low administrative cost. For example, to date, revenues from the airline ticket levy earmarked for the GAVI Alliance have tended to be relatively stable. Nonetheless, most resources collected by these mechanisms are still at risk of exhibiting forms of variability. The size of a financial transaction tax on domestic transactions will vary based on the extent of liquidity in a country, while a tax on currency transactions will vary by the size of global liquidity. The revenue obtained from a tax on certified emission reductions (CERs), or carbon credits, depends on the volume of Clean Development Mechanisms projects, which experience so far has shown to be highly variable.

Related measures of effectiveness include technical and political feasibility, and administrative simplicity. Since most of the taxes discussed would be collected on a national level, in most cases administration would be within the purview of domestic public sectors. However, to the extent that the "global reserves", as exploited, for example, through seabed mining, are to be taxed, funds would likely need to be collected by an international authority, which raises questions of both administrative and political feasibility. More broadly, as discussed above, there is political resistance to implementing many of these measures. The question then becomes to what extent this political resistance makes implementation of the mechanisms designed to finance global solidarity needs unlikely. As discussed in chapter II, there is strong reason to presume that if large revenues are collected, as from a carbon tax, they would mainly be used to meet domestic needs or reduce other taxes. Thus, the political feasibility of mobilizing resources for development from a proposed source is an important indicator.

In addition, taxes should be efficient. Standard economic analysis suggests that many forms of taxation create "distortions" to market operations and alter incentives, which may have negative effects on economic activity by, for instance, discouraging private savings or changing consumption or production patterns, thus possibly reducing efficiency.[7] However, there are forms of taxation whose aim is precisely to change behaviour, such as "sin taxes" and taxes on carbon emissions. In this case, tax policy has a corrective function and seeks to earn a "double dividend" by raising resources while correcting a negative externality, such as greenhouse gas emissions which undermine climate stability. Taxing goods that harm the environment tends to have a positive effect by encouraging consumers to buy goods that cause less damage to the environment (Atkinson, 2005). Thus, the question here is not whether taxes distort behaviour, but how that behaviour is impacted and whether the tax should be designed to encourage or minimize changes in behaviour.

Taxes should also be perceived as "fair", which is generally interpreted to mean that they impose higher tax burdens on the wealthy than on the poor. Fairness explores

Effective taxation should raise substantial, assured and predictable flows of finance at low administrative cost

Tax policy can seek to earn a "double dividend" by raising resources while correcting a negative externality

---

6   These are based on principles of taxation used in public finance, adjusted to the global level, as well as to specific issues that pertain to IDF. Principles of taxation include economic efficiency, fairness, administrative simplicity, transparency and flexibility (Stiglitz, 2000).

7   Economic efficiency arguments related to taxes generally assume a world with perfect competition and perfectly functioning markets. The global economy, on the other hand, is characterized by imperfect markets, externalities and other market failures. This being the case, taxes can potentially be used to help correct some of these failures, but it should be remembered that very well functioning markets may not necessarily achieve desirable public policy priorities.

the extent to which mechanisms are progressive or regressive, and whether they "unduly burden developing countries". For example, a financial transaction tax is likely to be a progressive tax since the rich make greater use of financial services than the poor. On the other hand, uniform carbon taxes can be seen as penalizing developing countries, since poorer countries would be taxed at several times the rate of developed countries, when measured as a proportion of their GDP (United Nations, 2011a). This is one reason why the Kyoto Protocol to the United Nations Framework Convention on Climate Change[8] and the Convention[9] itself only mandate that higher-income countries make specific targeted reductions.

Based on these measures, the *Survey* asks the following questions related to sources of financing: (a) what is the potential size of the resources?; (b) how stable and predictable is the financing?; (c) what are the implications of the mechanisms for economic efficiency?; (d) what are the implications for fairness and equity?; and (e) how feasible are the mechanisms, in administrative, technical, and political terms?

Identifying whether or not new funding is "additional" to existing ODA is difficult

A final question is whether IDF funds are additional to existing ODA. However, it is often difficult to determine whether IDF is in fact adding to existing ODA. A recent survey by the United Nations Development Programme (UNDP) (2012) found that, in the case of Benin, increasing flows of health-related IDF were accompanied by declining traditional ODA for the health sector; even though the two appear to be related, it is still difficult to ascertain whether the drop in ODA was in fact a response to the increase in IDF. The issue of how to measure additionality has also arisen in climate change negotiations. The Cancun Agreements[10] mandate that climate funds be "new and additional" to existing development aid. However, the parties to the United Nations Framework Convention on Climate Change have not been able to agree on a clear definition of additionality. As pointed out by Dervis and Milsom (2011), without a baseline against which to measure new commitments, it is impossible to determine additionality. They suggest that climate financing provided as ODA be counted as such only after countries have met their 0.7 per cent target. Although most donor countries are not close to fulfilling this target, the point is that the only way to ascertain whether mechanisms are indeed raising new sources of funds is to change accounting procedures. Similarly, to be able to adequately measure the additionality of IDF flows would require an agreement by countries regarding which mechanisms should be included in IDF accounting.

Innovative financial intermediation mechanisms

The effectiveness of intermediate financing mechanisms can be evaluated by comparing benefits with costs and potential risks…

Many innovations in intermediate financing mechanisms are based on innovations in financial markets. Hence, analysis of these mechanisms incorporates tools used in corporate finance, focused on the benefits of implementation as compared with the costs and potential risks, as well as public finance questions.

For example, IFFIm securitizes aid flows by issuing bonds backed by long-term pledges from donor countries with the objective of generating upfront financing. The main costs of securitization are the fees and the interest paid on the securitized bonds, which need to be weighed against the benefits of upfront financing, adjusted for risk. Note that securitizations, such as IFFIm, do not promise stable financing over time. They focus

---

8   United Nations, *Treaty Series*, vol. 2303, No. 30822.

9   Ibid., vol. 1771, No. 30822.

10   FCCC/CP/2010/7/Add.1, decision 1/CP.16.

on donor-Government approval of future earmarking of ODA outlays for principal and interest payments on bonds in exchange for a larger lump sum for immediate use upfront. Thus, there is a risk that issuing new bonds when additional financing beyond the initial upfront payment is needed will be difficult. This is especially true if market demand for the debt of donors is weak, as is the case today for some European sovereigns (see chap. III).

From a public finance perspective, additional questions relate to the potential size of these mechanisms and/or under what circumstances they would be replicable. The purpose of targeted funds is not necessarily to achieve a specific size, but rather to meet stated goals, such as combating a particular disease. The question is whether the mechanisms are replicable in other areas of policy concern and, if so, in what contexts. The main aim of programmes such as IFFIm, for instance, is to front-load resources. For certain vaccination programmes to be effective in serving public-health goals, such as containing the spread of contagious diseases, it is important that a certain level of coverage be quickly reached. Such front-loading of resources is also relevant for large investment projects characterized by indivisibilities, such as infrastructure or renewable energy investments. Aid securitization can bring such benefits which could be weighed against those of other financing options, as discussed in chapter III.

...as well as by determining whether a mechanism is scalable or replicable in other areas of development

Based on this analysis, the pertinent questions for analysis of these mechanisms are: (a) have the programmes met their objectives?; (b) what are the costs?; (c) what are the risks? (d) are the mechanisms scalable or replicable?; and (e) under what circumstances are they replicable?

Disbursement mechanisms

Principles of aid effectiveness are meaningful in assessing disbursement mechanisms related to IDF.[11] As discussed above, one of the main goals of IDF is to deliver stable and predictable financing. An important question is whether the stability of financial flows from a source translates into the stability of flows to recipients.

Disbursement mechanisms should be assessed against principles of aid effectiveness

A second relevant criterion is whether funds are adequately used to meet stated goals. This criterion is consistent with one principle of the Paris Declaration on Aid Effectiveness, which commits signatories to ensuring results-based aid delivery, based on "measurable outputs". Measurable outputs are important from the donors' perspective, since it tends to be easier to secure parliamentary approval in donor countries for programmes that have a clear results focus. Compliance with this principle should be pursued with some caution, however. There are several challenges associated with using measurable indicators, which need to be addressed when evaluating the effectiveness of IDF mechanisms. First, too strong an insistence on demonstrating visible results may cause limitations in the monitoring capacity of public management systems in recipient countries to be overlooked. Second, measurable short-term indicators are not necessarily indicative of development effectiveness over the medium term. Third, IDF may finance only a small portion of a programme, which makes it difficult to attribute results directly to IDF mechanisms.

The Paris Declaration also committed donors to working towards greater coordination and harmonization across programmes in order to address the issues of increased

---

11   The Paris Declaration on Aid Effectiveness committed both donors and aid recipients to adhering to five principles: (a) domestic ownership; (b) alignment behind national development strategies; (c) donor harmonization; (d) a results orientation, and (e) mutual accountability.

fragmentation of aid programmes and the exponential rise in the number of aid projects since the 1990s, which have resulted in increased bureaucratic and transactions costs in developing countries and inefficiencies in aid delivery (Knack and Rahman, 2004). As discussed in chapter IV, many IDF disbursements are currently administered through vertical funds that finance particular sectors, such as health or the environment, or narrowly defined elements within those sectors, such as AIDS, tuberculosis and malaria. Such vertical funds are, by nature, fragmented within the context of the rest of the aid architecture. Thus, the question to be addressed is how much additional pressure IDF mechanisms are putting on aid systems and whether the vertical funds through which they operate are exacerbating existing problems.

Country ownership is a core principle underpinning aid effectiveness. According to this principle, developing countries should set their own strategies for poverty reduction and commit to improving their institutions and tackling corruption, while donors should align aid programmes with developing-country national development strategies. Disbursement mechanisms, such as vertical funds, face the challenge of aligning their aid with national priorities, which is compounded by the "double conditionality" of earmarked funding and performance-related disbursement. However, as discussed in chapter IV, earmarking may also have certain benefits, such as facilitating aid budget approval by donor-country parliaments as well as additional fundraising. Earmarking may also be required to safeguard delivery of global public goods, such as control of contagious diseases. Thus, the related challenge is how to address international collective action goals, including those that necessarily encompass policies across countries, while still emphasizing individual-country ownership in the allocation process.

These challenges are compounded by the fact that donor countries and the institutions they control have various mechanisms for coordinating their activities, including country programming by the major institutions, and donor policy coordination and monitoring through the Development Assistance Committee (DAC) of the Organization for Economic Cooperation and Development. Coordination at the global policy level, which entails giving voice to recipient Governments and other stakeholders, is carried out at the United Nations, in particular in the Development Cooperation Forum. The coordination structure in programmes to advance international public goods is developed in specialized forums, on health and the environment, for example, and, on the broad policy level, at the United Nations. This raises questions regarding the adequacy of the governance structures of disbursement mechanisms. Such questions are even more critical when scaling up IDF and introducing new sources of financing, such as internationally coordinated tax revenue mobilized to finance global public goods and for defined development purposes.

Based on these principles, IDF disbursement mechanisms can be analysed in the context of the following questions: (a) how well does the mechanism meet its stated goals?; (b) how predictable and stable are disbursements for the end-user?; (c) is the mechanism contributing to further fragmentation of the aid architecture?; (d) how does the mechanism impact on local ownership and alignment of resource allocation with national development priorities?; and (e) is the governance structure of the mechanism adequate and supportive of achieving stated objectives?

IDF within the broader context of development finance

The potential of IDF

As discussed in chapter II, financial transaction taxes, including taxes on currency transactions, carbon taxes and SDRs for development purposes can technically be implemented so as to raise large amounts of resources for global cooperation. The total volume of financing collected by FTTs would depend on the size and breadth of the taxes, but estimates are of about $40 billion for a half basis point (0.005 per cent) CTT, whereas the proposed financial transaction taxes on domestic transactions in the European Union is expected to raise €55 billion.

At present, there is no internationally collected carbon tax. Many European countries have long-standing taxes on the consumption of fossil-fuel products, gasoline in particular. Australia introduced a carbon tax recently. A few countries are using part of the revenue to finance international climate and other environmental funds, but revenues mainly accrue to general Government revenue and only a fraction at best goes to domestic environmental programmes. As discussed in chapter II, a tax of $25 per ton of CO_2 emissions by developed countries could yield $250 billion annually, some of which could be used internationally.

Proposals for capturing global resources have significant potential. For example, there are proposals for SDR allocations that would generate about $100 billion or more per year, while some proposals project raising significantly higher levels of financing. However, as discussed in chapter II, there are political obstacles to their implementation.

In sum, these measures potentially account for a significant amount of financing. Nonetheless, the figures are considerably lower than some of the numbers published in the media, which have referred to potential revenues from an FTT of over $1 trillion per year (Chicago Political Economy Group, 2010)[12]—an amount that is a multiple of existing ODA. Understandably, advocates across sectors, from climate financing to education and agriculture, have sought to tap these mechanisms in order to meet their own priorities.

Although the potential size of financing raised through new sources could be substantial, it is likely to be too low to meet all development and climate change demands, given political realities. It is important for advocates to make a realistic assessment of the potential of mechanisms, and to incorporate that assessment into the broader discussion of development financing. IDF alone will not be able to meet broad-based needs. Development practitioners need to look to IDF in conjunction with other financing sources.

It is unlikely that innovative sources of financing will generate sufficient resources to meet all financing needs for development and global public goods provisioning

Strengthening domestic resources will also be crucial

IDF and other sources of development finance

Even though IDF has significant potential and can become increasingly important in financing global public goods, as discussed in chapter V, recipient countries should always weigh the potential of IDF against strengthening domestic resource mobilization and other forms of financing. In particular, as a form of international capital flow, significant IDF inflows into a country may lead to currency appreciation and widening current-account deficits in the recipient country, which could increase the risk of a financial crisis (Erten and Ocampo, 2012). Policymakers sometimes try to constrain exchange-rate appreciation

---

12 The studies in question assumed relatively large tax rates, which are unlikely to be politically feasible.

by buying foreign-exchange inflows (and building up reserves), while intervening in the market to manage the impact of the inflows on the money supply. However, the build-up in international reserves implies that at least a portion of the funds are not being invested in development. Further, managing the money supply through sterilization generally involves issuing government bonds to absorb excess liquidity, which raises domestic interest rates and could lead to an increase of the domestic public debt burden without a corresponding increase in domestic investment. Domestic resource mobilization, not subject to the risks associated with foreign inflows, is generally perceived to be a superior form of financing.

Multilateral development banks could contribute by lending in local currencies

In many developing countries, however, local capital markets have a short-term bias, so that countries might have difficulty financing long-term needs associated with necessary investments in sustainable development. Countries can try to lengthen domestic debt markets and multilateral development banks could help them to do this by, for example, providing loans in local currencies (Erten and Ocampo, 2012).

International tax cooperation could strengthen domestic resource mobilization by reducing tax evasion

Domestic resource mobilization through increased tax efficiency and other policies devised to increase tax receipts are an important means of public financing. International tax cooperation may support such efforts by reducing tax evasion. According to some studies, such cooperation could yield some $200 billion–$250 billion per year in additional fiscal resources for developing countries. This could be facilitated by an international tax commission such as that proposed in 2001 by the High-level Panel on Financing for Development (United Nations, General Assembly, 2001), built on existing institutions, without the need for a large organizational infrastructure.

Nonetheless, there is still an important role for international public financing in reducing poverty and disease, promoting development, and financing global public goods.

What lies ahead

The 2012 *World Economic and Social Survey* presents a flow-of-funds framework for understanding the role of innovative finance in global public finance. The structure of the 2012 *Survey* follows this mapping, with each chapter analysing another element in the flow of IDF, from the raising of resources to disbursements.

Chapter II examines proposals on sources of financing, including public sector revenues and proceeds from capturing global resources. It raises the question how much financing could be available and finds that currency transaction taxes and carbon taxes could technically raise substantial resources, although there are political hurdles that need to be overcome before implementation and, again, before any funds are allocated to international cooperation. SDRs could also be used to raise substantial amounts of development financing.

Chapter III discusses intermediate financing mechanisms, most of which already exist, and asks whether these can be scaled up or replicated in other areas. It finds that existing sizes are small and that there are difficulties in terms of replication. Nonetheless, several of the mechanisms do have potential in other areas, especially that of clean energy.

Chapter IV then looks at disbursement mechanisms. These mechanisms are primarily vertical funds for financing health- and climate-related global public goods. The chapter examines the challenges associated with allocating resources through earmarked funds while trying to maintain country ownership and adhere to principles of aid effectiveness. It also examines the global governance implications of scaling up financing for global public goods.

Chapter V looks at IDF from the perspective of recipients, assessing how much IDF countries have received, the benefits it has brought and the tensions to which it can give rise, focusing mainly on the health sector, where IDF has so far been concentrated.

Chapter II
Proposed sources of innovative international financing

Summary

♦ Half a century of calls for more substantial, assured and predictable resource transfers for development have largely gone unanswered. Recently, certain proposals are back in the agenda, a development triggered in part by needs to safeguard certain international public goods, such as financial stability and protection of the climate.

♦ In one such proposal, the International Monetary Fund (IMF) would issue more international liquidity in the form of special drawing rights (SDRs). Proposed amounts of regular SDR allocations are in the order of $150 billion to $300 billion annually. The "seigniorage" of such issuance, which now accrues to international reserve currency countries, could be skewed towards developing countries. Additional proposals in this category would convert over $100 billion per year of "idle" SDRs of reserve-rich countries into longer-term development finance.

♦ Internationally agreed taxes to discourage environment-damaging behaviour have been proposed, such as an additional tax of $25 per ton of carbon dioxide emissions to be paid in developed countries, which could raise $250 billion annually by 2020, while reducing carbon emissions. Channelling the funds to international cooperation would require a separate political agreement.

♦ Today's technology for international payments increases the feasibility of internationally coordinated taxes on financial and currency transactions. Many countries impose domestic financial transaction taxes and the European Union is considering a euro-wide tax. Revenue-raising capacity depends on which financial services are taxed and at what rates and by how many countries. A small currency transaction tax could collect up to $40 billion annually from major markets. Also, in this case, allocation of revenues to development would require a separate political agreement.

Introduction

The standard way in which States undertake international financial cooperation is through the Government's proposal and the legislature's approval of an allocation of funds for a particular purpose. The initiative may begin with one Government or as an initiative jointly agreed by several or all Governments acting together. While the Government commits itself to making the outlay, the actual outlay is contingent on legislative approval. This means that whether the outlay in question is a recurrent appropriation for a bilateral or multilateral initiative or a one-time outlay aimed at increasing the capital of an international financial institution, the process of ensuring national approval and disbursement introduces a measure of uncertainty, possibly entailing either a delay or the approval of an amount of funding different from that committed.

Policy thinkers have thus long asked, especially when considering the flow of resources for official development assistance (ODA), whether Governments might agree instead to a process resulting in more automatic and more assured payments. Could they, say, commit to payments for several years or set up a mechanism that would mobilize funds in a predictable manner and then earmark them for ODA financing or other international cooperation imperatives? The question was posed succinctly in 1980 by the Independent Commission on International Development Issues called the Brandt Commission after its chair Willy Brandt, the former Chancellor of the former Federal Republic of Germany, which called for: "automatic mechanisms, which can work without repeated interventions by governments". Noting that "(a)t present, the amount of aid depends on the uncertain political will of the countries giving it", the Commission asserted that "(w)ith more assured forms and methods, developing countries could plan on a more predictable basis, making aid more effective"; and that therefore "the donor governments should welcome the possibility of avoiding annual appropriations for a continuing cause" (Independent Commission on International Development Issues, 1980, p. 244).

As it turns out, the Brandt Commission model has rarely been adopted and when it was adopted, the model had limited scope, as illustrated in the case of the air passenger ticket levy (see below). National Governments consider it is their sovereign responsibility to determine both how to raise the revenues that finance their outlays (usually through domestic tax policy) and to what specific uses the allocated funds should be put. Governments channel most of their international cooperation outlays into the budget bucket known as "discretionary spending", whose details they usually legislate and present on an annual basis.

Nevertheless, the appeal of potential mechanisms for ensuring more automatic and assured flows of funds for international cooperation, especially if they can mobilize substantial amounts of resources, has led to a multiplicity of proposals on how to establish such mechanisms. These proposals generally encompass three broad categories of revenue sources: (a) proceeds captured from the global use of global resources; (b) internationally concerted taxes to be tapped without materially affecting (or "distorting") the behaviour of private actors; and (c) internationally concerted taxes levied for the purpose of capturing a "double dividend", that is, alteration in the particular behaviours of private actors and collection of revenues (Atkinson, 2005). Examples from the first category include new issuances of special drawing rights (SDRs) by the International Monetary Fund (IMF) and capturing proceeds from the exploitation of global commons (such as seabed mining in international waters). Examples from the second include levies on airline tickets or currency transaction taxes that are small enough not to significantly affect airline traffic or currency trading, but large enough to yield a meaningful amount of revenue. Examples from the third category include taxes on carbon dioxide (CO_2) emissions designed to slow global warming and taxes on short-term financial inflows to a country aimed at discouraging the entry of speculative "hot" money which exacerbates financial volatility.

While some of these proposals can be adopted unilaterally, all three types have also been suggested for adoption through international collaboration, but not necessarily international consensus. It was in this context that, as noted in chapter I, several like-minded nations agreed to experiment with various revenue-raising proposals by forming the Leading Group on Innovative Financing for Development. Indeed, the experimentation fostered by the Group may play a role in forging global consensus on new methods

Calls for more assured flows of development assistance have remained largely unanswered

A multiplicity of proposals for ensuring more assured flows exist...

...and several nations have agreed to experiment with proposals in the Leading Group on Innovative Financing for Development

of mobilizing substantial, assured and predictable public resource flows for development. The present *Survey* argues that efforts must be focused on overcoming the obstacles to mobilization of adequate resources for international cooperation for development and that revenues derived from the innovative mechanisms discussed in the present chapter can usefully complement the flows of the still-essential ODA provided through the commitment of the international community. Table II.1 provides an overview of the proposals discussed in this chapter.

Table II.1

Summary of proposed major sources of innovative international financing

Source	Description	Potential resource mobilization	Economic efficiency		Fairness	Feasibility
			Positive elements	Negative elements		
Proposals for capturing global resources for global use						
IMF issuance of special drawing rights (SDRs)	Regular annual allocations in favour of developing countries	Global issuance of SDR 150 billion-SDR 250 billion per year for three years could generate about $160 billion-$270 billion a year for developing countries if their allocation share was raised to two-thirds	Less need for reserve accumulation by individual countries; frees resources for domestic spending	Skewing allocations to developing countries requires IMF reform and may be resisted by major reserve-currency countries	Transfers seigniorage from reserve-currency countries to international community	Depends on political willingness to overcome obstacles such as required amendment of IMF Articles of Agreement
	Use SDRs of reserve-rich countries for investment in development	Proposals are in the order of $100 billion per year	Low-cost form of development finance	Need to carefully structure SDR use to protect its reserve status	Puts excess SDR holdings to internationally desired and supported use	Depends on political willingness to leverage SDRs for bond issuance and technical design so as to preserve status of SDRs as reserves
Ownership of global commons	Charge royalties for natural resource extraction beyond 100-mile exclusive economic zones	Undefined	Users of global commons should pay royalties in same way as users of national property	Will require enforcement regime	Royalties for use of global commons would be applied to global priorities	Requires agreement on regimes for managing global commons, such as the Seabed Authority
Proposals for internationally agreed taxes						
Carbon taxes	Tax on use of fossil fuels (and other emission sources) in accordance with contribution to CO_2 emissions	Depends on levy; a tax of $25 per ton of CO_2 emissions by developed countries could yield $250 billion annually, some of which could be used internationally	Double dividend: disincentive to greenhouse gas emissions and revenue raising	Tax may lead to higher production costs and affect income and employment growth	"Polluter pays" principle applies, but negative income effects need differential compensation so that low-income groups do not pay disproportionally. Tax to apply in developed countries	Technically feasible, as already implemented in some countries. Separate decisions needed to allocate a portion of tax revenues for development

(cont'd)

Table II.1 (cont'd)

Source	Description	Potential resource mobilization	Economic efficiency		Fairness	Feasibility
			Positive elements	Negative elements		
Cap and trade with the Clean Development Mechanism (CDM)	Emissions permits are traded among firms to ensure that they stay below a Government-defined cap of emission rights. Initial auction of permits yields revenue. Option to purchase "carbon offsets" under CDM	Depends on number of countries participating and initial price of emissions credits	Disincentive to greenhouse gas emissions and some revenue raising; CDM promotes carbon-efficient investment in developing countries	Trading volumes and prices of emission rights in existing systems have proved volatile, discouraging CDM investments	Same as above	Technically feasible, as already implemented in Europe. Allocating revenues from initial emission auctions for development requires separate decision. Need for proper oversight of emission trading market and CDM
"Billionaire's" tax	Tax of 1 per cent on individual wealth holdings of $1 billion or more	Estimated $40 billion-$50 billion per year (2012)	Non-distorting tax for international solidarity	Political resistance. Could provide incentive to tax evasion	A small transfer from the richest of the rich (about 1,000 people) for the benefit of humankind	No worked-out technical proposal exists. Unclear whether international agreement on collection of the tax and use of revenue is feasible
Air passenger levy	Small tax levied on airline tickets, proceeds earmarked for UNITAID	Imposed by nine countries thus far, yielding about $1 billion for UNITAID	Continuing and automatic source of funds, which can be earmarked for agreed purposes	Revenue fluctuates with air travel volume; tourism-dependent countries fear negative impact	Levy not really felt by air travellers while constituting source of funding for international solidarity purposes	Technically feasible, as already implemented. Politically attractive as a small tax earmarked for socially important use
Currency transaction tax (CTT)	Tiny tax on major currency foreign-exchange transactions, collectable through centralized clearing house (CLS Bank)	Could generate about $40 billion per year from major currency markets (for small tax rate of 0.005 per cent)	Double dividend: even tiny tax is likely to discourage potentially disruptive high-frequency currency trade, while generating additional public revenue	Revenues would possibly be volatile	Progressive tax, as most transactions on behalf of corporations and wealthy customers. Revenue would be allocated for international priorities	Requires participation of major trading centres of covered currencies; separate political agreement needed on using funds for development or global public goods
Financial transaction tax (FTT)	Tax on financial transactions, such as equity trades, bonds and derivatives	Depends on the size and coverage of the tax and the number of participating countries. The proposed European Union financial transaction tax is expected to raise up to €55 billion per year	Tax would discourage high-frequency trading; minimal distortions of the rest of financial sector at low rate for tax set	Revenues would be pro-cyclical and possibly volatile	Progressive tax (as rich make more use of financial services). Financial sector generally enjoys relatively low tax burden. Some of the revenue would be allocated for international priorities	Many countries already impose FTT. Allocation of (part of) revenues for international development would require separate agreement

Source: UN/DESA.

Capturing global resources for global use

Most of the proposals considered in this chapter involve taxation of the nationals of countries. Even if a number of Governments came together and agreed to impose a particular tax for a particular purpose, it is the individual cooperating Governments themselves that would most likely impose the tax, collect the funds and allocate them for the agreed purpose. While this approach can meet the need for automaticity and assured allocation, even with the funds passed through the Government, it does lead to the question whether resources of true global character—and thus not originating in national taxes or other national public sector revenues—could be tapped for international cooperation. Discussed below are two potential sources of such resources.

Resources of a global character can be tapped for international cooperation

Special drawing rights and development

Perhaps the earliest proposal for mobilizing international funds for development that did not "belong" to any set of taxpayers was the so-called SDR link, referring to the special drawing right, a reserve asset issued by IMF. The SDR was created in 1969 to help assure an adequate and internationally managed global supply of international liquidity. After a good start, it lay virtually fallow until the recent global financial crisis, when it attracted the attention of the Group of Twenty (G20), which in 2009 endorsed a large issue of SDRs. This meant that approval had finally been won for an SDR issue that was supposed to have been enacted in 1997 but which had been blocked by the United States Congress. The proposed development link had been the subject of multilateral discussion in the early 1970s, but was never agreed upon.

Special drawing rights were created to assure an adequate supply of international liquidity

SDR as a reserve asset

After the Second World War, the principal international reserves were gold, which was in limited supply and whose use in settling currency imbalances between central banks was inconvenient, and the United States dollar, which was universally accepted as a means of payment. Under the Bretton Woods system, the dollar was linked to gold at the fixed price of $35 per ounce and the exchange rates of other countries were fixed to the dollar (albeit adjustably). While central banks could settle international payments imbalances between countries in gold or any acceptable currency, the dollar served as the main official reserve currency. This meant that the United States gained—and largely still gains—the "seigniorage" benefit of providing the world's international currency.[1] However, the supply of dollars put into international circulation depended on the United States balance of payments. The world could thus go through periods of "dollar shortage" and periods of "dollar glut". During the latter, some Governments converted some of their growing dollar reserve holdings into gold, reducing the United States stock of gold and ultimately forcing the United States in 1971 to break the gold link, which in turn, after some years of failed negotiations, led to the end of the fixed exchange-rate system.

---

1   That is to say, because the global demand to hold dollar balances grows over time with the growth of the world economy and world trade, the United States is able to sustain a balance-of-payments deficit. Non-reserve currency countries ultimately have to repay their borrowings (a few other countries have reserve currencies, but none near the scale of the dollar).

So far, special drawing rights have played only a minor role as international liquidity

The original intention was that countries should increasingly substitute SDRs for dollars as an international reserve asset and gradually make the SDR the principal reserve asset of the international monetary system. That, of course, did not happen. After the first allocation of 9 billion SDRs in 1970–1972, which represented about 8 per cent of non-gold reserves in the final allocation year, a second allocation of 12 billion SDRs was made in 1979–1981, reaching about 6 per cent of reserves in 1981 (Boughton, 2001, p. 929). None were issued thereafter until 2009. A decision had been reached in 1997 to make a special allocation that would have doubled overall holdings and bring countries that had not been IMF members when the earlier allocations were made up to par with other members, but it was not implemented until 2009, as noted above. As a result of no issuance for almost 30 years while foreign-exchange reserves grew appreciably, the SDR became an insignificant reserve asset. In a way, this was not surprising, as the criterion for allocating new SDRs has been a finding by the Fund that there is a "global long-term need to supplement existing reserve assets" so as to "avoid economic stagnation and deflation as well as excess demand and inflation in the world" (IMF, 2011, Article XVIII, Section 1(a)).[2] As a result, the SDR has played a minor role as a reserve asset for settling obligations between central banks or with IMF and a limited number of other official institutions. The virtual rediscovery of the SDR in 2009 as part of the G20 response to the global financial crisis led to agreement to issue 161 billion SDRs (equivalent to $250 billion) and finally approve the pending 1997 allocation of 21.5 billion SDRs ($33 billion). The agreement raised the stock of SDRs to about 4 per cent of non-gold reserves.

The question now is whether the 2009 SDR allocation was a one-time event or whether SDRs will be issued more regularly. The original aim in creating an international reserve currency remains worthwhile and should be pursued, even though the attraction of the SDR as a monetary asset has been limited by design. In particular, central banks are not able to use the SDR directly in foreign exchange market interventions because there are no private holders of SDRs. But even if the SDR never becomes a private asset, it retains value as a usable reserve asset for settling inter-central bank claims as long as Governments can freely swap SDRs for hard currencies and this is guaranteed by IMF rules.[3] Moreover, experience shows that developing and transition economy countries have used their SDR allocations more intensively than developed countries for balance-of-payments financing, both historically (Erten and Ocampo, 2012, pp. 10–11) and during the current crisis (United States Treasury, 2010).

Special drawing rights are attractive reserve assets for developing countries

Indeed, the SDRs are attractive reserve assets for developing countries, as there are no conditions of international organizations attached to their use (Aryeetey, 2005, pp. 107–108). As a means of increasing their reserves, additional SDR allocations will be a significantly better alternative for these countries than borrowing the funds on international markets (available only to those countries enjoying such access) or running a balance-of-payments surplus and using the proceeds to buy reserve assets, particularly United States Treasury bonds (a point emphasized 25 years ago, for example, by Sengupta (1987)).

---

2   It is apparent that the criteria for SDR allocations ensured that the SDR would be the *residual* official reserve asset, preventing it from ever becoming the *principal* reserve asset.

3   As the allocations of SDRs have increased, IMF members have agreed to increase the size of their voluntary arrangements to accept SDRs in transactions with other members (and more countries have entered into such voluntary arrangements). In the event that members wish to sell more SDRs than agreed under the voluntary arrangements, IMF can activate a "designation mechanism", wherein members in strong external positions are required to buy SDRs from countries in weak external positions, paying in freely usable currencies, although thus far, there has not been a need to invoke the designation mechanism. Based on this practice, the size of the "market" for SDRs should grow pari passu with increased SDR allocations.

Not only could IMF create SDRs on a regular basis, as originally intended, but the SDR allocations could be skewed towards developing countries and economies in transition instead of according to IMF quota shares. For example, a revised allocation formula could take account of the fact that developing and transition economies tend to have a larger demand for reserves relative to gross domestic product (GDP) than countries with developed economies (Erten and Ocampo, 2012, p. 6). Admittedly, changing the SDR allocation formula would constitute a significant political undertaking, as it will require an amendment to the IMF Articles of Agreement. Amending the Articles, like decisions for a general SDR allocation under existing rules, requires an 85 per cent approval of member votes, giving the United States an effective veto. Indeed, United States support of regular SDR allocations would require that it exhibit a measure of global solidarity, as the seigniorage embodied in the new SDRs would be effected largely at the expense of a seigniorage no longer accruing to the United States. Nevertheless, such a change could significantly strengthen the international monetary system, which is an imperative that all IMF member countries support.[4]

In this context, it is also useful to recall the proposal of the Commission of Experts appointed by the President of the General Assembly in 2008 (Stiglitz Commission) to replace the global reserve system based mainly on the dollar with one based on an international currency, which could be the SDR. The Commission proposed annual allocations of from $150 billion to $300 billion of the international currency so as to render it unnecessary for countries to impart a deflationary bias in the growth of global demand by running balance-of-payments surpluses in order to mobilize the foreign exchange to add to official reserves (United Nations, 2009a, chap. 5). More recently, a prominent group of economists from the United States, China and other countries proposed that IMF establish a working group to study possible reforms of the SDR, including revising of the allocation formula and making it possible for members with excess SDRs to "deposit" them in the general resources account of the Fund, where they could be used to boost IMF lending to countries in need; in the meantime and as an interim measure, they proposed that the Fund allocate SDR 150 billion–250 billion (about $240 billion–$400 billion) annually for three years (Stiglitz and others, 2011). Based on the approved but not yet implemented revision of country shares in IMF quotas, this implies an increase of developing and emerging economy SDRs worth $101 billion–$169 billion. If the allocation instead favoured the countries, say, raising their share from 42 to 67 per cent, they would receive about $160 billion–$270 billion worth of SDRs.

SDR as financing for development

The SDR has no direct link to development finance, although the fact that an SDR allocation serves to create real purchasing power for the holder receiving the allocation has led numerous authors to ask whether that purchasing power could be captured for development or the financing of global public goods. In fact, a decade before SDRs came into existence, there was a proposed SDR link to development. In 1958, Maxwell Stamp proposed that IMF create special certificates—not cash, but essentially loans of indefinite maturity—and allocate them to developing countries, which would be free to use the certificates to pay for imports of goods and services. The commercial banks in the developed countries receiving the payments would pass them on to their central bank in exchange for national currency. The developed-country monetary authorities would thus end up holding the certificates and would consider them, as constituting claims against IMF, part of their official reserves (based on Machlup, 1964, pp. 326–329).

Additional SDR allocations could be skewed towards developing countries with larger reserve requirements

Proposals abound to capture the purchasing power of SDRs for development finance…

---

4   A view in a similar spirit was expressed by IMF staff in considering future annual SDR allocations of the equivalent of $200 billion a year (IMF, 2011, pp. 5–7).

...but have not gained
much political traction

The Stamp proposal did not receive much support at the time, but comparable proposals have been reiterated in academic and intergovernmental circles ever since, although none of these have gained much political traction either. Indeed, an SDR-aid link was officially considered but did not win backing during the major reforms of the international monetary system that were discussed in the IMF Committee of Twenty in 1972–1974 following the collapse of the Bretton Woods system. The developing-country joint position on the principal features of a fundamental international monetary reform included the recommendation that "a link should be established between the allocation of SDRs and development assistance", while the programme for immediate action urged "the early establishment of a link between SDR allocation and additional development assistance" (Group of Twenty–four, 1979, pp. 11 and 13). Developed countries opposed the link, fearing that there would be pressure for excessive and inflationary issues of SDRs.

Development financing
functions of SDRs should be
separate from their role as a
reserve asset

In any case, the possible development financing functions of SDRs allocated to developed countries should be clearly separated from their role in increasing the reserves of developing countries, as discussed above. In 2002, for example, George Soros proposed that SDR allocations be split into two parts, one for liquidity and one for development. He suggested that IMF allocate SDRs through the usual mechanism and that the SDRs received by developing countries be held as reserves. Developed countries would donate the SDRs that they received to non-governmental organization programmes that supported development or enhanced a global public good, with a committee of eminent persons compiling a list of acceptable recipients (Soros, 2002, pp. 181–186).

The equity capital of a
"Green fund" could be
drawn from SDRs

A more recent proposal envisaged the use of SDRs for development differently. Bredenkamp and Pattillo (2010) proposed the creation of a multilateral "Green fund" whose equity capital could be drawn from the 2009 allocation of SDRs, most of which had gone to developed-country members. However, given that equity shares with volatile prices do not normally qualify as a reserve asset and assuming that retaining reserve asset status was important, the authors also proposed that any shareholder should have the guaranteed ability to sell its shares to other shareholders at par.[5] What the proposal pointedly recommended, however, was not spending the SDRs but rather floating bond issues backed by SDRs (and thus backed, in effect, by the major developed-country Governments). The authors proposed a leverage ratio of 10 to 1, or $1 trillion in bonds backed by $100 billion in equity shares, once the Green fund reached full size. Clearly, this leveraging is the proposal's main attraction, given the large investment resources needed to address climate change.[6] The Green fund would collect market-based interest payments from at least some of its borrowers, which it would then use to pay its bondholders. As low-income countries could not afford such loans, the Fund would also receive additional annual contributions from donors to enable it to underwrite its concessional activities (as is largely the case for the concessional loan facilities of IMF).[7] The authors envisaged that substantial annual donor revenues would be needed, which according to their proposal might be mobilized from a carbon tax or some other international environmental revenue source.

---

5   It is not clear that any such guarantee by the other shareholders would suffice to make the participating Governments consider the shares as reserves; a commitment by IMF as unconditional global lender of last resort might be required.

6   In fact, the Green fund could be created by international agreement without the involvement of SDRs, which would require simply that enough Governments be willing to contribute sufficient equity capital, only a small portion of which, as in the case of the World Bank itself, would need to be paid in.

7   Moreover, assuming the Green fund was made a prescribed holder of SDRs, it would receive SDR interest income on its SDR balances, paid for by the shareholder donors whose SDR holdings would have been drawn down.

The main concept underlying the proposal, namely, that of using SDRs to purchase long-term assets, has been endorsed by some authors (see, for instance, Birdsall and Leo, 2011; and Erten and Ocampo, 2012), although reservations have been expressed by others (United Nations, 2010b, para. 89). The attraction for proponents resides in the ability to tap the large pool of "unused" SDRs, in order to invest them, for example, in equity shares in the Green fund, as noted above, or simply purchase multilateral institution bonds, or invest in a new multilateral development fund. Through regular substantial SDR allocations, over $100 billion in development financing could potentially be raised per year.[8] For others, the difficulty presented by such a proposal stems from the fact that SDRs were created solely for transactions of a monetary nature, as between central banks. Leveraging them in such a way as to expose their holder to risks of illiquidity would be to distort the purpose for which they were created. The question, then, is how much risk would be involved, which points to the need for careful design of the financial instrument so as to maintain its reserve nature. However, one could view leveraging "idle" SDRs, as proposed, as similar to the practice engaged in by a fair number of countries of moving excess foreign currency reserves into sovereign wealth funds, where the liquidity and risk characteristics of specific assets in the fund determine whether or not to declassify those assets as reserve holdings even though they are held by the central bank (International Monetary Fund, 2009).[9]

> Regular SDR allocations could raise $100 billion in development financing per year

Taking ownership of the global commons

Capturing seigniorage by issuing a global currency is not the only potential "global" source of funds. If corporations were to begin to mine the minerals on the seabed under international waters, they would be appropriating resources they do not own. Under national jurisdictions, developers of valuable resources—from minerals to bandwidth—license their exploitation rights from the private property owner or the State and usually pay royalties for their use. The oceans beyond territorial limits, outer space and Antarctica are considered the "global commons". As they lie outside national jurisdictions, any licensing and payment of royalties would have to involve an international authority that was recognized as the responsible agent for managing the specific commons. While fishing in international waters and other activities in the commons might be licensed in this way, only mining the seabed has thus far been perceived as a source of international public revenue.

> Royalties from the exploitation of the "global commons" are a potential source of international public revenue

Efforts over the period extending from the establishment of the Seabed Committee by the General Assembly in 1967 to the adoption of the United Nations Convention on the Law of the Sea[10] in 1982 enabled the principle of managing the seabed for the benefit of humankind to enter into international law (Treves, 2008). In the 1970s

---

8 The proposal assumes that IMF would allocate $240 billion–$400 billion worth of SDRs each year, of which about $144 billion–$240 billion worth of SDRs would be allocated to developed countries. Of that, $100 billion–$200 billion worth of SDRs would likely be unutilized and it would thus be deemed unnecessary to maintain this sum as a reserve (Erten and Ocampo, 2012, p. 18).

9 For example, if an international financial institution was a prescribed recipient of SDRs and if its board approved a bond issue denominated in SDRs and gave it seniority in repayment over other obligations coupled, say, with a repurchase guarantee by IMF, then the SDR-denominated bonds should qualify as a reserve asset. Indeed, IMF has itself issued SDR-denominated obligations to certain Governments as part of its emergency mobilization of funds to help address the global financial crisis.

10 United Nations, *Treaty Series*, vol. 1833, No. 31363.

and 1980s, when concerns about "limits to growth" and finite supplies of natural resources were in the ascendant, seabed mining seemed a near-term possibility. This meant that resources extracted from the seabed might serve as a source of financial revenue which could be used for the global good. Although 162 States have ratified the treaty, some 30 others have not, including the United States, owing in part to disagreements over how to manage seabed mining. The instruments concerning the other global commons do not contain provisions for capturing economic rents from their use by individual investors. However, the entry into force of the Treaty on Principles Governing the Activities of States in the Exploration and Use of Outer Space, including the Moon and Other Celestial Bodies,[11] in 1967 has signalled the beginning of collective responsibility for "orbital space", as has the entry into force in 1961 of the Antarctic Treaty,[12] which prohibits mining, for the Antarctic territory (see World Commission on Environment and Development, 1987, chap. 10).

As it turned out, improved resource extraction methods on land and within the enlarged exclusive economic zones of the seas have made the need to develop a full regime for overseeing investment in resource extraction in the global commons less urgent. Nevertheless, as prices of minerals may rise through time to accommodate the growing demand from emerging economies, mining the seabed in international waters, which is attractive from an economic perspective, may become more practical and an agreed regime may become more essential. The potential for mobilizing new sources of international financing for global development activities could be considered in that context.

"Incentive-compatible" taxes that can also raise international funds

Often, Governments impose taxes in order to change behaviour in specific ways while raising public revenue at the same time. Imposing a tax on the purchase of cigarettes is a common example of such a "double dividend" policy. Primarily, the objective is to discourage smoking, but the tax also raises public funds. The "justice" of raising revenue from a tax that discriminates against smokers regardless of their income lies in the fact that, upon developing lung cancer and other smoking-related ailments, they will later make disproportionate claims on public-health or health-financing systems. Similarly, in the environmental arena, the "polluter pays" principle (No. 16) set out in the Rio Declaration on Environment and Development, adopted at the Earth Summit (United Nations, 1992), points to pollution taxes as a means both to discourage pollution and to mobilize the financing that, at least to some degree, is made necessary by the pollution. Nevertheless, policymakers will examine more options than just taxes when seeking to address an environmental concern, as the primary goal is to change behaviour rather than raise tax revenue.

Climate protection policies

Perhaps the most discussed environmental policy intervention centres around how to reduce the global volume of CO_2 and other greenhouse gas (GHG) emissions released into

---

11   Ibid., vol. 610, No. 8843.

12   Ibid., vol. 402, No. 5778.

the atmosphere, so as to curtail the rise of the average temperature of the planet. A "carbon tax" levied on the use of fossil fuels is one option, but not the only one, and there is no sign yet of consensus on what policies to adopt globally. Other policy options address additional environmental and development concerns. For example, taxes on the timber trade and other forestry-related activities have been proposed to finance sustainable forestry programmes, but have yet to be taken into fuller consideration (see box II.1).

Box II.1

Options for raising new resources for sustainable forestry

At the request of the European Commission, the Overseas Development Institute (ODI) examined "innovative financial incentive mechanisms" that would support sustainable tropical forestry (Richards, 1999). The public good targeted in this case was not only the carbon-reduction benefit of forests as a "carbon sink", but also the preservation of the genetic diversity and biodiversity that are lost when forests—not to mention forest-based cultures—disappear. An additional domestic or regional benefit would accrue from the watershed protection provided by forests, as well as the long-term employment and other economic benefits from downstream processing of products of sustainably managed forests. In this context, forestry policy is part and parcel of development policy, as well as of a "global public goods" policy.

The word "incentive" was included within the context of the objective of the ODI study because if appropriate incentives lead to better private-sector forestry management, then less official financing will be needed. In addition, appropriate national fees and taxes on the sector can be a potentially significant source of the revenues needed to add to the resources to be made available for protecting and sustainably developing the sector and, if applied, would reduce the need for international support. The author nevertheless saw international support as warranted and proposed consideration of several specific proposals, including international taxes on the timber trade, fees on bioprospecting deals (licensing the search for medicinally beneficial flora), carbon offset trading (tied to trading carbon emission permits, as discussed in the main body of the present chapter) and creating internationally tradable forestry development rights (see Richards (1999) for details).

International discussion of such options is still a work in progress. In particular, an Open-ended Intergovernmental Ad Hoc Expert Group on Forest Financing was established by the United Nations Forum on Forests in 2009 to focus policy attention on the financing of sustainable forests (United Nations, Economic and Social Council, 2009, para. 3). The Expert Group met once in 2010 and will meet again before the 2013 session of the Forum. Ministers gathered at the high-level segment of the ninth session of the United Nations Forum on Forests in 2011 committed to taking "a meaningful decision on forest financing" at the 2013 session.[a] A full range of domestic and international actions to mobilize public and catalyse private financing are being considered in the context of a holistic view of forests, including making more effective use of existing international funds and the possible creation of a global forest fund.

One concern, for example, involves the United Nations Reducing Emissions from Deforestation and Forest Degradation plus Conservation (REDD+) initiative which entails payments by developed-country investors to developing countries for carbon offsets earned by maintaining standing forests (see main body of the chapter for a discussion of carbon offsets). While REDD+ is viewed as a useful source of financing for local communities, there is nevertheless concern that the focus is on carbon stocks and not on the rights and livelihoods of those communities (see United Nations, Economic and Social Council, 2011, annex III, para. 12).

Source: UN/DESA.

a See the ministerial declaration of the high-level segment of the ninth session of the United Nations Forum on Forests on the occasion of the launch of the International Year of Forests (United Nations, Economic and Social Council, 2011, chap. I.A, draft decision I, para.9 (d)).

Climate protection is a *global* public good in that greenhouse gas emission reductions wherever they occur will all contribute equally to containment of global warming. As all countries will benefit, all are expected to contribute to the effort, albeit with differentiated responsibilities (in accordance with principle 7 of the Rio Declaration) (United

Nations, 1992). Developed countries are expected to finance their own emission reductions and assist the efforts of developing countries. In addition, as temperatures are already rising and will rise further, countries will increasingly need to adapt to the higher temperatures as well as work to mitigate further warming. Most of the costs of this adaptation will be borne by households and businesses, which will also make most of the adaptive investments required. Governments will help shape the outcome, likely both directly, through climate-related expenditures and regulatory policies, and indirectly, through tax measures. As a large part of the required investments for climate change mitigation and adaptation will need to be made in developing countries—about half, by some accounts (United Nations, 2011a)—international cooperation also has an important role to play.

While the preceding scenario reflects principles that are universally agreed, the mechanisms for implementing those principles are not agreed. Discussion continues about policies both for rolling back carbon emissions and for mobilizing more automatic, assured and substantial additional flows to help finance carbon mitigation and adaptation. In this context, the Commission on Sustainable Development in 1996 considered the feasibility of a variety of innovative financing mechanisms for promoting sustainable development; examples included taxes on multiple sources of CO_2 emissions and auctioning of internationally tradable CO_2 emission permits (United Nations, Economic and Social Council Commission on Sustainable Development, 1996).

Carbon taxes

A carbon tax may yield a "double dividend": reducing greenhouse gas emissions and generating additional development financing

The most straightforward approach to reducing emissions through financial incentives would be to impose a tax on CO_2 emissions so as to encourage economic actors to reduce the emissions under their control, through shifting, for example, to less carbon-emitting activities and types of fuel. The price incentive should also stimulate increased output of more carbon-efficient products and services. However, there is little agreement on how much to tax, on what to tax (fuels, for example, are not the only source of greenhouse gases), or whom to tax (should it be, for example, the final consumer or the producer of the greenhouse gases) and on how to use the tax funds that would be collected.

A uniform global carbon tax would disproportionally affect developing countries

If global policy could be designed as if for a single economy, then a single global tax could be set (and adjusted over time) so as to steer overall emissions in the direction of a particular target to be achieved by a particular date; and economic actors would be left to decide for themselves how to respond to the tax. However, the world is made up of many countries which would experience different impacts on overall consumption and production from a single tax. Indeed, an IMF study of the impact of a uniform carbon tax indicated that, while the greatest reduction of carbon emissions would occur in China, the most severe reduction in investment and output would be found in the members of the Organization of the Petroleum Exporting Countries (OPEC); other developing countries would experience a smaller reduction in output but one nevertheless larger than that in the developed countries (IMF, 2008, pp. 164–168).

The differential impact of a uniform carbon tax would raise objections of countries and interfere with agreement on the tax, especially since it is unlikely that those making the smallest sacrifices under a uniform tax would fully compensate those making the largest. Indeed, a policy embodied in the 1997 Kyoto Protocol[13] to the 1992 United Nations Framework Convention on Climate Change[14] mandates only that higher-income

---

[13]   Ibid., vol. 2303, No. 30822.

[14]   Ibid., vol. 1771, No. 30822.

countries make specific targeted reductions, based on the fact that those countries are responsible for most of the industrialization-induced elevated level of CO_2 in the atmosphere and that they are best able to absorb the economic impact of transition.

This notwithstanding, carbon taxes can be an effective policy tool and generate large revenues; for example, a tax of $25 per ton of CO_2 emitted by developed countries is estimated to raise $250 billion a year in global tax revenues. Other tax rates would generate other revenue volumes (see box II.2). Such a tax would be in addition to taxes already imposed at the national level, as many Governments (of developing as well as of developed countries) already tax carbon emissions, in some cases explicitly and in other cases indirectly through taxes on specific fuels.

A tax of $25 per ton of CO_2 emitted by developed countries could raise $250 billion annually

---

Box II.2

What if? estimates of the revenue raising capacity of a carbon tax

The international community—developed countries in particular—have committed to helping transfer increasing volumes of financial resources to developing countries on an annual basis for climate change mitigation and adaptation, with the amount to have risen to $100 billion per year by 2020 (see paras. 95-112 of the Cancun Agreements (United Nations Framework Convention on Climate Change, 2010)). A significant portion of new multilateral flows would be mediated by a new Green Climate Fund, which could address the question often raised when proposals for innovative financing are discussed, namely, how will the newly collected funds be allocated. What remains to be decided (besides the issue of the concrete design of the new Fund) is how the funds should be mobilized.

A joint report by the World Bank, IMF, the Organization for Economic Cooperation and Development (OECD) and the regional development banks estimated that a carbon tax of $25 per ton applied in the developed countries would raise approximately $250 billion by 2020 (a separate OECD estimate yielded an even higher revenue flow). It was estimated that a tax of $15 per ton would raise $155 billion and a tax of $50 per ton would raise $450 billion (World Bank and others, 2011, para. 23). These funds would be collected by national tax authorities and primarily devoted to domestic expenditure or to offsetting tax reductions. Nevertheless, if only 10 per cent of the revenues in the medium-tax option were transferred to developing countries, this would meet 25 per cent of the $100 billion target.[a]

Other proposals focus on a carbon tax on international transportation. While such a tax is of course more limited than a tax on all carbon emissions, it is estimated that a globally coordinated charge of $25 per ton of CO_2 released by aviation fuel in international travel would raise about $12 billion per year by 2020, while a comparable tax on bunker fuel would raise $25 billion. To accord with the Kyoto commitments, the taxes paid by developing countries would need to be rebated (for example, to half the tax on travel between a developed and a developing country). It is thought this would absorb no more than 40 per cent of total revenues raised, thus leaving about $22 billion from both taxes for potential transfer to developing countries. It was said that a lower price of $15 per ton of carbon emitted would generate about $14 billion net for transfer (ibid., paras. 31-32).

The Secretary-General's Advisory Group on Climate Change Financing considered a wide range of scenarios for carbon prices on international travel, rates of carbon emissions and share of funds made available for climate finance, as well as alternative global economic models through which to make projections. It found that the 2020 revenues for transfer for climate financing ranged from $1 billion to $6 billion for the aviation sector and from $2 billion to $19 billion for shipping (United Nations, 2010b, pp. 45-47).

The issue of imposing carbon taxes on international transportation—indeed, on carbon emissions wherever they occur—requires further international consensus-building. At the moment, this is a work in progress.

Source: UN/DESA.

a The revenue estimates take into account that the higher prices faced by buyers would result in a reduction in their consumption. In the case of the $25-per-ton tax, consumption was expected to fall 10 per cent below the baseline.

It is estimated that explicit carbon taxes imposed by six small European countries have yielded aggregate annual revenues of about $7 billion in recent years (Buchner and others, 2011, p. 12). All of the funds collected are used domestically, although not necessarily to achieve carbon-related policy aims. Fuel or transportation taxes are often viewed as a user charge, imposed on users of highways and streets, for example, or as a means of discouraging road congestion; or they may be paid into a dedicated fund for maintaining and expanding highways and public transportation. In contrast, a number of fuel-exporting countries subsidize domestic fuel prices, with such subsidies having an effect opposite from that of carbon taxes.

While there is no prospect in the short term of international agreement with regard to imposing a global carbon tax, policymakers have discussed the possibility of adopting a carbon tax on *international* travel, which would target, say, aviation or maritime fuel (see box II.2). If a global initiative were undertaken jointly to impose these or general carbon-based taxes on all economic activity, quite substantial revenues could be mobilized. Given that some of those revenues would undoubtedly reduce other forms of taxation, a certain amount could be earmarked for development cooperation.

"Cap and trade" policies

The European Union limits its emissions through a "cap and trade" policy

Serious consideration of policies to discourage CO_2 or other greenhouse gas emissions is a fairly recent phenomenon. The European Union has acted to limit its emissions, primarily through a Union-level "cap and trade" policy rather than through a general carbon tax. In the European scheme, CO_2 emission ceilings are set and covered firms must either comply or purchase a right to emit above their limit from a firm that is producing less CO_2 than its allotment.[15]

While it was expected that countries would meet their Kyoto commitments mainly through national measures, it was also realized that some countries might achieve a greater-than-required emissions reduction and that others might underperform. The Kyoto Protocol thus created an international carbon market in which surplus countries can sell their excess annual emission reductions to deficit countries. Deficit countries can also earn carbon credits by purchasing ownership of emission reductions (called "carbon offsets") from investment projects undertaken in developing or transition economies.[16] Verification of the annual carbon emissions reduction and the credit accorded to the buyer is overseen by the so-called Clean Development Mechanism (CDM) for developing-country projects and by a parallel process for transition economy projects known as Joint Implementation, both established under the Kyoto Protocol.

It is apparent that the Kyoto carbon market provides an alternative means of bringing about much the same result as international carbon taxes in terms of reducing global greenhouse gas emissions, although the degree to which public revenues are mobilized under "cap and trade" depends on how the initial emission permits are allocated. That is to say, countries may allocate their emission permits for free, auction them to the highest bidders or sell them at a fixed price. The carbon market approach is also somewhat

---

15   Certain nitrous oxide (N_2O) emissions are also covered and additional gases will be added in 2013.

16   For example, a coal-burning electric power generator in a developing country might replace its ageing plant and equipment with new coal-burning capacity (the baseline) or switch, say, to biogas as fuel based on waste from a nearby farming community. A developed-country investor could agree to buy annually the reduction in CO_2 emissions arising from the switch to biogas, thereby helping to make the switch profitable for the power generating firm. The developed-country investor would find the agreement beneficial as long as it represented a relatively inexpensive means of obtaining emission credits and as long as that investor could sell the carbon offsets if it no longer needed them.

complicated and open to abuse—for example, through not valuing carbon emission savings in Clean Development Mechanism projects appropriately, which is why the Mechanism's monitoring function is essential. Moreover, there are other drawbacks, beginning with the fact that the global carbon market is small and prices are volatile, which can hinder long-term investments.[17] Although the cost per unit of carbon emissions reduction may be substantially lower for investments in developing rather than in developed countries, there appears to be a "home bias" reflected in the fact that most emissions reductions take place within domestic markets even though at higher cost. Moreover, although 77 developing countries had one or more Clean Development Mechanism projects as of 2010 and 15 transition economies had Joint Implementation projects, the geographical distribution of projects was quite skewed: China accounted for 40 per cent of the CDM total and India for another 25 per cent, but all of Africa accounted for only 2 per cent of such projects (World Bank, 2010b, p. 53). While the World Bank and other public entities may help design and finance CDM projects, success will depend on whether private firms from developed countries will want to purchase the carbon offsets produced by the projects once they are up and running. For this to occur, investors need to feel confident that the carbon offsets they are purchasing will continue to be created over a long period, i.e., that the investment will not be short-lived.

It would thus appear that a second initiative is needed to complement the existing international carbon market mechanism, one mobilizing a substantial volume of official funds that may be used for emission-reduction investments in developing countries, especially least developed and other low-income countries. One option is to draw more heavily from appropriately expanded traditional modalities of official development cooperation. A second option would consist in earmarking a share of the proceeds accruing to Governments if they auction carbon emission permits—an approach that Germany has already begun to adopt and one to which the entire European Union is committed—as opposed to the initial practice of allocating them for free.[18] Or the resources could come from a portion of the revenues derived from an internationally concerted carbon tax, should such a tax be one day agreed.

More resources are needed for emission-reduction investments in developing countries...

Finally, it should be noted that deeper international support is also required for climate change adaptation in developing countries. A small step in this direction was taken when the Kyoto process established the Adaptation Fund in 2007 (see FCCC/KP/CMP/2007/9/Add.1, decision 1/CMP.3), funded by a 2 per cent levy on the annual flow of carbon offsets in CDM projects. As noted by the World Bank, the levy is a tax on a global public good (carbon emissions reduction) rather than on a public bad (carbon emissions) and is thus the opposite of "incentive-compatible" (World Bank and others, 2011, p. 28). Nevertheless, it raised $168 million from May 2009 to September 2011, reflecting the modest volume and prices of carbon offsets. Future revenues could rise if carbon offset precies rose. For example, if a number of countries adopted additional carbon mitigation initiatives, prices could rise to $15–$25 per ton, leading to about $150 million per year for the Adaptation Fund by 2020. With further initiatives and a higher price, the levy could yield as much as $750 million (ibid, pp. 28–29). However, with actual prices having fallen and an uncertain outlook, it may be opportune to look for additional sources of resources for the Fund.

...and for adaptation

---

[17] Experience thus far comes primarily from the European system, where the volatility of forward—and especially of spot—prices of carbon have significantly exceeded that for stock market indices (United Nations, 2009b, pp. 161; Nell, Semler and Rezai, 2009, pp. 10–11).

[18] The European Union Emissions Trading System will shift from mainly freely allocating emission permits to mainly auctioning them off to the highest bidders, starting in 2013, (see http://ec.europa.eu/clima/policies/ets/auctioning/index_en.htm (accessed 24 February 2012)).

Currency transaction taxes to discourage exchange-rate volatility

A currency transaction tax is levied in a number of countries to limit exposure to exchange-rate volatility

A number of countries have sought to limit exposure to volatile movements of their exchange rate by levying a "currency transaction tax" (CTT), that is, a tax on financial inflows. Surges in financial inflows when a country is "hot" can appreciate the exchange rate, distorting normal prices in international trade and discouraging exports and import-competing industries. To prevent this, the monetary authority will usually seek to absorb the foreign-exchange inflow, taking those funds out of circulation, albeit at the expense of the larger circulation of domestic currency used to buy the foreign currency.[19] The currency transaction tax can be a useful complement to monetary authority policy. The currency transaction tax is usually levied on short-term capital inflows, with the aim of discouraging inflows of so-called hot money when the country is in favour with international investors, so that smaller amounts flee when the market psychology sours. Indeed, recent experience in Brazil, Colombia, the Republic of Korea and Thailand suggest that their CTTs, as part of a comprehensive policy approach, do discourage short-term inflows or encourage their conversion into medium-term inflows, at least for a certain period of time (Baba and Kokenye, 2011). The more effective (if somewhat cumbersome) alternative, still used in a number of developing countries, is to administratively limit short-term financial flows in and out of the country.

The currency transaction tax follows in the tradition of James Tobin's 1972 proposal, whose primary aim was to provide a disincentive to speculative exchange-rate movements, although Tobin did mention that national Governments would collect the tax and could pass the funds to IMF or the World Bank (Tobin, 1978, p. 159). What Tobin proposed was an internationally coordinated tax, while the CTTs implemented at national level have all been on the initiative of individual countries and the funds collected have been used domestically.

An internationally coordinated currency transaction tax could potentially raise vast revenues

Civil society organizations have called upon the countries hosting the major financial markets to impose a coordinated currency transaction tax. Initially, the belief was that a CTT could make a major contribution to reducing exchange-rate volatility, echoing the original claim of Tobin. However, there is little agreement on whether or to what extent this is true.[20] At the same time, there has been a growing appreciation of the fact that a small tax, even if implemented in only a portion of the global currency markets and at a tiny rate, could nevertheless raise a large volume of funds. In this regard, proposals for cooperative implementation of a tiny CTT belong to the class of minimally distorting tax proposals discussed directly below.

Minimally-distorting taxes for development cooperation

A number of proposals have been made, many of them decades ago, that seek to raise substantial amounts of revenue for international cooperation for development in assured and predictable ways (see box II.3). The taxes described in at least some of these proposals

---

19 Because the additional money supply in circulation can be inflationary, central banks will usually try to "sterilize" the monetary impact of the foreign-exchange purchases by simultaneously selling government bonds that it owns in the domestic market, thereby absorbing the additional currency in circulation. Not all developing countries have financial sectors deep enough to allow them to sterilize successfully.

20 See Matheson (2010) for a recent review of the literature.

fulfil the requirements set out by economists when defining a "good" tax for general revenue raising purposes, namely, that it should: raise a substantial, assured and predictable flow of funds at low administrative cost; be "fair", which is usually interpreted to mean "progressive", in the sense that the tax should fall relatively more heavily on more affluent people than on poorer people; and, in contrast to taxes whose aim is to change behaviour, minimally alter private behaviour.

Box II.3

The long history of international taxation proposals

After the Second World War and with decolonization gaining momentum, development cooperation began to be seen as a rising international imperative that had to be financed. Prominent economists devised proposals for efficient, fair and semi-automatic taxes for larger and more predictable development cooperation.

For example, in 1970, the United Nations Committee for Development Planning (now the Committee for Development Policy), chaired at the time by the first Nobel laureate in economic sciences, Jan Tinbergen, had proposed that Governments put a small ad valorem tax on selected consumer durables (0.5 per cent was suggested) to increase funds for development cooperation (Frankman, 1996, p. 813). The Committee was preparing its proposals for the Second United Nations Development Decade, including consideration of targets for international transfers of financial resources for development. The tax proposal was presented as a "world solidarity contribution" (United Nations, 1970, para. 68) and had a number of attractive features, in particular the request that richer people in all countries pay the tax. It would target the tax by restricting it to the purchase of "a limited number of goods, the possession of which is at present indicative of the attainment of a relatively high level of living by the purchaser: for example, cars (and aircraft and pleasure-boats), television sets, refrigerators, washing machines and dishwashers". The tax "would be collected by the tax authorities of each country and on their own responsibility" and "Governments would be considered to have fulfilled their pledges by submitting each year the receipts to international development organizations chosen by them from a list adopted by the General Assembly".

As it is now more than four decades later, the list of luxury durables might be somewhat different, but the sentiment reflected in the proposal can still be appreciated. Other proposals were made in other forums. For example, in a study prepared for the Club of Rome in 1976, Jan Tinbergen, Mahbub ul Haq and James Grant listed a number of international taxes that could increase the amount and automaticity of development assistance, while also progressively redistributing income internationally.[a] While these proposals might have changed behaviours in an "incentive-compatible" way, the authors' focus was on the revenue they might mobilize for development.

Indeed, while the Tobin tax proposal of the 1970s, noted in the main body of this chapter, sought to influence market behaviour, when Mahbub ul Haq along with Inge Kaul and others rediscovered it in the 1990s, they were highly interested in its potential as a large source of funds for development cooperation (Haq, Kaul and Grunberg, 1996). Indeed, current interest in the financial transaction tax as well as in the currency transaction tax is focused almost entirely on their utilization as a revenue source.

While the 1990s was a period of weakening donor Government commitment to development cooperation, at the same time a sequence of United Nations conferences had been concluding with calls for more international financial assistance to meet social and environmental as well as economic development goals. Several "new and innovative" financing proposals were thus discussed in the Commission on Sustainable Development and the Economic and Social Council, whose main thrusts ranged from seeking multiple-year pledges for United Nations operational activities, and pooling various extrabudgetary trust funds into a single "super" trust fund for international allocation, to more radical proposals such as the Tobin tax.[b] The current expression of interest in innovative mechanisms of financing for development attests to the continuing relevance of those concerns.

Source: UN/DESA.

a These included taxes on non-renewable resources, international pollutants, transnational enterprises, rebates of taxes paid in industrialized countries by workers trained in developing countries, commercial activities in the global commons, armaments spending and salaries of international civil servants (cited in Frankman, 1996, p. 813).

b See United Nations, Economic and Social Council (1996) and the references cited therein.

A billionaire's tax?

A tax on the wealth of the world's richest individuals would be both fair and efficient

Theoretically, the least distorting, most fair and most efficient tax is a "lump sum" payment, such as a levy on the accumulated wealth of the world's richest individuals (assuming the wealthy could not evade the tax). In particular, it is estimated that in early 2012, there were 1,226 individuals in the world worth $1 billion or more, 425 of whom lived in the United States, 90 in other countries of the Americas, 315 in the Asia-Pacific region, 310 in Europe and 86 in Africa and the Middle East. Together, they owned $4.6 trillion in assets, for an average of $3.75 billion in wealth per person.[21] A 1 per cent tax on the wealth of these individuals would raise $46 billion in 2012.

Would this hurt them? The "average" billionaire would own $3.7 billion after paying the tax. If that billionaire spent $1,000 per day, it would take him or her over 10,000 years to spend all his or her wealth. If the average billionaire did not spend the wealth but allowed it to accumulate (and lived off income produced independently of the accumulated wealth), the tax would slow the future growth of wealth by 1 percentage point per year. In fact, individuals enter and leave the list of billionaires, as their wealth does fluctuate, but the average billionaire has seen his wealth grow appreciably over the 25 years for which data on the world's wealthiest individuals have been gathered. The average wealth of billionaires in 2012 was virtually the same as in 2011 and the wealthiest underwent a substantial drop in the value of their assets in 2009; however, in the 20 years before the global financial crisis, the average billionaire's wealth had grown at the rate of 4 per cent per year. If that rate of growth returned, with no wealth tax, the average billionaire's wealth would double in less than 18 years. If the growth of wealth were reduced by an annual 1 per cent wealth tax, it would require over 23 years for the wealth to double. Thus, such a tax would seem not to be a major burden.[22]

Although the levying a 1 per cent annual tax on the wealth of the world's billionaires is an intriguing possibility, it has not been regarded as a means of raising revenues for international cooperation.

The air passenger ticket levy

In 1964, Dudley Seers proposed imposing a number of specific international taxes and earmarking them so as to achieve specific world social targets (Frankman, 1996, p. 812). Among his proposals was "a tax on airways tickets (a source of revenue hardly touched yet by national governments)", which he saw as having the desirable properties of being progressive in terms of its incidence, elastic in terms of the revenue that could be raised, and easy to collect (Seers, 1964, pp. 478–479). It took more than four decades, but that proposal has now been adopted by a limited number of countries.

Nine countries impose a small tax on air passenger tickets and donate the proceeds to UNITAID

In 2006, a number of Governments agreed to impose a small tax on air passenger tickets and to donate the proceeds to UNITAID, a special international facility created in 2006 to purchase, in bulk at low negotiated prices, drugs needed to treat HIV/AIDS, malaria and tuberculosis in developing countries. The tax, called a "solidarity contribution" to ease taxpayer discomfort, was imposed by nine countries as of September 2011. It supplied about 70 per cent of the funds donated to UNITAID in that year and has resulted in the transfer of over $1 billion to UNITAID since 2006.[23]

---

21   Based on data compiled by *Forbes* magazine. Available from http://www.forbes.com/special-report/2012/billionaires-25th-anniversary-timeline.html (accessed 19 March 2012).

22   See Herman (2011) for an earlier proposal for such a tax.

23   In 2011, the contributing countries were Cameroon, Chile, the Congo, France, Madagascar, Mali, Mauritius, the Niger and the Republic of Korea. In addition, Norway contributed part of the funds collected on a carbon-emissions tax on aviation fuel (information from UNITAID is available .

Although revenues from the tax will fluctuate with air travel volumes, they will provide a continuing, automatic and assured source of funds for procurement of a number of essential medicines. The tax rate differs in different countries but, being small enough, is not likely to discourage travellers, a distinct fear of a number of tourism-dependent countries that do not intend to introduce the levy. France's tax, for example, is 1 euro for a domestic flight in economy class and 6 euros for an international flight in the same class compared, with 10 euro for a business or first-class domestic flight and 40 euros for a comparable international ticket (UNITAID, 2011).[24]

It seems that parliaments in the participating countries have been willing to adopt the tax because it would be earmarked for a specific public benefit that is popularly supported. There has been no connection between the use of these tax revenues and their source. The tax is not a "user fee" or a payment to offset carbon emissions from a flight. Indeed, the amount of the tax is not even related to the duration of the flight. It is simply a small levy for a well-appreciated use that the flying public (nationals and foreigners) is deemed able to afford. The fact that participating Governments are adopting the tax in concert seems to further enhance its political appeal. There is a political cachet associated with being a global leader for a public good, as well as with being part of the Leading Group, which has promoted the tax.

Financial and currency transactions taxes

Until recently, there was no broad public support for jointly imposed financial or currency transaction taxes for development purposes. Some Governments, however, have collected such taxes for domestic use for years—indeed, for centuries. The United Kingdom of Great Britain and Northern Ireland, for example, first introduced a "stamp tax" in 1696, which today taxes sales or transfers of British company shares or the purchase or lease of land or property. The tax does in fact have an international dimension to the extent that even if a British security is sold by an investor in one foreign country to an investor in another, the transfer of ownership is recorded in the United Kingdom where the tax is paid. Taxes were also imposed on stock trading, as of 2010, in Australia (at State level); Brazil (on foreign issues by Brazilian firms); China, Hong Kong SAR; India; Indonesia; Italy (on shares traded off exchange); the Republic of Korea; Singapore; South Africa; Switzerland; Taiwan Province of China; Turkey; and the United States (by the Securities and Exchange Commission and New York State). Various countries also tax bonds and loans (see Matheson, 2010, pp. 148–149). In 1957, Sri Lanka had imposed a tax on debit transactions in commercial bank accounts, which it repealed in 1965, reimposed and repealed again, and then reintroduced in 2002. Several Latin American countries have imposed financial transaction taxes (FTTs) on a wide variety of banking and other transactions (Coelho, 2009).

In each of these cases, one of the attractions of the financial transaction tax has been that it acts as a progressive tax inasmuch as poor people engage in relatively few transactions with financial institutions and the rich engage in many. Also, the low administrative cost of the tax and the large number of financial transactions occurring, especially in middle- and high-income countries, mean that a low tax could raise substantial amounts of funds, which is important, given that a high tax increases financial sector incentives to evade the tax. Indeed, some analysts find that the financial sector becomes increasingly

The air ticket tax provides a continuing, automatic and assured source of funds

The tax was adopted because it was earmarked for a popular and specific public benefit

Financial transaction taxes for domestic resource use have existed for years

---

24 It was estimated that a tax of $6 uniformly applied to all air departures globally would raise $10 billion per year (Keen and Strand, 2007). There is little expectation, however, that all countries would adopt such a tax.

adept at finding ways to avoid the tax so that its revenue-raising ability is perceived to fall over time (Baca-Campodónico, de Mello and Kirilenko, 2006). Presumably, the smaller the tax, the less likely such an outcome.

According to the discussion in box II.4, a tax of one half of a "basis point" (0.005 per cent) on all trading in four major currencies (the dollar, euro, yen and pound sterling) might yield an estimated $40 billion per year. The discussion also indicates, however, that the revenue may not be scalable by raising the tax rate, because the higher rate is expected to affect the trading volume. It was also estimated that if France, Germany and Spain imposed a stamp duty that would be required for securities transactions to be enforceable, it would raise $15 billion with minimal distortion of financial markets. It was said that it could possibly raise as much as $75 billion if enough countries participated (Leading Group on Innovative Financing for Development, 2011b, p. 38).

> A currency transaction tax of one half of a basis point in four major currencies can yield $40 billion per year and a stamp duty could raise $15 billion-$75 billion

---

Box II.4

What if? estimates of the revenue raising capacity of the currency transaction tax

A tax on international currency transactions is deemed an attractive possibility principally because of the huge volume of daily transactions. While proponents assert that a very tiny tax would mobilize very substantial amounts of funds without materially affecting the market, opponents have argued that the banks that trade currencies work on very fine margins and that even a tiny tax would have a significant impact when all the layering of transactions underlying a final trade is taken into account, as banks continually adjust their currency exposures. Proponents reply that technological advances and investments in the infrastructure of international payments over recent years have significantly reduced the cost of making financial transactions and that the proposed tax would reverse that reduction only minimally. Now, therefore, the currency transaction tax is broadly considered feasible, although it might possibly reduce the earnings of individual banks.

In fact, the centralization of the global financial payments system over the past decade has made it easier to collect the tax and harder to avoid paying it. Indeed, an estimated 68 per cent of the wholesale foreign-exchange transactions in 17 major currencies are passed through the CLS Bank, which operates the Continuous Linked Settlement system.[a] By participating in the CLS Bank, financial institutions significantly reduce their annual operating costs and avoid "settlement risk" (the risk that payment to settle a transaction will not be received on a timely basis). The Continuous Linked Settlement system, when combined with the Society for Worldwide Interbank Financial Telecommunication (SWIFT) system for transferring financial messages across borders ensures that a very large and increasing share of international financial transactions can be tracked. As most payments have already passed through the CLS Bank, the tax could be automatically collected and channelled to national authorities or to a common pool.

Estimates of the revenue potential of a tax on global currency transactions, which reflect different assumptions about the rate of tax, the variety of covered transactions and the share of the global market assumed to participate, have ranged from $24 billion to $300 billion per year based on foreign-exchange transactions of about $1 trillion per day, which was the case around the start of the millennium (United Nations, General Assembly, 2009, para. 46). However, those massive revenue generation estimates did not take sufficient account of the impact that such a tax might have on the volume of currency trading on the market. On the other hand, trading in foreign exchange has grown to over $4 trillion per day, so that even estimates taking better account of the elasticity of trading volume should demonstrate the feasibility of mobilizing substantial sums from a currency transaction tax. Indeed, recent estimates put the revenue yield of a tax of one half of a "basis point" (0.005 per cent) on all trading in four major currencies (the dollar, euro, yen and sterling) at $40 billion per year. It was estimated that a tax of 1 basis point (0.01 per cent) would yield $39 billion, owing to a much larger reduction in trading volume (Schmidt and Bhushan, 2011, pp. 15-21).

Source: UN/DESA.

a Data as of April 2010, as reported by CLS Bank. Available from http://www.cls-group.com/About/Pages/default.aspx.

The pressure exerted over more than a decade by development-oriented and faith-based civil society organizations to adopt this tax has drawn various responses from Governments, some positive, and others, echoing concerns voiced by the financial industry, quite negative. Most of the criticisms have been of the proposed CTT, as it has been discussed since the 1990s. However the CTT is a type of FTT and thus answers to criticisms of the CTT apply to both. Firstly, the tax would fall on a sector that is not heavily taxed. Indeed, financial transactions are exempt from the value-added tax (VAT) of the European Union. Secondly, while a tiny tax would have minimal impact on transactions by non-financial customers, it might reduce the profitability and thus the volume of computer-operated high-frequency trades, such as proved so disruptive to the functioning of the United States equity market in the "flash crash" of 2010. Indeed, there is already concern that such high-frequency trading threatens to exacerbate volatility in major foreign-exchange markets (Bank for International Settlements, 2011). Thirdly, opposition to the tax seems tied to a fear by financial institutions based in countries possibly participating in the tax that they would be at a disadvantage in global competition for financial business. This concern would be alleviated if the tax were universally adopted, but there would also be less reason for concern if the tax rate were set very low, when it would mainly discourage the high-frequency trading that in any event should be discouraged.[25]

The deeper problem, however, in the view of some countries, seems to be the international nature of the tax, as it could take the form of an initiative of multiple Governments which would pledge to implement it jointly in order to mobilize substantial funds on an ongoing and assured basis, while earmarking at least an agreed percentage of the proceeds for international development cooperation (Leading Group on Innovative Financing for Development, 2011b). Perhaps an additional concern is that Governments might lose control of the use of the funds, although the model suggested by the former Committee for Development Planning in 1970 (see box II.3), which entailed pre-agreeing a list of acceptable recipients, might alleviate this concern, as could the proposal by an expert group to create, as part of an international financial transaction tax treaty, a jointly overseen and democratically governed common fund for allocation of the pooled resources for cooperation (ibid., pp. 28–29).

Today, one finds not only intensive and ever more widespread international advocacy efforts by civil society organizations for a financial transaction tax or a currency transaction tax as an international tax for development,[26] but also an increasingly sympathetic response on the part of some Governments, in particular among members of the Leading Group. The report of the expert committee convoked by the Group to study the feasibility and desirability of imposing a financial transaction tax to mobilize funds to support development, endorsed the concept (Leading Group on Innovative Financing for Development, 2010). France, a member of the Leading Group and 2011 Chair of the Group of Twenty (G20), put the FTT in the agenda of the G20 Leaders Summit in November 2011. In the concluding communiqué, Heads of State or Government agreed that "over time, new sources of funding need to be found to address development needs"

Financial and currency transaction taxes are gaining political traction…

---

25   One concern voiced regarding a proposed European financial transaction tax is that it would reduce economic growth; but recently revised estimates by the European Commission suggest that the reduction would be extremely small, and independent economists have argued that in fact the impact on growth could even be slightly positive (Griffith-Jones and Persaud, 2012b).

26   See, for example, the website on the European coalition Make Finance Work for People and the Planet (www.makefinancework.org) and that of the United States coalition Americans for Financial Reform (http://ourfinancialsecurity.org/).

and acknowledged "the initiatives in some of (their) countries to tax the financial sector for various purposes, including a financial transaction tax, inter alia, to support development" (Group of Twenty, 2011a, para. 28).

As may be seen from that statement, Governments of major economies acknowledge but have hardly acceded to the civil society organization campaign for taxation of international financial transactions *for development*. Indeed, the opposition to the financial transaction tax/currency transaction tax by some Governments had softened only when they came to recognize the massive mobilization of funds that had been needed to address the recent international financial crisis and grew concerned about the resources that might be needed in any future crisis. In particular, the Prime Minister of the United Kingdom, Gordon Brown, speaking at the meeting of G20 Finance Ministers and Central Bank Governors, held in St. Andrews, Scotland, in November 2009, reversed long-time British opposition and proposed the introduction of a financial transaction tax for financial rescue purposes.[27] As may be imagined, the financial sector in the City of London was not supportive; indeed, the successor British Government has not supported the tax, nor has the United States.

Nevertheless, responding to widespread public outrage at the huge cost of a crisis that had been imposed on the world by the mischief of the financial sector in some of the major economies, the G20 requested IMF to study options for raising funds from financial activities. The Fund did not recommend a financial transaction tax, but it did propose in its report, entitled "A fair and substantial contribution by the financial sector", that financial institutions should pay a tax based on their size and contribution to systemic risk plus, possibly, an additional tax on their profits (Claessens, Keen and Pazarbasioglu, eds., 2010, pp. 2–73).

While the G20 has not been ready to act on this or any other international tax proposal, the momentum building in recent years for the imposition of a financial transaction tax has led to its active consideration in the European Union. In March 2011, the European Parliament voted in favour of such a tax and in September the European Commission (2011) proposed a concrete initiative for adoption by member States. The European Commission proposed a minimum tax of 0.1 per cent on trades of bonds and shares, and of 0.01 per cent on derivatives (although individual EU members may impose higher rates), to be paid by buyer and seller if resident in EU. There would be no tax on spot currency exchanges, nor on issuance of stocks or bonds, home mortgages or loans to small and medium-sized enterprises. The estimated revenue (€57 billion per year) would be shared by the European Union and its member States. The matter is being considered in 2012 and the prospects for adoption should have been clarified by the time this *Survey* is published.

... but earmarking the proceeds for international development is encountering political obstacles

The European Commission has proposed a tax on bonds, shares and derivatives trading

---

27   Excerpts from the speech are available from www.cttcampaigns.info/gordonbrown1.

Chapter III
Existing mechanisms of innovative financing for development

Summary

♦ In general, existing innovative development financing mechanisms have been successful in fulfilling specific purposes, such as front-loading disbursements of official development assistance, mitigating risks and incentivizing the commercialization of new vaccines. However, they are relatively limited in scale, and generally do not provide additional resources.

♦ The International Finance Facility for Immunisation (IFFIm) has raised $3.6 billion for vaccine programmes since 2006 by front-loading ODA flows. Replication and scaling up are technically feasible, and may be useful where financing needs are temporary or investments are self-financing in the medium term; but prospects may be limited by fiscal constraints in donor countries and the recent downgrading of the IFFIm credit rating.

♦ While advance market commitments and the Affordable Medicines Facility - malaria are still at an early stage, initial results of the pilot projects appear promising. There may be potential for replication so as to induce technological innovation in renewable energy and/or sustainable agriculture, but scalability of this type of initiative may be limited by resource availability.

♦ The Caribbean Catastrophe Risk Insurance Facility has proved effective as a risk-pooling mechanism for member countries, with significant advantages over conventional insurance and with the potential for replication in some other regions.

♦ While resources mobilized through Product Red are additional to ODA, and may prove more predictable, the amounts raised have been small.

Introduction

The traditional view of innovative development financing (IDF) envisages mechanisms aiming primarily at generating substantial and predictable resources for development additional to traditional official development assistance (ODA). However, the development of such mechanisms has proved politically problematic, and achieving greater stability by avoiding dependence on discretionary donor budgets has become a daunting challenge. Consequently, the mechanisms that have been developed under the rubric of IDF have been of a very different nature and are broadly of three types:

• Mechanisms that aim to transform the time profile of development finance through the "securitization" of future ODA flows or the conversion of outstanding debts

- Mechanisms that seek to mitigate risk, either by providing guarantees or through insurance mechanisms
- Mechanisms that seek to harness additional voluntary contributions from the private sector to supplement official flows

The first section of the present chapter assesses two mechanisms of the first type: the International Finance Facility for Immunisation (IFFIm) and debt conversion schemes. The second section considers two guarantee mechanisms, advance market commitments (AMCs) and the Affordable Medicines Facility - malaria (AMFm), and one insurance mechanism, the Caribbean Catastrophe Risk Insurance Facility (CCRIF). The third section discusses two mechanisms for securing voluntary private contributions: Product Red and the short-lived MassiveGood voluntary solidarity contribution on air travel.

Mechanisms to transform the time profile of development finance

International Finance Facility for Immunisation

IFFIm is a mechanism for front-loading ODA...

The International Finance Facility for Immunisation (IFFIm), a mechanism for front-loading aid disbursements, was initiated in 2006 to accelerate the availability of funds for immunization. It converts binding pledges by donors over a long period into immediate financial resources by securitizing part of future ODA budgets: IFFIm issues bonds in the international capital markets, to be serviced and repaid from ODA allocations earmarked in advance for this purpose. This allows development finance to be increased in the medium term at the expense of a reduction in the longer term. The resources generated are used to support immunization programmes through the GAVI Alliance. The structure of IFFIm is presented in figure III.1.

Ten countries have so far contributed to IFFIm (the United Kingdom of Great Britain and Northern Ireland, France, the Netherlands, Sweden, Japan, Norway, Italy, Spain, Brazil and South Africa), and have pledged a total of $6.2 billion for periods of between 5 and 23 years. The United Kingdom and France account for 72.4 per cent of the total amount pledged. On the basis of these pledges, IFFIm has undertaken 19 bond issues in five markets, raising nearly $3.6 billion, of which $1.9 billion had been disbursed in 70 low-income countries by the end of 2010 (GAVI Alliance and World Bank, 2012). This represents 49.2 per cent of the total disbursements of the GAVI Alliance since its establishment in 2000, and 64 per cent since the establishment of IFFIm in 2006 (Pearson and others, 2011).

The World Bank has supported IFFIm by executing its capital-raising programme and managing the proceeds of bond sales to ensure the maintenance of sufficient liquidity for timely debt-servicing and to meet funding commitments. Several legal and banking entities have also provided pro bono legal and investment banking services. An independent evaluation of IFFIm found it to have been highly successful in keeping both borrowing and administrative costs low, the former being considerably below donors' original expectations (ibid.). It has also managed its liquidity well in the face of the unpredictability of its funding requirements associated with market uncertainty and the country demand-led nature of GAVI Alliance activities. While start-up costs were relatively high, this is largely a reflection of the innovative nature of the mechanism.

Initially, the resources generated by IFFIm were devoted to six "investment cases": projects with a particular need for front-loading, which were developed specifically to use the proceeds of the first $1 billion IFFIm bond issue. Subsequently, funds have been used in parallel with other GAVI resources for general immunization programmes, mostly for pentavalent vaccine[1] since 2008. Up to September 2010, IFFIm provided about two thirds of total GAVI resources for health system strengthening programmes, and half of its resources for pentavalent vaccine, the latter accounting for 51.4 per cent of total IFFIm funding (see figure III.2). In other areas, IFFIm funding has been up to one quarter of total GAVI funding (Pearson and others, 2011).

IFFIm funding has unquestionably added to the substantial contribution of GAVI to increasing vaccination coverage in low-income countries. Overall, it is estimated that IFFIm-funded programmes up to end–2011 will eventually save some 2 million future lives (Pearson and others, 2011).

…and has contributed substantially to the success of the GAVI Alliance

Figure III.1
Structure of IFFIm

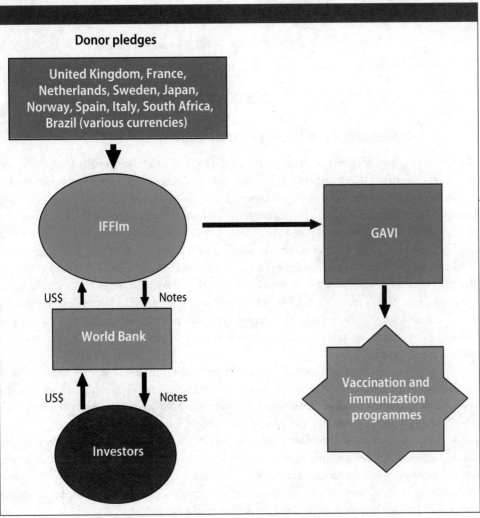

Source: GAVI Alliance (2011a).

---

1. Pentavalent vaccine combines vaccines for diphtheria, pertussis (whooping cough) and tetanus (DPT3) with those for hepatitis B and *Haemophilus influenzae type B* (Hib) disease. It is recommended by the World Health Organization (WHO) in preference to the individual vaccines.

Figure III.2
GAVI disbursements of IFFIm funds as of December 2011

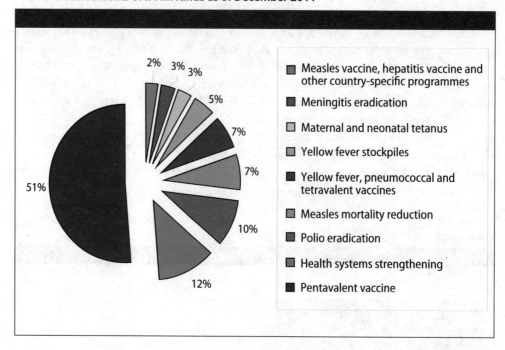

Source: UN/DESA, based
on GAVI Alliance and
World Bank (2012).

Additionality, front-loading and predictability

IFFIm increases
development finance
now, but reduces future
ODA flows

While IFFIm provides a net increase in funding in the medium term, this is offset by the diversion of future ODA budgets in later years, which means that it does not provide additional resources in the long term (see figure III.3). Its justification is thus based on front-loading a given stream of financing rather than on increasing funding. Thus far, payments to the GAVI Alliance have exceeded ODA commitments to IFFIm; but from around 2013, in the absence of further bond issues, the annual cost to ODA budgets of servicing IFFIm bonds will exceed the resources that IFFIm provides to the GAVI Alliance, so that the net effect on development finance will be negative. The negative balance will become substantial ($194 billion-$372 billion per year) from 2016 to 2026, becoming marginally positive again only in 2027-2031 as IFFIm winds down its liquidity. This is a matter of potential concern in light of the growing funding gap of the GAVI Alliance (Pearson and others, 2011, figure 39).

Even without additionality, such front-loading may still be beneficial in particular cases. In the case of immunization, for example, the rationale is based on the concept of "herd immunity". Immunization protects each individual directly, but with a high enough vaccination rate the risk of contracting a disease is also reduced for those not vaccinated, as there will be fewer infected people. When immunization coverage rates reach a threshold level (estimated at between 75 and 95 per cent for different diseases, according to their particular characteristics) a herd immunity effect is achieved, effectively interrupting transmission of the disease. If sustained, this can greatly increase the effectiveness of immunization programmes in reducing disease prevalence.

This phenomenon provides a strong rationale for front-loading resources for investment in rapidly expanding immunization coverage, particularly by vaccinating older

Figure III.3
ODA Commitments to IFFIm and IFFIm funding of the GAVI Alliance, 2006-2031

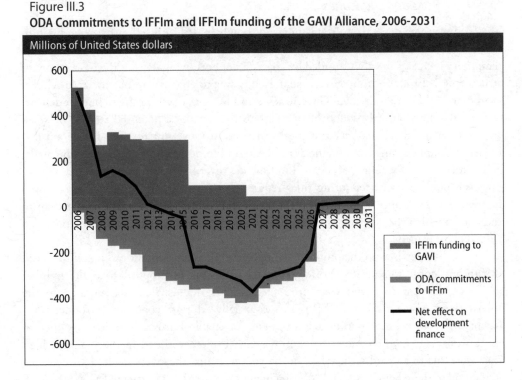

Millions of United States dollars

IFFIm funding to GAVI
ODA commitments to IFFIm
Net effect on development finance

Sources: Data (to 2011) and projections (2012-2031) are based on GAVI Alliance (2012b; 2012c). Projections for IFFIm funding to the GAVI Alliance are available only as averages for 2011-2015, 2016-2020 and 2021-2031.

children who were not vaccinated at the usual age, although the case for front-loading is less clear in the case of routine immunization programmes, which need to be sustained over a prolonged period to have lasting benefits.

In practice, however, the extent of front-loading under IFFIm has been restricted by the Treasury Management Agreement with the World Bank, which requires IFFIm to retain 30.3 per cent of its resources as a financial cushion in order to maintain its credit rating. This leaves only 69.7 per cent of resources raised available for disbursement, with further limits resulting from annual ceilings on IFFIm disbursements imposed by donors under the Finance Framework Agreement, which sets the parameters for their financial participation. These constraints, together with the limited capacity of the GAVI Alliance to use front-loaded resources, have led to the failure of IFFIm to realize its full potential for front-loading (Pearson and others, 2011), giving rise to a substantial difference between the funds generated by IFFIm and the resources provided to the GAVI Alliance.

Predictability of disbursements, as well as front-loading, has been presented as an advantage of IFFIm (GAVI Alliance, 2011a): by increasing demand and making it more predictable, the availability of stable and predictable financing for vaccination over the medium term allows a reduction in vaccine prices. A prospective study (Barder and Yeh, 2006) estimated the benefits of predictability to be of a similar order of magnitude to those of front-loading. However, large and variable (20–45 per cent) shortfalls of actual disbursements (GAVI Alliance, 2012b) as against those anticipated in that study between 2007 and 2012 raise some questions as to whether the anticipated level of predictability was in fact achieved. Setting aside the issue of front-loading, IFFIm reliance on financial markets means that its disbursements are inevitably less predictable than the stream of legally binding future ODA commitments on which they are based, as the resources generated depend on market conditions at the time of bond issues.

There are limits to the front-loading and predictability of IFFIm financing

Risks and challenges

The IFFIm model depends on the issuance of bonds by IFFIm itself rather than by individual Governments. Without this feature, it would amount to no more than a source of temporary increases in ODA, funded by government borrowing. Part of the motivation for structuring IFFIm as an intergovernmental body was to enable it to borrow at lower cost than that available to individual Governments and without contributing to budget deficits.

However, this structure gives rise to the issue of a potential tension between the financial needs of markets and the fiscal rules of Governments. For future aid disbursements to be securitized, financial markets need to be certain that they will be made, which means that they must be legally binding on Governments. In most donor countries, however, public sector accounting rules require that such binding commitments should be treated as expenditures in the year in which the commitment is made rather than in the year in which the cost is incurred. This would give rise to serious fiscal constraints on IFFIm commitments.

To get around the problem, a "high-level financing condition" was introduced in funding commitments to IFFIm, reducing payments in proportion to the number of GAVI-recipient countries with protracted arrears (longer than six months) to the International Monetary Fund (IMF). This essentially arbitrary condition introduced sufficient uncertainty into funding commitments to enable Eurostat (Statistical Office of the European Union) to allow the commitments to be accounted in the year in which they were due to be paid rather than in the year in which they were made. However, the likelihood of there being enough GAVI-recipient countries with protracted arrears to IMF to affect the ability of IFFIm to service its debts under this clause was sufficiently remote to ensure that investor confidence was not significantly weakened (Moody's Investors Service, 2011).

In the event, however, subsequent occurrences in the financial market have posed a greater risk to the credit rating of IFFIm. At its inception, IFFIm had a AAA rating, founded upon four factors: its status as an intergovernmental body; the fact that AAA-rated Governments accounted for almost 85 per cent of total pledges; the politically compelling nature of the use of funds (child vaccination in low-income countries), which bolstered confidence in continued political commitment; and the choice of the World Bank as treasurer.

Since the financial crisis, three IFFIm donors accounting for some 41.3 per cent of pledges (France, Italy and Spain) have lost their AAA credit ratings with one or more ratings agencies, and the possibility has emerged of a similar downgrade for the United Kingdom of Great Britain and Northern Ireland (accounting for a further 47.5 per cent of pledges). Declining confidence in the financial position of funders contributed to Moody's downgrading of the IFFIm credit rating from AAA to Aaa in December 2011 and to Standard and Poor's downgrade from AAA to AA+ in January 2012 (Moody's Investors Service, 2011; Standard and Poor's Ratings Services, 2012). This could limit the ability of IFFIm to generate additional funds through further bond issuance, and/or increase its borrowing costs, particularly if other ratings agencies follow suit. Ketkar (2012) proposes third-party guarantees or excess coverage as a means by which the IFFIm could regain its AAA credit ratings, although these approaches would also increase costs.

Budgetary pressures in all IFFIm contributor countries also pose a risk, limiting the prospects of further pledges of future ODA. For euro-area countries in particular, the requirement under the Stability and Growth Pact of maintaining budget deficits below 3 per cent of gross domestic product (GDP) and gross public debt below 60 per cent of

GDP, implies a strong focus on expenditure reduction in the coming years, potentially putting significant pressure on future ODA budgets.

Scalability and replicability

Replicability of IFFIm—the possibility of an international financial facility (IFF) for other uses—is limited by its nature as a mechanism for front-loading resources rather than for generating additional resources over the long term. While this may be beneficial for some aspects of immunization, it is not appropriate for the many other development-related undertakings that require more sustained financial support. In the context of education, for example, an international financial facility could finance investment in building schools and training additional teachers, but this would provide little long-term benefit, without additional funding for recurrent costs such as teachers' salaries, teaching and learning materials, maintenance of buildings and equipment and ongoing training (Ketkar, 2012).

IFFIm is replicable, but suitable only for some purposes…

Nonetheless, there may be some contexts in which such a mechanism would be useful—primarily where there is a temporary need for capital investment, and where associated recurrent costs are minimal or essentially self-financing. Examples might include investments in a transition to renewable energy, climate change adaptation and some infrastructure projects.

Since such uses would require substantially greater resources than those for immunization, the question of replicability is closely related to that of scalability. Pearson and others (2011) are optimistic on the subject of scalability of the IFF mechanism, suggesting that it could comfortably be increased to the size originally envisaged ($40 billion) and arguing that the scale of IFFIm has been constrained by donor preferences rather than by technical constraints. It should be noted, however, that a much larger IFFIm would require commensurately larger ODA commitments, which may be problematic at a time of fiscal austerity, as well as magnify the effect on future ODA disbursements for other purposes. The scale of commitments required would be further increased substantially if interest costs were higher, as a result either of higher market rates or of higher spreads. The downgrading of the IFFIm credit rating (which post-dates the Pearson evaluation) may also make donors more cautious about developing new IFFs.

…and its scalability may be limited in the coming years

In sum, the international financial facility is potentially replicable as a mechanism, and there is no technical obstacle to its being replicated on a substantially larger scale. However, current economic and market conditions make it unlikely that IFF-type mechanisms could operate on a larger scale than IFFIm for the foreseeable future; and the potential usefulness of the mechanism is limited to contexts where the primary need is the front-loading of funds. Where the primary need is for stable, sustainable and predictable financing, this could more satisfactorily be achieved by channelling binding pledges of future ODA directly to recipient countries rather than by securitizing them through financial markets so as to concentrate resources in a more limited period. As Pearson and others (2011, p. 5) observe, IFFIm represents only "a very efficient second-best solution" to the problem of how to effect fulfilment by donors of their international aid commitments.

Debt-conversion mechanisms

Debt conversion entails the cancellation by one or more creditors of part of a country's debt in order to enable the release of funds which would otherwise have been used for debt-servicing, for use instead in social or environmental projects. Where debt is converted at a discount with respect to its face value, only part of the proceeds fund the projects,

Debt conversion can generate resources for developmental and environmental projects…

the remainder reducing the external debt burden, typically as part of a broader debt restructuring.

While early debt swaps entailed the conversion of commercial bank debt purchased at a discount on the secondary market, often by non-governmental organizations, swaps of bilateral debts owed to Governments have predominated since 1991, when the Paris Club of bilateral official creditors introduced a framework for debt conversion into its rescheduling agreements. Discounts under such transactions vary between creditors: Germany, for example, applies a discount of between 50 and 80 per cent (Buckley, 2011b), while Spain applies a discount of 60 per cent for countries qualifying for the Heavily-Indebted Poor Countries (HIPC) Initiative, but converts debt at face value for other countries (United Nations Educational, Scientific and Cultural Organization, 2011).

...but not all debt conversion qualifies as innovative development finance

Debt *cancellation* (for example, under the HIPC Initiative or the Multilateral Debt Reduction Initiative) does not represent innovative development financing, as discussed in chapter I, but rather recognition by creditors that their past loans are not recoverable. Debt *conversion*, by contrast, does qualify as IDF, to the extent that it diverts resources to development purposes that would otherwise have been devoted to debt servicing. However, this effect is limited to the conversion of debts that would otherwise have been serviced. As discussed in box III.1, this makes estimation of the IDF component of debt conversion very difficult.

Debt-for-nature swaps

Debt-for-nature swaps date back to the 1980s...

Debt conversion first emerged, in the guise of debt-for-nature swaps, during the 1980s debt crisis, following an opinion article by Thomas Lovejoy, then Executive Vice-President of the World Wildlife Fund (WWF), in the New York Times in 1984. Lovejoy argued that a developing country's external debt could be reduced (also providing tax relief to participating creditor banks) in exchange for the country's taking measures to address environmental challenges. Estimates based on Sheikh (2010) and Buckley, ed. (2011) suggest that between $1.1 billion and $1.5 billion of debt has been exchanged through debt-for-nature swaps since the mid–1980s, although it is not possible to assess how much of this constitutes IDF, for the reasons discussed in box III.1.

There have been two basic forms of debt-for-nature exchanges (Buckley and Freeland, 2011). In the first, part of a country's external debt is purchased by an environmental non-governmental organization and offered to the debtor for cancellation in exchange for a commitment to protect a particular area of land. Such transactions occurred mainly in the late 1980s and 1990s and were generally relatively small-scale. An early example was a 1987 deal under which Conservation International, a Washington, D.C.-based environmental non-governmental organization, bought $650,000 of the commercial bank debt of Bolivia (now Plurinational State of Bolivia) in the secondary market for $100,000, and exchanged this for shares in a company established to preserve 3.7 million acres of forest and grassland surrounding the Beni Biosphere Reserve in the north-east part of the country.

In the second form, debt is exchanged for local currency (often at a discount), which is then used by local conservation groups or government agencies to fund projects in the debtor country. Swaps of this kind are generally much larger, and have predominated since the 1990s. The largest such swap came in 1991, when a group of bilateral creditors agreed to channel principal and interest payments of $473 million (in local currency) into Poland's Ecofund set up to finance projects designed to counter environmental deterioration. The EcoFund financed 1,500 programmes between 1992 and 2007, providing grants

| | Box III.1 |

When is debt-conversion IDF?

Debt conversion for developmental purposes only provides additional resources for development, and thus only qualifies as IDF (as defined in this present publication), in cases where the debts converted would not otherwise have been cancelled. This is clear-cut in the case of the conversion of bilateral debts (either under Paris Club agreements or through Debt2Health) owed by countries not eligible for debt cancellation. Because the debt would otherwise have been serviced in full, all proceeds from the conversion can be considered IDF.

In other cases, however, the issue is more problematic. Where debt is converted as part of a debt restructuring which would otherwise have resulted in partial cancellation of the debt, only that part of the funds generated that would otherwise not have been cancelled can be considered IDF. For example, if a debt is converted at a discount rate of 50 per cent, but would otherwise have been reduced by 75 per cent in net present value terms, it is only the part corresponding to the uncancelled part of the debt that qualifies (that is, 25 per cent of the value of the debt, or half of the funds generated). The remainder is, in effect, additional financing provided by the debtor from its own resources as a counterpart to the creditor's contribution. This introduces a serious complication in respect of estimating the contribution of debt conversion to IDF.

Still more complex is the case of conversion of commercial debts purchased on the secondary market. These debts were not, in general, converted as part of an overall debt restructuring agreement; neither were they eligible for reduction or conversion at the time of conversion. In many cases, however, they would have been included in subsequent commercial debt restructurings (for instance, under the 1989 Brady Initiative) or debt buy-backs, which would have reduced the debt if it had not previously been converted. In the former case, the effective debt reduction (and hence the IDF component of debt conversion in each case) would also depend on the specific restructuring option chosen by the individual creditor whose debt was converted. This makes estimation of IDF provided by this type of debt conversion virtually impossible.

Source: UN/DESA.

for conservation projects relating to cross-border air pollution, climate change, biological diversity and the clean-up of the Baltic Sea (Buckley and Freeland, 2011).

However, most debt-for-nature swaps have been much smaller, so that the funds generated are generally limited relative to environmental financing needs, providing funding, instead, for individual projects. Critics also argue that monitoring mechanisms are often insufficient to ensure that debtor countries fulfil their environmental obligations, and that swaps may be detrimental to national sovereignty in cases where they result in the transfer of landownership to foreign entities. In view of the latter concern, conservation organizations involved in three-way swaps (involving the debtor Government, the creditor and a third party) often refrain from buying land directly with funds generated by swaps (Sheikh, 2010).

...but their scale has generally been limited

Debt2Health

Since the development of debt swaps in the 1980s, there has been a diversification of their uses to encompass social projects, most recently in the area of health under the Debt2Health initiative, which was launched by the Global Fund to Fight AIDS, Tuberculosis and Malaria in 2007 to harness additional resources for its programmes. Under Debt2Health, a donor country agrees to reduce part of a loan ineligible for debt relief under global initiatives such as the HIPC and Multilateral Debt Reduction Initiatives, in exchange for a commitment by the debtor to invest (in local currency) half of the nominal value of the debt in programmes approved by the Global Fund. The Global Fund is committed to

Debt2Health provides innovative financing for the Global Fund

devoting all of the funds thus generated to financing programmes in the country rather than overhead costs (Buckley, 2011c).

Germany was the first donor country to participate in the Debt2Health programme, cancelling €50 million of its debt with Indonesia to provide €25 million of funding for Global Fund activities in that country over a five-year period from 2008. In total, Pakistan and Côte d'Ivoire have received a further €59 million of debt relief from Germany, generating €29.5 million for Global Fund projects; and Australia has cancelled €54.6 million of bilateral debt with Indonesia, generating €27.3 million (Leading Group on Innovative Financing for Development, 2012). In June 2011, in a new type of "triangular" agreement, Germany also agreed to write off €6.6 million of Egypt's debt, in return for Egypt's contribution of half of that amount to Global Fund anti-malaria programmes in Ethiopia (see table III.1) (Buckley, 2011b).

Other debt swaps: debt-for-development and debt-for-education

Debt conversion has multiple uses…

In addition to the uses described above, debt swaps have also been successfully implemented for education and development.[2] Clear delineation among the various types of swaps is often problematic, however, as debt-for-development swaps typically provide funding for environmental, health and/or education projects.

Based on Buckley, ed. (2011), the cumulative amount of debt-for-development and debt-for-education swaps appears to be in the order of $3 billion, including 18 debt-for-education swaps in 14 countries since 1998, the proceeds of which were in most cases directed to funding for local schools (Buckley, 2011c). Again, however, the proportion of this total that has provided additional funding—and may therefore be considered to constitute IDF—cannot readily be estimated. In particular, $865 million of the $3 billion total represents Debt Reduction-Development Contracts with the Agence Française de Développement, covering debts arising from past ODA loans from France which would otherwise be eligible for cancellation under multilateral debt reduction programmes such as the HIPC Initiative. Although nominally debt-conversion operations, these Contracts stipulate that debtor countries are to continue to service these debts in full, while receiving, however, an equivalent amount of new ODA grants tied to specific programmes when they do so (Agence Française de Développement, n.d.). Thus, resources are not redirected from debt servicing to other uses; rather, potential fiscal savings from debt-service reduction are forgone, the resources instead being directed to specific uses (Buckley, 2011a). These transactions thus cannot be considered to constitute IDF.

Some other debt-for-development programmes, such as that of Germany, more clearly qualify as IDF, and the Government of Germany has earmarked €150 million of bilateral debt for conversion per year since 2008 (including for debt-for-nature and Debt2Health) (Buckley, 2011b).

Potential and challenges

…but has generated limited additional resources

Debt conversion has existed as a means of funding development and environmental projects for some 25 years, and has evolved considerably during this period. While relatively few

---

2   Similar mechanisms have also been widely used for commercial debt-for-equity swaps, although these do not fit the definition of IDF.

cases have generated substantial resources, the cumulative amount is significant. However, debt conversion does not generally provide additional resources for development, to the extent that the cancellation of bilateral debts (on which most debt swaps are now based) is generally classified as ODA; and the scale of those resources that *are* provided remains insufficient to make a meaningful contribution to solving the debt problems of developing countries or improving their creditworthiness. In the case of Debt2Health, there are also potentially significant cash-flow implications for recipient Governments, in that the financing of Global Fund projects occurs within a shorter time frame than that of the payments profile of the debt that is converted. This also reduces the real value of the debt relief (Cassimon, Renard and Verbeke, 2008).

Debt swaps have shown great malleability as regards replication in different sectors. The evolution of debt conversion demonstrates the considerable flexibility associated with its use, the main limitation being that the funds generated are in local currency rather than foreign exchange, which effectively limits use to activities of a domestic nature. However, the relative maturity of debt conversion as a financing mechanism suggests that the potential for further scaling up (with the possible exception of Debt2Health) is likely to be limited: constraints arise from factors such as the availability of debt not eligible for cancellation under existing multilateral mechanisms, the willingness of creditors to engage in debt swaps using such debt, and country eligibility criteria (particularly under Paris Club agreements), including the requirement of participation in an IMF Poverty Reduction and Growth Facility (PRGF) programme.

> Debt conversion is replicable, but the potential for scaling up may be limited

The funding generated by debt swaps is closely tied to their designated end use (although the effectiveness of this depends on monitoring mechanisms). While this effective earmarking of budgetary funds indicates a trade-off with policy space, the debt relief provided by converting debt at a discount (where the debt would otherwise have been serviced) releases resources for use in accordance with national priorities. However, the exclusion of relevant ministries and limited civil society participation in the design and implementation processes may undermine coherence with medium-term national development strategies.

As can be seen from the examples cited above, the scale of debt swaps is highly variable, ranging from less than $1 million (particularly in the case of non-governmental organization-intermediated swaps of commercial debt) to hundreds of millions in the case of some swaps involving bilateral debts. This is an important consideration, as administrative costs are significant, indicating the importance of economies of scale. Thus, large-scale swaps, such as that involving the $473 million multi-country EcoFund in Poland (where operational costs were further reduced by coordination among donors), are likely to be much more cost-effective than smaller projects.

Overall, debt swaps may be expected to continue making a modest contribution to development finance. Their impact could be enhanced if creditor countries: provided higher discount rates (at least equivalent to the extent of debt cancellation that would otherwise be applicable); widened eligibility criteria and increased their transparency; improved the alignment of the programmes supported with national development priorities; and strengthened coordination through the use of multilateral funds such as the EcoFund in Poland.

Risk-mitigation mechanisms

Pull mechanisms

Pull mechanisms are designed to overcome market failures and promote innovation by rewarding successful innovations ex post. By providing assured public funding for goods that embody socially beneficial technologies for which private demand is inadequate (for example, vaccines, pharmaceuticals and renewable energy technologies), they aim to turn notional into effective demand, thus allowing investors to capture more fully the social value of their research and investments. Predictability of funding is a key factor: ensuring a specified level of demand greatly reduces risk and uncertainty, making socially beneficial investments more commercially viable.

Pull mechanisms can also help to reduce adverse effects of oligopolistic markets by decreasing entry barriers: substantially increasing the scale of a market can draw in new producers, increasing competition and lowering prices. A patent buyout for the purpose of making certain intellectual property available to a wide range of producers may have a similar effect.

While this chapter focuses on advance market commitments, three other pull mechanisms should also be noted:

- **Standard prizes**, which reward achievements in a technology development contest. They may be designed as a winner-takes-all prize or may also reward runners-up.
- **Proportional prize structures**, which reward innovations in proportion to their impact, offering a fixed per-unit reward proportional to the total benefits achieved, while the overall size of the award is variable.[3]
- **Patent buyouts**, which are a direct form of the pull mechanism, under which the public sector pays private holders of an existing patent to transfer ownership to the public domain.

Advance market commitments

Advance market commitments aim to make socially beneficial technologies profitable

The function of advance market commitments is to offer a time-limited public subsidy for goods and services that the intended beneficiaries want to buy so as to increase market size and make returns more certain for producers, while requiring a commitment from producers to provide the product at a viable long-term price for an agreed period after public support ends. The concept of global AMCs was developed by Kremer (2000) as a response to market failure in research and development (R&D) for new vaccines against malaria, tuberculosis and the strains of HIV common in Africa, although similar mechanisms had previously been deployed at the national level for other purposes in a number of developing countries (Department for International Development, 2009).

An advance market commitment represents a legally binding contract guaranteeing a specified level of demand at a specified price for a specified period to producers that develop and bring to the marketplace a new product meeting previously agreed product specifications. While producers still bear the risk that their R&D efforts will fail to generate a product that meets those specifications, AMCs guarantee that, if they succeed, a viable market will be available for a known period.

---

3   An example is the Haiti Mobile Money Initiative (HMMI), a partnership between the Bill and Melinda Gates Foundation and USAID, which will award $6 million to participating mobile operators once 5 million mobile money transactions have been executed in Haiti. The prize money will be distributed according to the relative contribution of each operator to the total number of transactions.

The pneumococcal vaccine AMC

Thus far, advance market commitments have mainly been used to accelerate access to new vaccines in developing countries, which is often delayed by a decade or more after their arrival on the market owing to their high costs (Cernuschi and others, 2011). In 2007, five donor Governments (Canada, Italy, Norway, the Russian Federation, and the United Kingdom) joined with the Bill and Melinda Gates Foundation to commit $1.5 billion to the commercialization of new pneumococcal vaccines for use in low-income countries, leading to the establishment of a pilot AMC programme for pneumococcal vaccine in 2009, with co-financing (of up to $6.3 billion) from the GAVI Alliance. The GAVI Alliance also acts as the secretariat of the AMC, co-leading both the design of the pilot (with the World Bank) and its implementation (with the United Nations Children's Fund (UNICEF) and the World Health Organization (WHO)).

A pilot AMC programme is under way for pneumococcal vaccines

The choice of pneumococcal vaccine to test the viability of the AMC concept was based on consideration of two factors: the considerable potential health benefits to target populations and the existence of vaccines in advanced stages of development providing the potential for rapid results (Cernuschi and others, 2011). Pneumococcal disease is the largest single vaccine-preventable cause of death among young children globally, killing more than 800,000 under-fives every year, with more than 80 per cent of these deaths occurring in GAVI-eligible countries (Snyder, Begor and Berndt, 2011).

The pricing structure under the AMC for pneumococcal vaccine is shown in figure III.4. Based on demand forecasts, a target was set of providing 200 million doses of vaccines annually by 2015, and participating manufacturers are required to make a 10–year supply commitment to contributing an agreed proportion of this target level. Vaccine in the first 20 per cent of each manufacturer's supply is priced at $7 per dose, to make AMC participation more attractive and allow rapid recovery of a proportion of R&D costs. The remaining 80 per cent is purchased at a "tail price" of $3.50 per dose, close to the marginal cost of production (ibid.). The difference between the price of $7 per dose and the tail price is met through donor commitments under the AMC; the tail price (and the corresponding part of the $7/dose price) is shared between the GAVI Alliance and the recipient country throughout the AMC period, the level and rate of increase of each country's share varying according to its per capita income.

Two pharmaceutical companies, GlaxoSmithKline and Pfizer, each agreed in March 2010 to provide 30 million doses of pneumococcal vaccines annually for 10 years to GAVI-eligible countries, with each company receiving a pro rata (15 per cent) share of the available funding ($225 million of $1.5 billion). These commitments represent 30 per cent of the target level, leaving 70 per cent of the funding available for further commitments (Cernuschi and others, 2011). As of December 2011, a total of 37 countries had been approved to receive funding for the vaccines, and 16 countries had introduced them with GAVI support (GAVI Alliance, 2012a).

Risks and challenges

Risks and challenges associated with AMCs arise on the levels of funders, producers and recipient countries. For funders, the key issue is the need for assured payments over a prolonged period. In the case of pneumococcal vaccine, the problem is relatively limited for the AMC funders themselves, since their commitment covers only the first two years of supply by each funder; but even here, payments from GAVI need to be maintained over the whole 10–year period, which is potentially more problematic.

Advance market commitments require assured financing and demand

Figure III.4
Price structure of the pneuomococcal vaccine AMC, 2013-2022

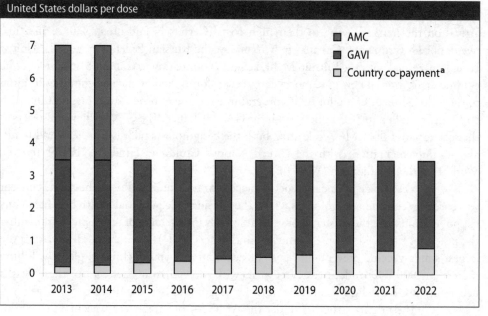

Source: Snyder, Begor and Berndt (2011).

a The country co-payment represents a weighted average, taking account of differential terms according to income levels.

From the producers' perspective, while AMCs can provide predictable funding for the purchase of products after their development, they do not provide funding to support R&D expenditures or product development. This may represent a major obstacle to participation by smaller companies and for products at an earlier stage of the R&D process.

Producer uptake of the AMC for pneumococcal vaccine has so far been relatively limited, with commitments to date reaching only 30 per cent of the target level. However, this may in part reflect potential demand constraints. Besides co-payments by often resource-constrained recipient countries (and their need to bear additional costs, for example, for cold chains and other distribution-related factors), full operation of the AMC would require $6.3 billion of funding from GAVI over the next 10 years, in addition to the $1.5 billion of funding for the AMC itself. Lack of demand has been identified by pharmaceutical companies and non-governmental organizations as a major concern in relation to participation in the AMC. To allay these concerns, UNICEF has agreed to purchase 20 per cent of supply commitments for the first year, 15 per cent for the second and 10 per cent for the third (Snyder, Begor and Berndt, 2011).

The pilot AMC programme has brought significant health benefits

Notwithstanding these issues, the AMC has been successful in accelerating the availability of pneumococcal vaccine in low-income countries, possibly by as much as 10 years, although, as yet, on a more limited scale than was originally envisaged; and the health benefits accruing therefrom are clearly considerable. The GAVI Alliance estimates that acceleration in the production and distribution of pneumococcal vaccine could avert 650,000 future deaths by 2015 (GAVI Alliance Secretariat, 2011). The cost per disability-adjusted life year (DALY)[4]—a measure of cost-effectiveness of medical interventions—is expected to be in the order of $33–$36, well below the threshold value of $100/DALY used by the World Bank to define highly cost-effective medical interventions (Department for International Development, 2009).

---

4   The disability-adjusted life year (DALY) is a measure of the number of years lost due to ill health, disability or early death. It extends the concept of potential years of life lost due to premature death by including, with a lesser weight, years spent in poor health or disability.

Replicability

In some respects, vaccines (and, to a lesser extent, pharmaceuticals) represent a relatively straightforward case for AMCs. This is partly because (as in the case of the IFFIm) the strong political support for vaccination programmes generates greater faith in the long-term donor pledges that are required to give producers confidence. At least as important, however, is the specificity of the product, the relatively straightforward nature of product specification and the readily quantifiable nature of benefits. In the case of vaccines, it is simple to specify that a qualifying vaccine should provide a specified degree of immunization against a specified disease; and estimating the feasible level of coverage at a given price and the health benefits of this level of coverage is relatively straightforward. While this may also be feasible in the case of improvements to some existing technologies (for example, more efficient or lower-cost solar panels), for wholly new technologies (for example, in agriculture and other productive sectors), the exercise may be considerably more complex. It is noteworthy that pull mechanisms currently under development by the World Bank rely on prize mechanisms, rather than on advance market commitments, with the exception of one project involving the development of a vaccine for livestock (see box III.2).

Even in the field of vaccines, however, some caution is needed in extrapolating the experience of pneumococcal vaccine to other disease contexts. While AMCs were originally envisaged as a means of promoting research into new technologies, the pneumococcal vaccines being supplied under the AMC had already been in late stages of development in 2003, six years before the AMC itself was initiated (Snyder, Begor and Berndt, 2011). It therefore remains to be seen how successful this type of mechanism could be for products at earlier stages of the R&D process, when uncertainty regarding development costs and the prospects of fulfilling product specification requirements can generate potentially important additional disincentives to participation.

Further lessons applicable to global advance market commitments may be drawn from experiences of similar programmes at the national level. A report of the Department for International Development (2009) calls attention to three key points in this regard:

(a) The demand created by AMCs will stimulate investment only if suppliers respond to the changed market conditions. If there are constraints or bottlenecks in respect of accessing inputs, AMCs may lead merely to higher prices and the creation of rents with no developmental benefit;

(b) Investors require a degree of certainty that the policy will not be reversed. A less ambitious—but credible—policy is therefore more likely to promote investment than more ambitious policies that are perceived to be unsustainable;

(c) Since AMCs are by nature temporary, lasting benefits require additional action to remove the longer-term barriers to widespread diffusion of the technologies promoted.

Such barriers may include, for example, inadequacy of the resources needed to finance public goods at the national level, and perverse incentives arising from the international intellectual property regime in relation to technologies providing primarily social rather than commercial benefits.

> Advance market commitments are replicable, but other applications may be more complex

Affordable Medicines Facility - malaria

The Affordable Medicines Facility - malaria (AMFm) is an initiative of the Global Fund to Fight AIDS, Tuberculosis and Malaria aimed at reducing the prices of artemisinin-based combination therapies (ACTs) as paid by end-users. ACTs constitute a recently developed

> AMFm seeks to reduce the cost of artemisinin-based combination therapies for malaria

treatment for malaria which is significantly more effective than the alternatives; but prices are higher, and ACTs continue to be underused in many low-income countries. In only 2 of 13 countries with survey-based data on ACT coverage for 2007–2008 were more than 15 per cent of children under age 5 with fever treated with ACTs (World Health Organization, 2009a). A more recent study found treatment rates of between 3 and 10 per cent in four of six malaria-endemic African countries in 2008-2010 (Littrell and others, 2011).

To increase access to quality-assured ACT and minimize the threat of parasite resistance (thus prolonging the lifespan of the treatment), AMFm negotiates with manufacturers to reduce ACT prices for private and public sector users, while also making a co-payment on behalf of first-line buyers. The aim is to reduce the price per treatment from $6–$10 to $0.50 (Matowe and Adeyi, 2010), in order to make ACTs competitive against other, less effective anti-malarial treatments.

Funding for the programme has come from UNITAID, the United Kingdom and the Bill and Melinda Gates Foundation. As of April 2012, a total of $312.1 million had been pledged, of which $243.6 million had been received by the Global Fund (Global Fund, n.d.b). This has financed a pilot project, scheduled to extend from 2010 to 2012, covering eight countries: Cambodia, Ghana, Kenya, Madagascar, the Niger, Nigeria, Uganda and the United Republic of Tanzania. A decision is expected in December 2012 on whether to continue, accelerate, expand or terminate the programme, based in part on an independent evaluation (Sabot and others, 2011).

It has taken time to achieve the subsidization of ACTs

Subsidization of ACTs was proposed as long ago as 2004, and is justified on the basis of the perverse incentives and adverse public-health implications of high prices for ACTs relative to less effective alternatives (Institute of Medicine of the National Academies, 2004). The long delay before the establishment of AMFm partly reflects the impact of a number of controversies about the modalities of such a programme, particularly surrounding subsidization of supplies to the private-for-profit sector. While the private sector is a major source of supply of antimalarials in many developing countries, concerns included the risk that subsidized ACTs would be purchased by people without malaria, and that the benefits of the subsidy would be captured by middlemen rather than reflected in a reduction of end prices (Sabot and others, 2011).

Early results of the AMFm pilot programme appear promising

While it is too early to assess the effects of AMFm, most ACT subsidy programmes and pilot schemes have had broadly positive effects, contributing to wider availability of ACTs relative to other antimalarial treatments at the desired price level, with significantly greater market share (Schäferhoff and Yamey, 2011). Early results of price-tracking surveys in six African countries commissioned by the Global Fund and undertaken to provide continuous information on the impact of AMFm also indicate that AMFm-subsidized medicines are sold at prices much lower than those of non-AMFm antimalarial treatments (Health Action International, 2012). Nonetheless, concerns regarding the role of the private sector are not without justification: in Zanzibar (United Republic of Tanzania), for example, private buyers have ordered 150,000 subsidized doses of ACTs, compared with an average of 2,000 cases of malaria treated in the private sector annually (Sabot and others, 2011).

There are also questions whether results could be improved, for example, by prioritizing ACT subsidies in high-incidence areas, where cost-effectiveness is greater, while placing greater emphasis on diagnosis in low-incidence areas, where subsidized ACTs are otherwise more likely to go to people without malaria, particularly in the private sector (ibid.).

Any definitive judgement on the merits of AMFm must await the independent evaluation scheduled for 2012.

Caribbean Catastrophe Risk Insurance Facility

The Caribbean Catastrophe Risk Insurance Facility (CCRIF), created in 2007 by the members of the Caribbean Community (CARICOM) with the assistance of the World Bank and financial support from Japan, is the first multi-country catastrophe insurance pool. The Facility is capitalized through a multi-donor trust fund financed by the European Union, the World Bank, the Caribbean Development Bank and the Governments of Bermuda, Canada, France, Ireland, and the United Kingdom, in addition to receiving the premiums paid by the 16 participating countries and territories.[5] CCRIF provides rapid financial support to Governments in the event of a catastrophe arising from an earthquake or hurricane,[6] principally to support the re-establishment of basic government functions.

Such insurance is of particular importance in the Caribbean region, where countries are prone to common risks associated with earthquakes and hurricanes, and the small size of national economies means that their impact typically exceeds an individual country's ability to deal with them. A major hurricane occurs in the region on average every two years, typically affecting between one and three countries. The experience of Hurricane Ivan in 2004, which caused losses approaching 200 per cent of GDP in both Grenada and the Cayman Islands (United Nations, 2008), was a major motivation for the establishment of CCRIF.

CCRIF enables member countries to purchase insurance coverage under which payments of up to $100 million are triggered by a once-in-15-year hurricane or a once-in-20-year earthquake. Payouts are determined according to a formula applied to data from the National Hurricane Center (Miami, Florida) (for hurricanes) and the United States Geological Survey (for earthquakes). This allows for immediate payment and eliminates the wait for detailed impact assessments and costings. Payment is intended to approximate 20 per cent of the costs to Governments arising from damage to Government buildings and infrastructure, loss of tax revenue and relief expenditures.

Each country's premiums are determined by the amount of coverage it decides to take, the deductible for that coverage, and its risk profile. Since each country thus pays in proportion to the amount of risk it transfers to CCRIF, there is no cross-subsidization among members. Country premiums range between $200,000 and $4 million per year (United Nations, 2008); and eight payouts totalling $32.2 million were made to seven countries and territories between 2007 and 2010 (Caribbean Catastrophe Risk Insurance Facility, 2011c).

By pooling risks among the member countries, CCRIF allows them to secure insurance at about half the cost that would be incurred if each country accessed the re-insurance market individually. CCRIF retains part of the risk, and keeps a minimum of $20 million in reserve to allow immediate payouts, while contracting commercial reinsurance for a further tranche ($132.5 million in 2009–2010). A catastrophe swap between CCRIF and the World Bank Treasury covers $30 million of the top layer of risk (Caribbean Catastrophe Risk Insurance Facility, 2010).

The Caribbean Catastrophe Risk Insurance Facility allows Caribbean countries to pool disaster-related risks

CCRIF reduces insurance costs substantially…

---

5 The members of CCRIF are Anguilla, Antigua and Barbuda, the Bahamas, Barbados, Belize, Bermuda, the Cayman Islands, Dominica, Grenada, Haiti, Jamaica, Saint Kitts and Nevis, Saint Lucia, Saint Vincent and the Grenadines, Trinidad and Tobago and Turks and Caicos Islands.

6 Beginning in 2012, CCRIF plans to offer coverage also for excess rainfall (Caribbean Catastrophe Risk Insurance Facility, 2011c).

Box III.2

Proposals for pull mechanisms

Apart from their involvement with the pilots for AMCs and the Affordable Medicines Facility - malaria, some donors are seeking to develop pull mechanisms to tackle other development-related challenges, such as climate change and food insecurity, by encouraging investment in renewable energy and agricultural technology.

The World Bank is currently developing agricultural projects based on pull mechanisms through the Agricultural Pull Mechanism (AGPM) initiative, with the objectives of increasing production, reducing losses and enhancing food security for small farmers. There are six pilot programmes currently being developed, which are expected to be launched in June 2012. Their objectives are:

- To develop distribution networks for bio-fortified crop varieties (high pro-vitamin A cassava, maize and sweet potato, and high in iron beans) in Africa
- To promote the development and use of new hybrid rice varieties in South Asia
- To develop improved fertilizers and fertilizer production processes
- To promote adoption of improved post-harvest storage technologies
- To incentivize the use of biocontrol mechanisms against aflatoxin contamination of crops
- To promote development and use of a vaccine against *peste des petits ruminants* in livestock in Africa

Only the pilot with the last-mentioned goal is based on an AMC-type mechanism (a purchase guarantee linked to the distribution of vaccines), all the others relying on various combinations of differently structured prizes.

The Department for International Development (DFID) of the United Kingdom, one of the funders of the pneumococcal vaccine AMC, has also taken a lead role in exploring how AMCs could be used to drive private sector investment in low-carbon and climate-resilient technologies, such as renewable energy (Department for International Development, 2009). Projects currently under consideration encompass, inter alia, medium-scale deployment of biogas for schools and hospitals; assistance in rolling out mini-grids in remote areas of India with limited prospects for connection to the central electricity grid; and the offer of guarantees to private developers of large-scale grid-connected renewable energy projects in the United Republic of Tanzania (based on a proposal of the Private Infrastructure Development Group) (Department for International Development, 2010a; 2010b). Elliot (2010) has proposed the use of AMCs to engage the private sector in the development of new technologies to deal with problems of land and water scarcity, climate change, and declining crop yields.

Source: Department for International Development (2009) and World Bank (2011).

In addition to providing insurance, CCRIF has also been active in assessing climate change adaptation (Caribbean Catastrophe Risk Insurance Facility, 2010), through allocation of resources for the development of a quantitative knowledge base to assist in the reduction of climate change risks and enhance adaptation strategies across the region (Caribbean Catastrophe Risk Insurance Facility, 2011b). This includes regional implementation of the Economics of Climate Adaptation methodology developed by Swiss Re and McKinsey and Company, with the support of key regional partners including the Caribbean Community Climate Change Centre and the Economic Commission for Latin America and the Caribbean (ECLAC).

...and allows for much faster payouts

The Caribbean Catastrophe Risk Insurance Facility offers two advantages to its members over individual insurance on a commercial basis: it provides substantial financial savings and allows for much faster payouts in the event of hurricanes or earthquakes, so that assistance is received quickly, before other relief funds are available. Haiti, for example, received $7.75 million just 14 days after having been struck by the devastating 2010 earthquake (Caribbean Catastrophe Risk Insurance Facility, 2011a).

CCRIF has also shown some flexibility in adjusting to the needs of its members. In 2007, heavy rainfall and a tropical storm surge due to Hurricane Dean, a hurricane with Category 5 status, caused significant damage in Jamaica, Dominica, Saint Lucia, Antigua and Saint Kitts and Nevis. However, the losses were insufficient to trigger payouts to any of these Governments, partly because of the high deductible for hurricanes, and partly because the main impact was on the agricultural sector (which is not covered by CCRIF, as damage to that sector does not entail a cost to the Government). This pointed to the desirability of an extension of CCRIF coverage to include excess rainfall. Such coverage has since been developed, and is expected to become available to member countries in 2012.

Replicability

Risk-pooling and insurance are of particular importance to small countries (which do not have the potential for risk-pooling at the national level), especially in regions prone to natural disasters. The regional basis of such a scheme is not ideal, as there is a higher level of correlation among the risks faced by the countries concerned; but inasmuch as the islands of the Caribbean are spread across a sufficiently wide area, and the impacts of the risks covered are sufficiently localized, this joint risk appears to be manageable.

Similar mechanisms may be beneficial in other regions

These factors would need to be taken into account in any attempt to replicate CCRIF in other regions, particularly for other risks. A similar mechanism might be beneficial for earthquakes and/or tropical storms among the smaller Pacific islands, for example; but insurance against tsunamis is likely to be less viable, because of their potentially much wider geographical scope. Similarly, drought insurance could be beneficial for many countries in sub-Saharan Africa, but a risk-pooling scheme would almost certainly need to be region-wide rather than subregional, owing to the high correlation of risk within subregions.

Nonetheless, given an appropriate combination of geographical scope and risk coverage, there would seem to be some potential for replicating CCRIF in other regions; and the need for such mechanisms might be expected to increase over time as a result of climate change. If the Risk Insurance Facility were replicated more widely, risk-pooling between similar mechanisms across different regions could help to lower costs further.

Private voluntary contributions

Product Red

Product Red was founded in 2006 by the singer Bono and Bobby Shriver to provide a sustained flow of funds from the private sector to the Global Fund to Fight AIDS, Tuberculosis and Malaria, for support of HIV/AIDS programmes in Africa, while also raising awareness of the issue. Product Red is a brand licensed to several private companies, each of which creates a product with the Product Red logo, and donates a portion of the profits made from selling this product to the Global Fund. Participating companies include Nike, American Express UK, Apple, Starbucks, Converse, Bugaboo, Gap, Hallmark (United States) and Dell.

Product Red provides genuinely additional resources…

At the time of writing (April 2012), the initiative had raised $189.6 million for AIDS-related activities of the Global Fund in six countries in Africa: Ghana, Lesotho, Rwanda, South Africa, Swaziland and Zambia[7] (Global Fund, n.d.a; n.d.b). While this

7   See www.theglobalfund.org/en/privatesector/red/ (accessed 10 January 2012).

Table III.1
Summary of mechanisms for innovative international financing

Source	Description	Donors; partnerships	Funds committed (estimated)	Resource mobilization	Predictability	Scalability	Replicability	Additionality to ODA
		Mechanisms that transform time profile of development finance						
International Finance Facility for Immunisation (2006-2011)	Securitization of long-term ODA commitments of donor countries, to front-load resources, proceeds being allocated to the GAVI Alliance	United Kingdom, France, Netherlands, Sweden, Japan, Norway, Italy, Spain, Brazil, South Africa	$6.2 billion over 5-23 years	Raised: $3.6 billion Disbursed: $1.9 billion	Yes	Yes, in principle; currently uncertain in practice	Yes where front-loading is appropriate (that is, where recurrent costs are minimal or self-financing)	No (financed from future ODA budgets)
Debt-for-nature (1984-2011)	Cancellation of payments on one or more foreign currency loans, part or all of the associated debt-service payments being used (in local currency) to fund public and/or non-governmental environmental projects (note: only payments corresponding with that part of the debt which would not otherwise have been cancelled qualifies as IDF)	Examples: Netherlands/Costa Rica, 1989 ($9.9 million); Sweden/Costa Rica, 1989 ($3.5 million); multiple bilateral creditors/Poland, 1992 ($473 million); Italy/Egypt, 2001 ($149 million); Italy/Kenya, 2006 (€44 million); Germany/Madagascar, 2003; (€13.8 million); Germany/Indonesia, 2006 (€6.25 million); Switzerland with Bulgaria in 1995 (Sw F 20 million); France/Madagascar, 2008 ($20 million); France/Cameroon, 2002 ($25 million); United States/Peru, 2002 ($40 million); United States/Indonesia, 2009 ($19.6 million)	–	$1.1 billion - $1.5 billion	No	Yes, but constrained by availability of debt not eligible for cancellation	Yes	No (counted as ODA)
Debt2Health (2007-2011)	Cancellation of payments on one or more bilateral official loans, 50 per cent of the associated debt service being used (in local currency) to finance projects of the Global Fund to Fight HIV, Tuberculosis and Malaria	Germany/Indonesia (€50 million); Germany/Pakistan (€40 million); Germany/Côte d'Ivoire (€19 million); Germany/Egypt (€6.6 million); Australia/Indonesia (€54.6mill) (amounts of debt, of which 50 per cent goes to the Global Fund programmes)	–	$107 million	No	Yes, but constrained by availability of debt not eligible for cancellation	Yes	No (counted as ODA)

(cont'd)

Table III.1 (cont'd)

Source	Description	Donors; partnerships	Funds committed (estimated)	Resource mobilization	Predictability	Scalability	Replicability	Additionality to ODA
Mechanisms to mitigate risk								
Advance market commitments (2007-2011)	Temporary public subsidy to technology-intensive products to incentivize research and development, subject to a negotiated price. Pilot programme for pneumococcal vaccine	Canada, Italy, Norway, Russian Federation, United Kingdom and Bill and Melinda Gates Foundation	$1.5 billion	$450 million	Predictable payments to suppliers	Potentially scalable, but pilot constrained by the GAVI Alliance co-financing capacity	Yes	No (funded from ODA budgets and philanthropic sources)
Affordable Medicines Facility - malaria (AMFm) (2010-2011)	Subsidy to suppliers of artemisinin combination therapy in the form of a co-payment on behalf of purchases, subject to a negotiated price. Pilot stage	UNITAID, United Kingdom, and Bill & Melinda Gates Foundation	$312 million	$243.6 million	Predictable payments to suppliers	Yes	Uncertain, pending outcome of pilot programme	No (funded from ODA budgets, philanthropic sources and IDF; but IDF component counted elsewhere)
Caribbean Catastrophe Risk Insurance Facility (2007-2012)	Provides fast-disbursing financial assistance to Governments in the event of a catastrophe following earthquakes or hurricanes, to re-establish basic Government functions	Partnership of 16 Caribbean countries and territories: Anguilla, Antigua and Barbuda, Bahamas, Barbados, Belize, Bermuda, Cayman Islands, Dominica, Grenada, Haiti, Jamaica, Saint Kitts and Nevis, Saint Lucia, Saint Vincent and the Grenadines, Trinidad and Tobago and Turks and Caicos Islands	$67.5 million	$67.5 million	Yes	Yes	Potentially replicable for some risks in some regions	No (capitalized from donor funds, including ODA; recurrent finance from members)
Mechanism to harness voluntary contributions								
Product Red (2006-2012)	Brand that may be licensed by suppliers for specific products in return for allocation of a proportion of the profits on those products to the Global Fund to Fight HIV, Tuberculosis and Malaria	Nike, American Express UK, Apple, Starbucks, Converse, Bugaboo, Gap, Hallmark (US), Dell, Penguin Classics (UK and International) and Emporio Armani	$190 million	$190 million	Moderate	Dependent on demand	Potentially (but there is risk of competition among alternative brands)	Yes

Source: UN/DESA.

represented only about 1.2 per cent of total contributions received by the Global Fund since Product Red's establishment in 2006, the Global Fund estimates that the programmes financed have reached more than 7.5 million people, for example, providing antiretroviral therapy (ART) to more than 122,000 people living with HIV in Rwanda and Lesotho, including more than 50,000 pregnant women (thereby reducing the risk of mother-to-child transmission) (Global Fund to Fight AIDS, Tuberculosis and Malaria, 2011a).

Product Red has been criticized for being less efficient and less transparent than direct charitable contributions by the companies concerned (Yuvraj, 2009). While this may indeed be the case, the financial value provided to participating companies by the brand offers an additional motivation for contributions. Thus, unlike most other existing forms of IDF, Product Red has the advantage of providing genuinely additional resources which would not otherwise have gone to development or related uses.

...and has some potential for replication and scaling up

Product Red also has some potential for both scalability and replicability. However, it is reasonable to assume that its current scale is a reflection of the current level of demand (although this may well grow over time); and the benefits of widespread replication could be substantially reduced by the effects of competition among alternative "social responsibility" brands.

MassiveGood

...but a voluntary levy on air ticket sales proved unsuccessful

In 2010, the Millennium Foundation for Innovative Finance for Health (a non-profit foundation created by UNITAID in 2008) launched MassiveGood, a voluntary counterpart to the airline ticket levy. The objective was to seek voluntary micro-contributions of $2 or more from people purchasing travel reservations in order to raise funds for UNITAID (Millennium Foundation, n.d.a). Like Product Red, this mechanism generates resources independently of traditional aid, which would not otherwise have been used for development purposes.

A pilot scheme was launched in Spain, jointly with the Spanish Red Cross; but attempts to replicate this in other countries proved problematic, and MassiveGood was formally abandoned in November 2011. The Millennium Foundation attributed this failure to the effects of the financial crisis, which occurred in the period between the conceptualization of the scheme and its implementation. However, the technology behind MassiveGood remains potentially available for future use (Millennium Foundation, n.d.b).

Conclusion

IDF mechanisms have achieved specific financial objectives but have generated few additional resources

Existing IDF mechanisms have generally been successful in fulfilling their specific purposes, such as front-loading ODA disbursements, mitigating risks and incentivizing the commercialization of new vaccines. However, they have generated few genuinely additional resources for development, primarily bringing forward ODA from later years or diverting it from alternative uses. While some of the mechanisms have potential for expansion or replication, the additional resources generated would remain limited in quantitative terms. Table III.1 summarizes the main mechanisms, their current and potential scale and their key features.

Where ODA is diverted, benefits of IDF must be set against opportunity costs

The issue of additionality is critical to any evaluation of these mechanisms; but it also makes such evaluation seriously problematic. Where innovative financing mechanisms harness current or future ODA (as exemplified by AMCs and IFFIm, respectively), their direct benefits will be at least partly offset by the opportunity cost to development of the alternative uses from which ODA is diverted. Even where aid is diverted contemporaneously, identifying which activities are reduced and evaluating the opportunity cost they represent would require considerable research; in the case of future aid, it will be possible only retrospectively.

The relatively limited potential of existing mechanisms to generate additional resources, together with the limited prospects for further major increases in ODA and the political obstacles to the implementation of larger-scale IDF mechanisms such as those as discussed in chapter II, limits in turn the likely increase in overall financing for development in the near future. This has led to increased attention to other options such as growth-indexed bonds; efforts to harness remittances and diaspora resources for development; and tax coordination (see box III.3).

Box III.3

Other mechanisms for harnessing resources for development

The need for additional resources for development has led to increased attention to a number of other potential sources of financing, in addition to the mechanisms discussed in the main text of this publication. While these sources do not strictly meet the criteria for IDF as set out in chapter I, they are nevertheless sometimes included in discussions of IDF.

Growth-indexed bonds are bonds on which the interest rate in any given year is adjusted according to the issuing country's rate of economic growth in that year. For example, a country with a trend growth rate of 5 per cent per year which can borrow in the market at 10 per cent per year might issue bonds paying 1 per cent above or below 9 per cent for every 1 per cent by which growth exceeds or falls short of 5 per cent. The yield thus varies systematically with the gap between the actual and trend growth: payments decline when growth is slow, but increase when it is faster, so that payments have a counter-cyclical effect (Griffith-Jones and Sharma, 2006). If a sufficient proportion of a country's debt were indexed to GDP in this way, it could also reduce the risk of default or problems in debt servicing.

While the idea of growth-indexed bonds has been implemented only to a limited extent, in the context of debt restructurings (notably in Argentina and Greece, but also under the 1989 Brady Initiative), it gained impetus following the financial crisis of the late 1990s; and the current crisis has again focused attention on possible counter-cyclical financing instruments. However, growth-indexed bonds do not qualify as IDF in themselves: rather, they are a commercial instrument through which Governments with access to international financial markets could borrow, without any need for external official support.

Similarly, *diaspora bonds* have been proposed as a potential source of funding for developing-country Government bonds (although these also do not qualify as IDF, for similar reasons). However, while such bonds have in the past been issued successfully by Israel and India, it is far from clear that the conditions that allowed this success—large, well-established and relatively high-income diasporas, with a relatively positive attitude towards, and a high level of trust in, their respective Governments—are replicated widely enough for this to be a major source of funding for more than a handful of countries. Nonetheless, Ethiopia has recently launched a second diaspora bond, despite the failure of its first attempt in 2009, while Kenya and Nigeria are receiving support from the World Bank for pilot bond issues, despite the former's unsuccessful attempts to promote diaspora participation in an infrastructure bond issue in 2010. Nigeria is also receiving support from the African Development Bank, as is Rwanda; and Uganda is planning to issue a diaspora bond in 2013 (This is Africa, 2012).

Other means of *tapping diaspora resources* may have more potential, although mainly for funding of small-scale private investment rather than for the public sector. While occasionally

(cont'd)

Box III.3 (cont'd)

included in discussions of IDF, migrants' remittances clearly do not qualify as such: they have existed for centuries, and are private transactions between individuals for their own personal purposes, generally with little or no development dimension.

Nonetheless, national diasporas represent a potentially significant source of financing for many developing countries. Multilateral development institutions and national development banks could help to tap these resources for development by facilitating investment in productive activities by members of the diaspora[a] and/or remittance recipients. This could provide a source of small-scale foreign direct investment (FDI), whose developmental benefits would be enhanced (relative to more conventional FDI) by being more deeply rooted in local economies.

Some regional development institutions have already undertaken such projects. For example, the Multilateral Investment Fund (MIF), an organ of the Inter-American Development Bank, has, since 2000, offered grants, primarily for technical cooperation, to projects designed to increase remittances and channel them towards development goals. The programme has focused on housing, policy and regulatory frameworks, banking the unbanked, productive investments, financial education, entrepreneurship training, and research and knowledge dissemination (Inter-American Development Bank, 2010).

There is also significant potential to increase developing countries' own public revenues through ***international tax cooperation***. This would have the advantages of sustainability, not creating liabilities, and maintaining policy space and alignment with national priorities and strategies. An important first step could be achieved through information exchange between jurisdictions so as to allow the full application of existing tax codes, which would not require new institutions (other than for norm-setting and monitoring) or tax rate coordination.

Based on data for the mid-2000s, the potential tax gain for developing countries has been estimated to be in the order of $200 billion–$250 billion per year. However, the distribution of these resources varies broadly in line with levels of economic activity, so that the primary benefits would accrue to emerging market economies, while relatively few benefits would accrue to low-income and least developed countries. Nonetheless, the potential gain to sub-Saharan Africa (estimated at $6 billion–$11 billion per year) would represent a substantial benefit[b] (FitzGerald, 2012). The benefits to development could be greatly enhanced if developed countries were to devote some part of their gains from international tax cooperation (estimated at some $475 billion) to development finance (ibid.).

Information exchange is central to tax cooperation, and more comprehensive information exchange under existing treaties would be an essential component. However, the effectiveness of such measures would be undermined by the use of offshore centres both for tax avoidance and as transfer pricing points (Organization for Economic Cooperation and Development, 1977).

Source: UN/DESA.

a Investment by members of the diaspora (nationals resident in other countries) strictly speaking constitute capital flows, although they may in practice be misclassified as remittances.

b These estimates are based on a very conservative methodology using mid-2000s data and are therefore likely to constitute a significant underestimate.

Chapter IV
Using innovative financing for health and climate change mitigation and adaptation

Summary

♦ Most resources raised through existing mechanisms of innovative development financing are channelled through global vertical funds, primarily financing health- and climate-related international and global public goods.

♦ Global funds, helped by a clear link between funding and visible outcomes, have been very successful in mobilizing resources for health. However, only one quarter (about $5.5 billion) of the resources mobilized between 2002 and 2010 came through innovative funding mechanisms.

♦ In the area of climate change, there has been a great proliferation of funds and a less visible link between funding and outcomes, limiting the contribution of innovative mechanisms of financing to about $3 billion between 2002 and 2011, although such financing is expected to increase considerably in the coming years.

♦ The proliferation of global funds has contributed to the fragmentation of the international aid architecture; and the link to targeted outcomes poses challenges in respect of aligning the additional funding with national policies and priorities. Such problems could be magnified should innovative financing increase substantially, particularly through purpose-specific instruments.

♦ To address these problems, consideration should be given to: (a) consolidating global funds in health and in environmental protection, so as to reduce fragmentation and transaction costs; (b) improvements in the governance structures of global funds so as to ensure adequate representation of the interests and priorities of recipient countries; and (c) compliance with agreed aid effectiveness principles, ensuring ownership through alignment with national development strategies and priorities.

♦ Large-scale innovative finance mechanisms represent a potentially more viable route to filling the large financing gaps for development and global public goods, if the political obstacles can be overcome.

Introduction

Innovative development finance (IDF) has to date been focused on specific uses, most notably in the health sector and, more recently, in confronting climate change. The present chapter examines the uses and disbursement dimension of the existing IDF mechanisms, with a view to assessing their effectiveness and the allocation of funds. It adopts a sectoral perspective, focusing primarily on health (as the sector in which innovative development finance is most developed) and climate change mitigation and adaptation (as the sector in

Innovative development finance is most developed in the area of health and has the greatest potential in climate change mitigation and adaptation

which it has the greatest potential in the near future). Based on the lessons drawn from these experiences, this chapter also seeks to assess the implications for global governance of scaling up IDF mechanisms or implementing larger-scale IDF mechanisms, such as international taxation, tax cooperation and allocations of special drawing rights (SDRs) by the International Monetary Fund (IMF).

Uses of innovative development finance for development and global public goods

Each of the innovative finance mechanisms that have been successfully implemented so far (reviewed in chap. III) has been driven by a very clear-cut earmarking of funds for a specific purpose. For funders, this serves the dual purpose of facilitating fundraising, particularly where the results are highly visible and politically popular, and ensuring that funds are allocated at the recipient level in accordance with donor priorities (Adugna, 2009). This has been the key to securing agreement with regard to such mechanisms and their ability to attract funds. From the recipient's perspective, however, earmarking reduces policy space and thus risks undermining some aspects of aid effectiveness, particularly national ownership and alignment with national development strategies.

Innovative finance mechanisms focus on the production of global public goods

The emphasis of actual and potential innovative finance mechanisms on climate change and health reflects in part an increasing focus on the delivery of global public goods (Kaul, Grunberg and Stern, 1999; United Nations Development Programme, 2003). The massive financing needed for climate change mitigation and adaptation looms large in current debates on development finance, while increasing cross-border health risks associated with globalization, and the fight against the HIV/AIDS pandemic in particular, have increased the attention given to global public goods in the health arena (Smith and others, 2003).

The development and global public goods agendas are complementary…

The development and global public goods agendas are clearly complementary. Development is an essential requirement for many global public goods in both the health and environmental spheres, while global public goods, such as limiting climate change and controlling the HIV pandemic, have very considerable developmental benefits. However, there is, as noted in chapter I, an important conceptual and practical distinction to be made between development finance and finance for global public goods. Traditionally, one important underlying rationale for official development assistance (ODA) has been a distributional principle, namely, that it is morally incumbent on the better off to support those who face multiple serious deprivations. The rationale for financing the delivery of global public goods, on the other hand, is based primarily on considerations of allocative efficiency, and includes a substantial element of self-interest: enabling resource-constrained countries to make their necessary contributions to the production of a global public good benefits the donor as well as (and potentially as much as) the recipient.

…but need to be assessed against separate criteria

In consequence, while many forms of external finance have dual development and global public good objectives, levels of financing in these two categories need to be assessed separately (Dervis and Milsom, 2011). Development finance from Development Assistance Committee (DAC) donors should continue to be judged against the United Nations ODA target, whereas financing for global public goods should be based on relevant agreements, such as the 2009 Copenhagen Accord commitments on climate financing,[1] where such agreements exist (United Nations Development Programme, 2012).

---

[1] See FCCC/CP/2009/11/Add.1, decision 2/CP.15.

Like ODA, innovative finance for development should also be assessed against aid effectiveness principles as agreed in the Paris Declaration on Aid Effectiveness and in the outcomes of other international forums (see chap. I), whose focus was not only on improving the stability and predictability of financial resources, but also on decreasing fragmentation and conditionality in the use of funds and facilitating local ownership and alignment with national development strategies. While financing for global public goods should also seek to be so aligned, in this case there may be a rationale for earmarking funds for a particular purpose on the basis of its cross-border externalities. The challenge is to reconcile global priority-setting with national priorities and effectiveness of spending at the national level, and to ensure that national systems are strengthened rather than weakened.

Differentiating between these two agendas is also important in the context of analysing the allocation of innovative finance. While aid allocations, motivated by equity considerations, are largely based on needs, financing for global public goods is driven mainly by efficiency considerations, with the primary concern being the potential impact on production of the global public good concerned. In some areas, such as communicable disease control, needs and potential impact may be closely related; in others, such as carbon emissions reduction, the relationship is likely to be much weaker.

The distinction between funding for development and funding for global public goods thus plays a key role in appraisal of the experience of innovative mechanisms for health and climate financing to date, in terms of both allocation and assessment against aid effectiveness criteria.

Innovative finance in health

Financing needs for health

Universal access to health care is a key goal of the global community, and in the last decade, health—and, more particularly, the health-care sector—has been increasingly prioritized both by national Governments and by donors. However, it is unlikely that the health-related Millennium Development Goals will be reached, let alone that broader global health needs will be fulfilled. Life expectancy remains very low and child mortality rates remain extremely high in many low-income countries, especially in sub-Saharan Africa.

While many of the factors underlying ill health in the developing world—undernutrition, lack of access to safe water and sanitation, poor living and working conditions, and low education levels—are rooted in poverty, health improvements also require access to effective health services able to meet a population's needs. Yet, access to health services and their quality remain poor in many developing countries, owing largely to an insufficiency of financial and human resources for national health systems.

Currently, annual government health expenditure in low-income countries averages $12 per capita. Private expenditure accounts for an additional $13 per capita, but most of this comes from out-of-pocket spending at the point of service delivery or for self-medication in the absence of affordable access to adequate health services. External assistance, which funds both private and public expenditure, amounts to $6 per capita on average, almost one quarter of total spending (Taskforce on Innovative International Financing for Health Systems, 2009).

The health sector has been increasingly prioritized by national Governments and donors

While it is difficult to quantify precisely the financing needed to address the remaining gaps in global health, it is clearly considerable. In a study carried out for the Taskforce on Innovative International Financing for Health Systems, the World Health Organization (WHO) found that merely achieving the health-related Millennium Development Goals—a much more limited objective than fulfilling global health needs—would require an additional $29 per person per year of health sector spending in low-income countries by 2015, or more than a doubling of total current health spending (ibid.).

While these figures have to be interpreted with caution, there is arguably a considerable funding gap relative to needs. Some 40 per cent of the $251 billion of total additional spending necessary between 2009 and 2015 would finance capital investments; 60 per cent would pay for additional recurrent costs, the latter primarily for expansion of the health workforce and increased pharmaceutical expenses. The fact that spending requirements are greatest for supporting health systems, and substantially less for combating specific diseases, partly reflects the sharp increase in external assistance for disease-specific programmes over the last decade (figure IV.1).

Figure IV.1
Total ODA to health, from all donors reporting to OECD, 1995-2010

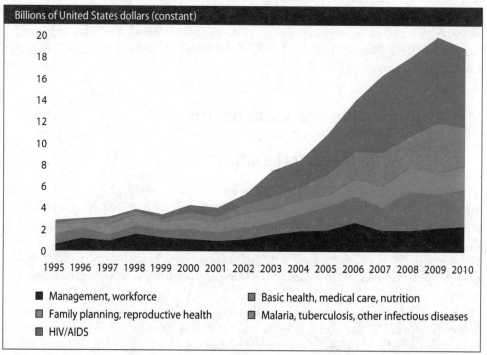

The predominance of recurrent costs in health system financing means that additional funding must be stable, predictable and sustainable. The higher level of recurrent spending necessary to achieve the health-related Millennium Development Goals would also have to be maintained beyond 2015 merely in order to sustain the health benefits achieved. Ideally, these resources would come from domestic sources; however, economic and fiscal constraints limit the potential of many low-income countries to generate or reallocate resources on this scale, so that for the foreseeable future, external finance will continue to play an important role.

The role of innovative finance in the health sector

Most innovative financing mechanisms covered in this publication have targeted interventions in the health sector. As shown in chapter I and figure I.3, virtually all innovative development finance for health—from innovative sources and from innovative intermediate financing mechanisms—has been disbursed through three global initiatives: the Global Fund to Fight AIDS, Tuberculosis and Malaria, the GAVI Alliance and UNITAID (table IV.1). These initiatives have been key drivers of the surge in development assistance for health and because of their innovative governance structures and allocation mechanisms and their vertical (disease-specific) orientation, they have dramatically changed the architecture of development cooperation in health in the last decade.

Innovative finance in health is disbursed through global health initiatives

Table IV.1
Major global health Initiatives

Initiatives	Focus of operations and modalities	Sources of funding	Disbursement
Global Fund to Fight AIDS, Tuberculosis and Malaria	Provides grants for HIV/AIDS, tuberculosis, malaria programmes, and the health system strengthening linked to these diseases Submission of funding proposals by Country Coordinating Mechanisms; selection by expert panel; implementation at the country level by governments, non-governmental organizations and international organizations	US$19 billion in contributions between 2002 and 2010: 94 per cent from traditional bilateral funds, 3.5 per cent from the Gates Foundation and 1.9 per cent from innovative sources (UNITAID, Product Red, Debt2Health)	Disbursements of US$14.4 billion for grants in 150 countries between 2002 and 2011[a]
GAVI Alliance	Grants for programmes to improve immunization and access to vaccines in countries with gross national income below $1,520 Implementation by national authorities in cooperation with United Nations organizations	US$5.2 billion in contributions between 2000 and 2010: 39 per cent from bilateral ODA, 23 per cent from the Gates Foundation and 36 per cent from IFFIm	Disbursements of US$3.5 billion between 2000 and 2011[a]
UNITAID	Global drug purchasing facility using its market power to lower prices of effective HIV/AIDS, malaria and tuberculosis treatments	US$1.3 billion in contributions between 2006 and 2010: 75 per cent from innovative sources (68 per cent from the Solidarity Levy on Airline Tickets; and 7 per cent from Norway's CO_2 levy), 23 per cent from bilateral contributions; and 3 per cent from the Gates Foundation	Disbursements of US$955 million between 2006 and 2010

Sources: Global Fund to Fight AIDS, Tuberculosis and Malaria (2011a); GAVI Alliance (2011a and 2011b); and World Health Organization (2010).

a Data from Global Fund to Fight AIDS, Tuberculosis and Malaria (http://portfolio.theglobalfund.org/en/DataDownloads/Index); and GAVI Alliance (http://www.gavialliance.org/results/disbursements/). See also table IV.2.

The Global Fund, created in 2001 as an initiative of the United Nations and the Group of Eight (G8) to finance programmes targeting the three priority diseases, is by far the largest of the three funds, having received more than $19 billion in contributions from donors between 2002 and 2010. Funding for the Global Fund comes overwhelmingly from traditional bilateral ODA, while most of the remaining financing (3.5 per cent) has been provided by the Bill and Melinda Gates Foundation. Up to 2010, three IDF mechanisms— UNITAID, Product Red and Debt2Health—together accounted for 1.9 per cent of its total funding (Global Fund to Fight AIDS, Tuberculosis and Malaria, 2011a).

The GAVI Alliance, launched at the World Economic Forum in 2000, aims to provide predictable and sustainable resources to countries for adoption of new vaccines and increased coverage of existing ones, while also seeking to lower vaccine prices for low-income countries by aggregating demand and procurement and promoting competition among suppliers. GAVI received $5.2 billion from its funders between 2000 and 2010, 36 per cent of which came from an innovative source, the International Finance Facility for Immunisation (IFFIm).[2]

UNITAID, launched in 2006 as a drug purchasing facility, seeks to supply affordable medicines for HIV/AIDS, malaria and tuberculosis to low-income countries by using its purchasing power to lower market prices of drugs of proved quality, and to create sufficient effective demand for niche products with large public-health benefits. Uniquely, the majority of UNITAID funding—$1.3 billion in total between 2006 and 2010—comes from innovative sources, primarily the Solidarity Levy on Airline Tickets, an integral part of its operating model, which, in 2010, accounted for 63 per cent of UNITAID funding (World Health Organization, 2010). Norway's contribution to UNITAID is funded by a tax on its carbon dioxide (CO_2) emissions; and the remaining funding comes from bilateral contributions (23 per cent) and the Gates Foundation (3 per cent).

Overall, IDF mechanisms raised $5.5 billion for health initiatives between 2002 and 2010 (United Nations, General Assembly, 2011). However, as discussed in chapter III, most of the IDF mechanisms have limited additionality to the ODA provided by DAC members. IFFIm brings forward future ODA disbursements; Debt2Health swaps are funded with bilateral ODA; and contributions to UNITAID are channelled through ODA budgets. In all, only $0.2 billion of the $5.5 billion raised to date through IDF mechanisms in the health sector is additional to ODA in the narrow sense of representing funds not classified as or sourced from ODA (ibid.). The Global Fund and the GAVI Alliance in particular have thus been effective primarily in channelling ODA and private charitable contributions into the health sector (either directly or through innovative mechanisms) rather than in generating new and additional resources for development finance.

> Innovative finance mechanisms raised $5.5 billion for health between 2002 and 2010

Governance of innovative disbursement mechanisms

> Global health partnerships rely heavily on traditional sources of finance...

The global health programmes, albeit largely funded, directly or indirectly, from traditional public and private sources, have nevertheless been innovative in their governance structures and allocation strategies. This institutional innovation was born from a sense of urgency generated by the HIV/AIDS crisis and skepticism about the potential of traditional aid modalities to deal with this and other large-scale health crises (Hardon and Blume, 2005). The new global partnerships were to be evidence-based and guided by independent scientific review, and to be focused on quantifiable results, while the delivering institutions

---

2   Since its inception in 2006, IFFIm has become an increasingly important funding source, accounting for 64 per cent of its total funding during this period.

themselves were to remain lean and transparent and to include the private sector and civil society in their governing structures (Isenman and Shakow, 2010).

The three initiatives were thus set up as public-private partnerships, with the private sector, civil society and philanthropic donors, as well as Governments represented at the board level. They do not implement programmes on the ground but rather finance programmes and projects of developing-country Governments, multilateral organizations and non-government organizations.

A key common feature of the global health funds is their focus on specific diseases or interventions which has been critical to their success in fundraising. As discussed in chapter V, the vertical approach is far from new in development assistance for health. Tackling infectious diseases and pandemics has long been a priority in international development, and donors have tended to view vertical approaches as the most direct means of targeting them. However, there has been a debate regarding the appropriateness of the vertical approach and its relationship with health system development, which dates back to the 1960s and beyond.

There are three particular reasons for the vertical approach adopted by the global funds. First, it reflects a strong political consensus on the need to address specific health issues on a global level—a consensus much stronger than that on health in a broader sense. This is most obvious in the case of the HIV/AIDS pandemic, which is seen as a global health emergency with potential repercussions not only in the most strongly affected countries, but in donor countries as well (Ooms and others, 2011). Second, disease-specific interventions hold the promise of quick, demonstrable and readily quantifiable results which can be directly linked to funding. This is a particular concern not only for philanthropic donors, which value clear success indicators, but also for official donors seeking to demonstrate the impact of ODA. Third, all three mechanisms are strongly oriented towards global public goods (which provide benefits to all countries) or international public goods (which provide benefits to a large subset of countries).

Innovative development finance for health has focused on two types of global public goods. The first type, associated with the Global Fund, encompasses dimensions of health that themselves have global or international public-good attributes—primarily the control of communicable diseases of global scope, notably HIV/AIDS and tuberculosis[3] (particularly multidrug resistant tuberculosis). In addition to its considerable importance within each country, reducing the prevalence of these diseases brings substantial benefit to other countries (including donors), by reducing the risk of their spread across borders. Their effective control is thus a global public good which can be produced only by the collective efforts of all countries.

The second type consists of global or international public goods that require only one producer, while providing generalized health benefits, notably the technologies embodied in vaccines and pharmaceuticals for the prevention or treatment of diseases of global (or wide international) scope. Allowing low-income countries to access these goods has been the primary focus not only of the GAVI Alliance and UNITAID, but also of advance market commitments and the Affordable Medicines Facility-malaria.

At the national level, however, progress in health outcomes—in terms of both global public goods of the first category and national health priorities—can be sustained only if strong health systems are in place to provide reliable access to high-quality health

...but are innovative in their governance structures and allocation strategies

Global health funds adopt a vertical approach focusing on specific interventions that address global public goods

---

3   GAVI Alliance support for polio myelitis vaccination, as part of global eradication efforts, also falls within this category. Since the scope of malaria is not global, its control can be considered only an international— but not a global—public good.

services. Such systems can also substantially reduce the cost of delivering the interventions supported by global funds and other donors. From an aid effectiveness point of view, the key challenge for vertical programmes is thus to strengthen existing health systems, or at least to avoid damaging them, through their more narrowly focused interventions (Unger, de Paepe and Green, 2003).

Allocation of resources raised by innovative finance for health

The Global Fund allocates resources based on national proposals

The global health initiatives vary greatly in their approaches to balancing inter-country equity and efficiency considerations in their resource allocation. The Global Fund has the strongest bias towards efficiency, operating as a challenge fund rewarding the best project proposals within the context of a process of competitive tendering for a fixed amount of resources on a global level (Isenman, Wathne and Baudienille, 2010). Proposals are submitted to the Global Fund through the Country Coordinating Mechanism, a country-level partnership in which key stakeholders are represented, and assessed and selected for funding by a technical expert panel. Once approved, the funds are disbursed to the principal recipients (usually ministries of finance or health, international agencies or non-governmental organizations), which are nominated and overseen by the Mechanism, and implement the projects. There is also a results-based element in funding: an evaluation after two years determines whether targets have been met and whether funding should be continued for a second phase. While both low- and middle-income countries are eligible for funding, proposals in middle-income countries must address specific populations with severe disease burdens in their proposals and a higher level of co-financing is required in their case.

This allocation model is in line with two core principles of the Global Fund: ownership of programmes and a focus on performance. Disbursements are always tied to country-based funding proposals so as to ensure national ownership, and the selection of proposals is conducted at the global rather than at the national level on the basis of their quality.

By comparison, GAVI Alliance and UNITAID allocation strategies place a stronger emphasis on equity. GAVI provides funding only to countries with a gross national income (GNI) per capita below a certain threshold which is annually adjusted (in 2012, the threshold is $1,520), while the current strategy of UNITAID includes a commitment to spend at least 85 per cent of its resources in least developed countries.

GAVI announces funding windows in vaccine support based on country needs

The GAVI Alliance announces funding windows in new and underused vaccine support, immunization services support and health system strengthening support. Countries can access these funds by submitting funding proposals through an Inter-Agency Coordinating Committee comprising representatives from government, civil society, WHO and the United Nations Children's Fund (UNICEF) provided that they fulfil the eligibility criteria (including multi-year immunization plans, costing and financing analysis, and coverage rates for specific existing vaccines in cases where funding is sought for introducing new vaccines). In contrast to the Global Fund, GAVI provides a de facto indicative allocation of funds for countries based on the number of children in age cohorts in eligible countries (Isenman, Wathne and Baudienille, 2010).

Resource allocations for diseases and interventions are determined by the global health partnerships' respective mandates. More than half of the Global Fund's grants are dedicated to HIV/AIDS programmes, while malaria accounts for slightly less than one third and tuberculosis for the remainder. Funding for health systems is linked to disease-specific grants (Global Fund to Fight AIDS, Tuberculosis and Malaria, 2011a). UNITAID drug purchasing programmes show a similar pattern, with HIV/AIDS accounting for more than half of its total spending, and malaria and tuberculosis for 22 per cent and 16 per cent, respectively (World Health Organization, 2010). The largest share of GAVI resources—almost 70 per cent—is allocated to the introduction of new and underused vaccines in eligible countries, the remainder being dedicated to supporting immunization services and health system strengthening (GAVI Alliance, 2011a).

Table IV.2

Cumulative disbursements of the Global Fund to Fight AIDS, Tuberculosis and Malaria and of the GAVI Alliance to selected regions and the top five country recipients in each region, by amount and share of global total, 2000–2011

Region		Global Fund (cumulative disbursements, 2000-2011)			GAVI Alliance (cumulative disbursements, 2000-2011)	
		Amount (millions of US dollars)	Share of global total (percentage)		Amount (millions of US dollars)	Share of global total (percentage)
East Asia and the Pacific		**2063.0**	**14.3**		**255.4**	**7.3**
of which:	China	601.1	4.2	Viet Nam	74.3	2.1
	Indonesia	384.6	2.7	Indonesia	49.4	1.4
	Thailand	292.5	2.0	China	38.7	1.1
	Cambodia	278.2	1.9	Cambodia	27.3	0.8
	Viet Nam	130.9	0.9	Myanmar	26.3	0.8
South Asia		**1284.7**	**8.9**		**725.3**	**20.8**
of which:	India	801.6	5.6	Pakistan	309.5	8.9
	Bangladesh	189.7	1.3	Bangladesh	186.6	5.3
	Pakistan	90.2	0.6	Afghanistan	97.7	2.8
	Nepal	70.8	0.5	India	59.0	1.7
	Iran (Islamic Republic of)	45.0	0.3	Nepal	48.6	1.4
Sub-Saharan Africa		**8505.9**	**59.1**		**2306.4**	**66.1**
of which:	Ethiopia	1142.1	7.9	Ethiopia	317.5	9.1
	United Republic of Tanzania	759.0	5.3	Democratic Republic of the Congo	247.6	7.1
	Nigeria	614.6	4.3	Kenya	214.0	6.1
	Rwanda	575.5	4.0	Uganda	133.6	3.8
	Malawi	477.4	3.3	Nigeria	118.1	3.4
Latin America and the Caribbean		**1074.2**	**7.5**		**44.6**	**1.3**
of which:	Haiti	208.3	1.4	Honduras	17.1	0.5
	Peru	116.3	0.8	Nicaragua	12.6	0.4
	Dominican Republic	99.5	0.7	Bolivia (Plurinational State of)	10.5	0.3
	Guatemala	84.8	0.6	Guyana	2.4	0.1
	Honduras	78.2	0.5	Haiti	1.8	0.1
Other regions		**1471.9**	**10.2**		**156.1**	**4.5**
Global total		**14399.7**	**100.0**		**3487.8**	**100.0**

Sources: Global Fund to Fight AIDS, Tuberculosis and Malaria (http://portfolio.theglobalfund.org/en/DataDownloads/Index); and GAVI Alliance (http://www.gavialliance.org/results/disbursements/).

Figure IV.2
Regional distribution of cumulative disbursements from health and climate funds since 2000

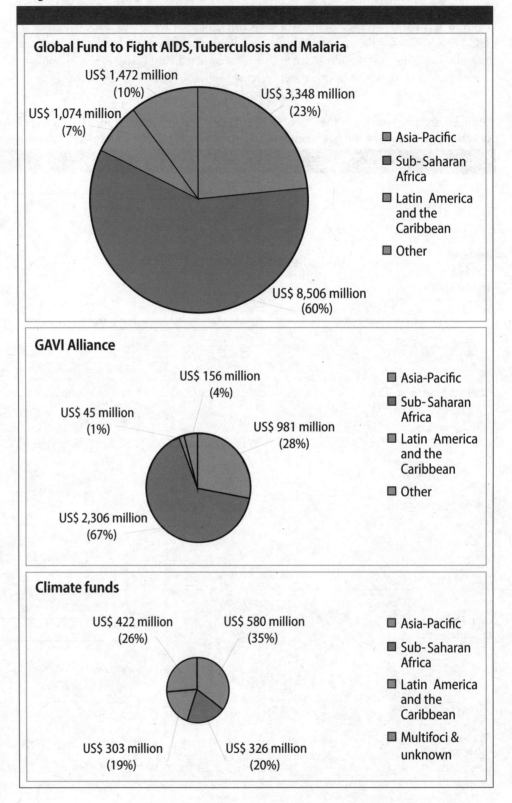

Sources: The Global Fund to Fight AIDS, Tuberculosis and Malaria (http://portfolio.theglobalfund.org/en/DataDownloads/Index); GAVI Alliance (http://www.gavialliance.org/results/disbursements/); and Climate Funds Update (www.climatefundsupdate.org).
Note: Each pie chart is scaled in proportion to its total disbursements.

Geographically, about 60 per cent of Global Fund flows have gone to Africa, 23 per cent to Asia and 7 per cent to Latin America; GAVI allocations follow a very similar pattern (see table IV.2 and figure IV.2). The strong emphasis on Africa reflects its particularly high disease burden and the focus of the global partnerships on low-income countries and least developed countries. GAVI in particular has targeted the poorest and most fragile low-income countries, which have received relatively large disbursements per child (CEPA, 2010). UNITAID supports projects in 94 countries, covering most of sub-Saharan Africa and 26 Asian countries as a priority. However, the geographical allocation of funds cannot readily be estimated owing to the global nature of its approach and the nature of its relationship with implementing partners.

The absence of predefined and needs-based country allocations in the Global Fund contributes to a relatively weak, though positive, relationship between disease-specific needs and disbursements: countries with a higher incidence of HIV or tuberculosis have on average received only marginally more funding for programmes for these diseases in the last decade (see figure IV.3).[4] While this may in part be due to income thresholds, it is also possible that lack of capacity to formulate effective programmes and/or obstacles to project implementation have limited access in some high-incidence countries.

There is no strong link between the disease-specific needs of countries and disbursements

Despite the greater emphasis of the GAVI Alliance on equity and its indicative country allocations, there is no discernible relationship between its disbursements and immunization needs (figure IV.4). This may reflect in part the eligibility requirements relating to coverage rates. By far, the largest component of GAVI Alliance activities entails support for the introduction of new and underused vaccines. However, access to this funding requires at least 70 per cent coverage of diphtheria, pertussis and tetanus (DPT3) immunization.[5] While countries below this threshold can apply for immunization services support, less funding is available within this window; moreover, a strong performance-based component is included, with funding after the initial investment being based on the additional number of children receiving immunization. This has made it difficult for low-income countries with weak institutions, in particular, to access these resources (Chee and others, 2007).

Effectiveness of innovative finance for health

Examining the overall effectiveness of innovative development finance is a challenging task, as IDF funds are disbursed in combination with more conventional development finance from bilateral and private donors. In the present section, we focus on the principal channels through which IDF is disbursed, namely, the Global Fund and the GAVI Alliance.[6]

Both these institutions emphasize their commitment to the aid effectiveness agenda and to the Paris Declaration on Aid Effectiveness, the Accra Agenda for Action[7] and the Busan Partnership for Effective Development Cooperation. In some areas—notably transparency, innovative and more inclusive governance structures, and emphasis on results—they are sometimes considered exemplary. However, tensions exist between the earmarking of funds for specific purposes and other aid effectiveness principles, particularly country ownership. The present section assesses the Global Fund and the GAVI

Both the Global Fund and the GAVI Alliance are committed to the aid effectiveness agenda

---

4   A similar analysis for malaria has not been possible owing to inadequate data.

5   Under GAVI phase 1, the minimum coverage rate required for DPT3 was 50 per cent.

6   UNITAID is considered only in selected parts of this section, as it disburses its funds to multilateral implementing partners. Direct assessment of effectiveness at the country level would thus be difficult.

7   Document A/63/539, annex.

Figure IV.3
Allocation of Global Fund resources (2000-2010) versus country needs

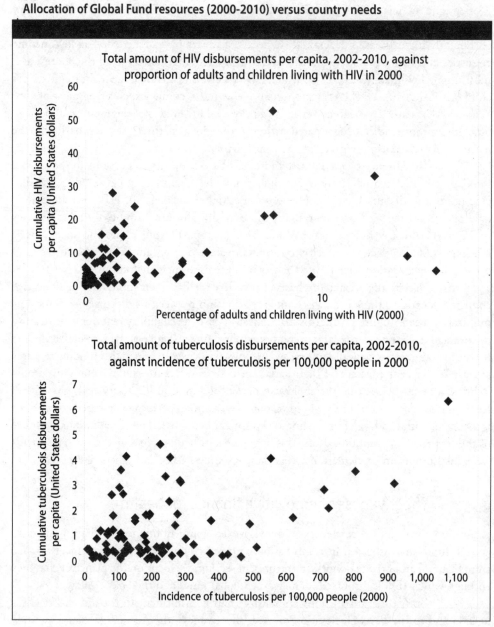

Sources: Global Fund to Fight AIDS, Tuberculosis and Malaria (http:// portfolio.theglobalfund. org/en/DataDownloads/ Index); and Health Nutrition and Population Statistics Database, World Bank (http://databank.worldbank. org/ddp/home.do).

Alliance from a global perspective, in terms of ability to meet stated goals, stability and predictability of disbursements, fragmentation and country ownership and alignment with national strategies. Chapter V considers the perspective of recipient countries.

Meeting stated goals

Vertical funds have achieved visible results in their priority areas

The major strength of vertical funds is generally perceived to be their ability to achieve rapid and visible results. Both the Global Fund and the GAVI Alliance report strong progress in their priority areas of intervention, quantified in millions of lives. The GAVI Alliance claims that its vaccination programmes have prevented more than 5 million future deaths since its inception in 2000. The Global Fund reports that more than 3 million people receive antiretroviral treatment financed by its grants. The simplicity and tangibility of such indicators have played an important role in enabling the Global Fund and the GAVI Alliance to secure funding.

Independent evaluations largely confirm the positive impacts of the two institutions in their respective areas of intervention. An external evaluation carried out in 18 countries found the Global Fund to have contributed to rapidly increasing funding for HIV/AIDS, a major expansion in access to services, large increases in treatment coverage, and similar progress in the distribution of bed nets and other preventive measures against malaria (Global Fund Technical Evaluation Reference Group, 2009a). The GAVI Alliance flagship programme, which provides support for new and underused vaccines, has allowed countries to scale up their vaccination programmes, and has also contributed to increasing the supply stability of underused vaccines and to creating viable markets in low-income countries (CEPA, 2010).

Figure IV.4

Allocation of GAVI Alliance resources (2000-2010) versus country needs

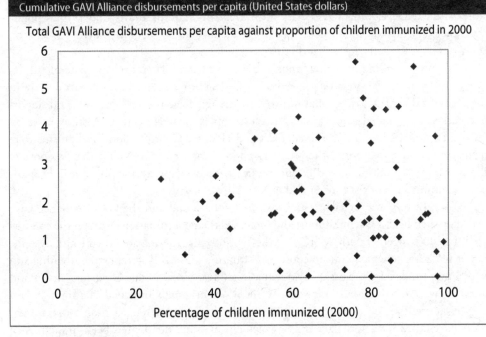

Total GAVI Alliance disbursements per capita against proportion of children immunized in 2000

Percentage of children immunized (2000)

Sources: GAVI Alliance (http://www.gavialliance.org); and Health Nutrition and Population Statistics Database, World Bank (http://databank.worldbank.org/ddp/home.do).

Stability and predictability

Greater stability, sustainability and predictability of resource flows for recipient countries have long been important motivations for IDF mechanisms. These considerations are of particular importance in the health sector, which is characterized by substantial recurrent costs over longer time periods. Dependence on short-term aid therefore carries significant risks of financial disruption (Dodd and Lane, 2010). However, while some innovative mechanisms have the potential to provide funding more predictably than ODA, as discussed in chapter III, greater predictability of fundraising at the international level does not necessarily translate automatically into more predictable delivery at the country level.

Health partnerships have contributed to increased predictability of aid for health

Overall, the health partnerships are able to make longer-term commitments for support, on average, than bilateral donors, and have thus contributed to increased predictability of aid for health in recent years (Dodd and Lane, 2010; see also Organization for Economic Cooperation and Development, 2011b). However, the Global Fund's overwhelming reliance on bilateral contributions leaves it highly vulnerable to funding cuts. In November 2011, it was forced to cancel its eleventh funding window, reflecting budgetary pressures in main donor countries. As a result, it will fund only projects already approved and not issue new grants until the end of 2013. Similarly, the independent evaluation of the International Finance Facility for Immunisation noted concerns about the financial sustainability of the GAVI Alliance in the context of its dependency on IFFIm (Pearson and others, 2011).

Fragmentation

In recent decades, the number of donors and aid projects in all areas of development cooperation has risen sharply, while the average project size is on the decline. More than 30 countries now have to deal with over 40 active bilateral and multilateral donors, while not a single country had to deal with this degree of fragmentation just two decades ago (International Development Association, 2007). This state of affairs undermines policy coherence, raises transaction costs and imposes substantial administrative burdens on countries with limited capacity and human resources.

The pooling of donor funds and a move from bilateral to multilateral aid delivery clearly have the potential to reduce fragmentation. However, and particularly in the case of HIV/AIDS, the global health partnerships have not replaced bilateral donors but, rather, have added actors to an already complex aid architecture. A study in seven recipient countries found that the Global Fund Country Coordination Mechanisms were increasingly integrated with other country coordination structures, but that in some of those countries, multiple coordination bodies with overlapping membership and mandates continued to coexist (Spicer and others, 2010).

Health system support has been scaled up and is becoming better coordinated in order to reduce fragmentation

In response to such criticisms, the Global Fund and the GAVI Alliance have scaled up their health system support and increased their coordination efforts at the country level. In 2009, together with WHO and the World Bank, they created the Health Systems Funding Platform, which aims to coordinate funding for health system strengthening and to disburse funds on the basis of a single national health plan, fiduciary arrangement and monitoring and evaluation framework. While it was originally intended that there should also be substantial new resources to fund joint health system strengthening programmes, these have failed to materialize; and engagement by other donors has been limited. As a result, the emphasis has shifted towards coordinating the health system strengthening programmes of the participating organizations (Hill and others, 2011).

Even in this attenuated form, the Platform has some potential to increase aid effectiveness and to reduce transaction costs associated with fragmentation. As it becomes operational in more countries, however, it will have to address a number of challenges. The Global Fund and the GAVI Alliance maintain separate procedures and timelines for receiving and approving grant applications, which renders joint applications less attractive for countries (Evidence to Policy Initiative, 2011). There is also a significant degree of uncertainty centred around the amount of funding that will be available for health system strengthening, given the current fiscal environment and the preference of certain constituencies on the boards of both institutions for focusing on their core mandates.

Local ownership and alignment

Country ownership of national development strategies and donor alignment with such strategies are at the core of the aid effectiveness agenda. These goals are best realized through general budget support and sector-wide approaches. In development assistance for health, however, sector-wide approaches have so far played a relatively minor role—accounting for less than 8 per cent of total aid for health between 2002 and 2006 (Piva and Dodd, 2009).

Disease-specific mandates constrain global health partnerships in respect of aligning their funding with country priorities

The ability of the global health partnerships to act in conformity with those goals is constrained by their disease- and intervention-specific mandates, reflecting global health priorities, which may limit the scope for alignment with national health priorities. Measured in disability-adjusted life years (DALYs)[8], HIV/AIDS, tuberculosis and malaria account for 5.2 per cent, 2.7 per cent and 4 per cent, respectively, of the total disease burden in low-income countries (World Health Organization, 2008). In comparison, diarrhoea, and maternal and perinatal conditions, account for 7.2 per cent and 14.8 per cent, respectively, of the disease burden. While non-communicable diseases account for almost one third of the disease burden, they are largely ignored by donors and draw less than 3 per cent of overall aid to health (Nugent and Feigl, 2010).

Some degree of ownership is ensured within the constraints of the vertical approach by funding proposals from countries and implementation by nationally nominated principal recipients (Radelet and Levine, 2008). Nonetheless, this strengthens the case for further extending health system support so as to allow recipient countries greater flexibility in allocating health spending in line with national priorities; and to ensure that disease-specific interventions are set up in such a way as to strengthen national systems instead of undermining them, for example, by drawing health workers out of the general public-health system into vertical programmes. To address these concerns, the GAVI Alliance and the Global Fund could usefully fund investments in the educational infrastructure and the training of new health professionals, instead of focusing only on in-service training on disease interventions of existing staff (Vujicic and others, 2012).

Conclusion

Innovative disbursement mechanisms in the health sector target specific diseases and interventions, generally with global public-good characteristics. The earmarking of funds for a highly visible purpose with global appeal and the potential to demonstrate measurable results has arguably been integral to those mechanisms' success in channelling substantial resources into their priority subsectors and enabling large-scale measurable progress in specific areas of health.

The earmarking of funds for a visible purpose was integral to channelling resources into priority areas

While it can represent a departure from national priorities, provision of additional resources for particular diseases or interventions may be justifiable to the extent that it corrects underfunding of global public goods. However, it is important that, in delivering such funds, a further increase in the fragmentation of the aid architecture and disbursement mechanisms—and thus in the transaction costs of aid delivery—be avoided. This can best be achieved by consolidating bilateral and multilateral disbursement mechanisms.

---

8   Disability-adjusted life years take into account both premature death and disability caused by disease.

It is also important to ensure that the ability of health systems to deliver on local needs as well as global priorities is enhanced rather than impaired. This implies a need for integration of financing for disease-specific programmes into health systems, and greater funding for health systems (including budgetary support) in addition to disease-specific funding. While the Global Fund and the GAVI Alliance have themselves taken some important steps in this direction, notably through the establishment of the Health Systems Strengthening Platform, their specific mandates set a limit to these efforts.

Climate change

While the funding mechanisms that have thus far been established under the rubric of innovative development finance have focused mainly on health, there is a growing emphasis on climate change. As in the case of health, where innovative mechanisms have mainly funded particular health-related interventions with strong global public-good attributes, such as communicable disease control, climate-related innovative development finance has similarly concentrated on the global public good of mitigation rather than adaptation.

The unprecedented global improvements in average living standards over the last two centuries have come at the cost of serious degradation of the natural environment. The most serious environmental threat is climate change, brought about by global emissions of carbon dioxide and other greenhouse gases. In addition to considerable expenditure for adaptation, climate change necessitates a fundamental shift in development strategies towards a much less carbon-intensive model, and a major reduction in reliance on fossil fuels.

While climate change arises overwhelmingly from historical emissions in developed countries, it impacts disproportionately the well-being and livelihoods of people in developing countries. This makes a compelling case for the assumption by richer countries of the costs of mitigation and adaptation.

Financing needs for climate change mitigation and adaptation

Financing needs arising from climate change in developing countries are large

Estimates of the financing needs arising from climate change in developing countries are seriously complicated by methodological issues and the inherent uncertainties surrounding climate change impacts and associated mitigation and adaptation needs, and vary widely according to geographical and sectoral coverage, timescale and assumed objectives (Buchner and others, 2011). However, it is generally recognized that the costs are considerable.[9]

The World Bank (2010c), for example, reports estimates of additional annual investment needs in developing countries by 2030 at $140 billion–$175 billion for mitigation (plus additional upfront investments of $265 billion–$565 billion) and $30 billion–$100 billion for adaptation. Other studies produce broader estimates of the financing needed to achieve sustainable development objectives. *World Economic and Social Survey 2011* (United Nations, 2011a), for example, estimates incremental green investment needs

---

[9]   Reports estimating climate financing needs include those of Stern (2007); United Nations Framework Convention on Climate Change (2007); United Nations Development Programme (2007); International Energy Agency (2008); McKinsey & Company (2009); United Nations Conference on Trade and Development (2010); World Bank (2010c); United Nations Environment Programme (2011); and United Nations (2009b; 2011a).

for achieving sustainable development objectives in a context of climate change and global carbon constraints at about 3 per cent of world gross product (WGP).[10] Assuming that some 60 per cent of such investment will occur in developing countries, this implies a little over $1 trillion per year in additional investment, which will require domestic and external financing from the public and private sectors.

At the 2009 United Nations Climate Change Conference in Copenhagen, developed countries pledged $100 billion annually to developing countries by 2020 to finance climate change adaptation and mitigation,[11] this compared with total aid from DAC countries for climate change-related programmes of $42 billion between 2000 and 2009 (Organization for Economic Cooperation and Development, 2011c). While DAC commitments increased to almost $23 billion (15 per cent of total ODA) in 2010, one third for adaptation and two thirds for mitigation (Organization for Economic Cooperation and Development, 2011d), this amount remains short of the commitment, and well below the level of international assistance required.

> Developed countries have pledged $100 billion annually to developing countries by 2020 for climate change adaptation and mitigation

The role of innovative finance in climate change funding

Despite the considerable potential of the innovative financing proposals discussed in chapter II—notably, international carbon taxes, emissions trading, financial and currency transaction taxes, and allocations of special drawing rights (SDRs)—innovative development finance has thus far made a limited contribution, estimated at something over $1 billion to climate change financing.[12]

As discussed in chapter II, the one tax mechanism developed to date is a 2 per cent levy on transactions of the Clean Development Mechanism (CDM), a global emissions trading scheme established by the 1997 Kyoto Protocol[13] to the United Nations Framework Convention on Climate Change[14] as a means of transferring finance and technology to developing countries for exploitation of low-carbon development opportunities (see Article 12 of the Protocol). To date, the proceeds amount to $168 million, providing two thirds of the cumulative cash receipts of the Adaptation Fund[15] (the remainder coming from voluntary government contributions). So far, utilization of these resources has been minimal: of about $258 million available, just over $30 million had been disbursed for projects in 12 countries by 2011, and almost half of this covered fund administration costs (Nakhooda and others, 2011).

> So far, innovative development finance has made only a limited contribution

Separately from the Clean Development Mechanism, Germany allocates part of the proceeds from the sale of tradable emission certificates under the European Union Emission Trading Scheme (EU ETS) to fund its own International Climate Initiative and thereby support international projects for climate change mitigation and adaptation and climate-related biodiversity. To date, the International Climate Initiative has received

---

10   These estimates are broadly in line with those of the United Nations Environment Programme (2011), but do suggest that the investments needed to induce a green energy transformation would be higher.

11   See FCCC/CP/2009/11/Add.1, decision 2/CP.15, para. 8.

12   The present discussion focuses on mechanisms designed primarily to channel resources to climate-related programmes rather than risk-mitigation mechanisms such as the Caribbean Catastrophe Risk Insurance Facility. Mechanisms in the latter category are discussed in chapter III.

13   United Nations, *Treaty Series*, vol. 2303, No. 30822.

14   Ibid., vol. 1771, No.30822.

15   See FCCC/KP/CMP/2007/9/Add.1a, decision 1/CMP.3.

pledges of $841 million and $582 million of financial support has been approved. However, it is unclear how much has been disbursed as of early 2012 (Climate Funds Update, n.d.).

Debt-for-nature swaps constitute the longest-standing innovative financing mechanism for environmental projects (see chap. III). Since their emergence in the 1980s, it has been estimated that some $1.1 billion–$1.5 billion worth of debt has been swapped for environmental causes (Sheikh, 2010; Buckley, ed., 2011). However, it is difficult to determine how much of this has been for climate change mitigation and adaptation.

Despite the limited contribution of innovative mechanisms to climate finance to date, the urgency and global nature of the climate change threat make this the area most likely to generate a scaling up of existing flows in the near future, and the issue most likely to stimulate progress on larger-scale mechanisms.

Substantial progress may already be anticipated in the coming years. From 2012, the Government of Germany will allocate 100 per cent of the proceeds derived from auctioning EU ETS permits to a Special Energy and Climate Fund, established in 2010 to finance national and international climate-related expenditures. This is expected to generate $780 million in 2012, and some $3.2 billion annually in 2013–2015, approximately 15 per cent of which (about $500 million per year) is to be directed to international climate financing from 2013. Activities to be supported include forest protection and biodiversity and enhancement of existing climate-related activities (including the International Climate Initiative), as well as a new German climate technology initiative (German Watch, 2011).

From 2013 onward, the European Union as a whole has agreed to auction emissions allowances (in some sectors up to 100 per cent), which is expected to generate revenues in the range of $20 billion–$35 billion per annum. While member States have been reluctant to make a collective decision to earmark these resources for climate financing, many individual countries have indicated their intention to allocate at least 50 per cent for this purpose (I-8 Group/Leading Innovative Financing for Equity (L.I.F.E.), 2009). However, it remains unclear what proportion of these resources, if any, will be used to finance climate change action in developing countries. Since Germany has been the most willing EU country to devote the proceeds of emission allowance sales to international climate-related activities, average allocations of post–2013 revenues are unlikely to exceed Germany's commitment of 15 per cent. This would imply IDF from EU ETS trading in the order of $1 billion to $5 billion per annum.

The Reducing Emissions from Deforestation and Forest Degradation plus Conservation (REDD+) initiative is another potentially important IDF mechanism for climate change mitigation in developing countries. While the Programme currently acts as a coordinating mechanism for conventional bilateral and multilateral funding, it is proposed that REDD+ should evolve into an innovative carbon trading-based mechanism that would issue tradable carbon credits to countries with tropical forests for saving and planting trees, which could then be sold to other countries to offset their own carbon emissions. A number of pilot projects testing REDD+ principles and procedures have been launched, and some $450 million of financing has been approved between 2008 and 2011, with disbursements of $250 million (Nakhooda, Caravani and Schalatek, 2011).

REDD+ is considered a key component of the post–2012 international climate change regime; and with deforestation accounting for an estimated 17 per cent of greenhouse gas emissions (Intergovernmental Panel on Climate Change, 2008), its financial potential is considerable. It has been estimated that markets for emission reduction credits from REDD+ could generate some $30 billion per annum for developing nations,

The urgency and global nature of the climate change threat make it the area most likely to generate a scaling up of innovative finance

REDD+ could evolve into an innovative mechanism by issuing carbon credits to countries for preserving tropical forests stimulating an exponential increase in demand for carbon sequestration services, particularly from South-East Asia (Nakhooda, Caravani and Schalatek, 2011). Potential receipts for Indonesia alone could amount to $2 billion per year (Figueroa, 2008).

However, despite support from a number of countries, notably Norway, and from the United Nations and other multilateral organizations, no international agreement has yet been reached on the implementation of such a carbon offset approach. At the seventeenth session of the Conference of the Parties to the United Nations Framework Convention on Climate Change, held in Durban from 28 November to 11 December 2011, significant progress was made towards agreement on important preconditions for the design and operation of a REDD+ emissions trading scheme, including reference levels for forest-related carbon emissions, environmental safeguards, and monitoring, reporting and verification. However, the absence of agreement on identifying sustainable means of financing represents a major obstacle to the establishment of a REDD+ market mechanism in the near future. Other problems include the lack of reliable information on the highly variable opportunity costs of forest protection in different local contexts and the carbon content of forests (Nakhooda, Caravani and Schalatek, 2011). The voluntary nature of REDD+ may also limit its scope and undermine effective project delivery; and trade-offs may arise between the necessity of preventing deforestation, and the need to tailor REDD+ activities to local circumstances, including potential adverse effects on forest-dependent communities and indigenous peoples.

In scaling up existing IDF mechanisms and implementing new ones, it is important to ensure that resources are not diverted away from development assistance. Among the existing mechanisms, however, only the levy on CDM transactions devised to finance the Adaptation Fund is truly additional to traditional ODA: proceeds from the sale of ETS emission certificates, support to climate-related risk insurance mechanisms and debt-for-nature swaps are all included in ODA.

Allocation of innovative climate finance

In the climate change sector, innovative financing is disbursed mainly through multilateral, bilateral and national special-purpose funds which earmark resources for particular adaptation and/or mitigation activities. The distinction between adaptation and mitigation is critical: while support to adaptation benefits primarily the recipient country (although it may arguably be considered compensation justified by the historical responsibility of developed-country emissions for climate change), financing of mitigation in developing countries is more appropriately viewed as supporting production of a global public good of universal benefit (climate stability). Thus, while there is a strong case to be made for a needs-based allocation and national administration of funds for adaptation, the key considerations in mitigation are potential for and cost of mitigation.

The Adaptation Fund, which is funded principally through innovative finance, allocates resources according to need. The Fund takes into consideration the level of vulnerability and urgency, while seeking to ensure equitable access to funds (for example, by capping overall resource allocations to each country). Unusually, its board, comprising 16 members representing the parties to the Kyoto Protocol to the United Nations Framework Convention on Climate Change, includes a majority of developing countries, in line with the compensatory nature of adaptation flows.

Innovative financing is disbursed largely by special-purpose funds for specific adaptation or mitigation activities

In principle, Adaptation Fund projects are implemented by national implementation entities, thus providing national Governments with direct access to funds (Dervis and Milsom, 2011). In practice, however, national implementation has so far been the exception (United Nations, General Assembly, 2011). Moreover, the Adaptation Fund's allocation criteria have not always been clear, and low-income and resource-scarce countries often lack the human and technical capacity to tap these funds effectively.

Despite a commitment to balanced allocation, resources for adaptation trail behind resources for mitigation

This low level of funding reflects a more general lack of resources for adaptation, which dramatically trail behind resources for mitigation, despite the commitment to balanced allocation set out in the Copenhagen Accord (Nakhooda and others, 2011). Despite a commitment to splitting resources equally between sustainable energy on the one hand and adaptation and biodiversity on the other, Germany's International Climate Initiative (funded from auctions of certified emissions reductions (CERs)) in practice devotes a larger share of funds towards the former. This results from its selection of projects on the basis of their mitigation potential; innovative nature; and their complementarities with partner countries' national strategies, Germany's climate policy and the conservation of other global environmental goods.

The Green Climate Fund is envisaged as the main multilateral financing mechanism for disbursement of climate finance

The Green Climate Fund, agreed in Cancun in 2010,[16] could dwarf all the existing funding channels in the coming years. It is envisaged as the main multilateral financing mechanism for disbursement of the additional resources pledged in Copenhagen. It may also be a channel for innovative finance flows: for example, the European Union is currently exploring options for the pricing of carbon emissions from the shipping and aviation industries in order to finance the Fund.[17]

Because of its potential importance, the Green Climate Fund's governance structures and its allocation and disbursement principles were strongly contested. While developing countries insisted on financing from new, additional and predictable sources, and (as in the case of the Adaptation Fund) on direct access to these funds, developed countries argued for the Fund's primary role to be as a catalyst of private investments, and for basing disbursements on measurable results (Schalatek, Nakhooda and Bird, 2012). At the seventeenth session of the Conference of the Parties to the United Nations Framework Convention on Climate Change, held in Durban in November–December 2011, it was decided that developed and developing countries should have equal representation on its Board, and that allocation would broadly follow the model of the Adaptation Fund, allowing developing countries direct access to funding (Nakhooda and Schalatek, 2012).[18]

Since it is envisaged that the Green Climate Fund will channel tens of billions of United States dollars annually, an appropriate balance between equity and efficiency is critical. Allocation mechanisms could usefully draw on the experience of the funds set up under the Global Environment Facility (GEF), including the Least Developed Countries Fund and the Special Climate Change Fund. The Facility determines country envelopes based on a formula that includes per capita income (so as to ensure that poor countries receive sufficient resources), past institutional performance as measured by the World Bank Country Policy and Institutional Assessment (CPIA) and past performance on GEF projects, and a measure of the likely environmental benefit of the investment (Global Environment Facility, 2010).

---

16   See FCCC/CP/2010/7/Add.1, decision 1/CP.16, para.102.

17   http://www.euractiv.com/climate-environment/finance-ministers-eye-transport-levies-feed-climate-fund-news-510986.

18   See FCCC/CP/2011/9/Add.1, decision 3/CP17.

It is not clear that existing climate funds are allocating resources either in accordance with efficiency criteria or in function of needs. Asia and the Pacific has been the largest recipient of climate finance, receiving about one third of the funds, with the main country recipients being China, India and Indonesia. Sub-Saharan Africa and Latin America and the Caribbean each received one fifth of climate funds (see figure IV.2 and table IV.3). The geographical allocation of climate funds may in part reflect their focus on mitigation (adaptation accounting for only 25 per cent of the total) and the greater potential for mitigation in more industrialized regions; but even in respect of adaptation, the share of sub-Saharan Africa is relatively limited (35 per cent, as compared with 27 per cent for Asia and the Pacific and 20 per cent for Latin America). Similarly in forestry, where sub-Saharan Africa has considerable potential, its share of funding is relatively limited: only 15 per cent of REDD+ funding has gone to sub-Saharan Africa, representing approximately half the shares of Latin America (32 per cent) and Asia and the Pacific (29 per cent).

The geographical allocation of climate funds partly reflects the focus on mitigation

Table IV.3
Climate funds disbursements by region and the top five countries in each region, 2002–2011

Region	Cumulative climate funds disbursements	
	Amount (millions of US dollars)	*Share of global total (percentage)*
Asia and the Pacific	**580.5**	**35.6**
of which:		
China	187.3	11.5
India	143.6	8.8
Indonesia	86.6	5.3
Cambodia	33.5	2.1
Viet Nam	33.4	2.0
Sub-Saharan Africa	**326.2**	**20.0**
of which:		
South Africa	28.0	1.7
Ghana	20.0	1.2
United Republic of Tanzania	14.0	0.9
Ethiopia	12.0	0.7
Zambia	11.0	0.7
Latin America and the Caribbean	**302.7**	**18.6**
Other regions	**422.4**	**25.9**
Global total	**1631.8**	**100**

Sources: Region and global totals taken from Climate Funds Update website (www.climatefundsupdate.org); country data for East Asia and the Pacific and South Asia from Sobhan (2012); figures for sub-Saharan Africa from Noman (2012).

Effectiveness of innovative climate finance

Assessing the effectiveness of innovative climate finance requires, as in the case of health, an examination of the global funds through which it largely flows. The following discussion is not limited to those funds currently receiving IDF flows since existing as well as new climate funds are likely to be a preferred channel for future IDF resources, including those from new large-scale mechanisms. However, the scope for assessment of these funds is limited, as most are still in their infancy: 19 of the 23 funds monitored by the Climate Funds Update have become operational only within the past five years (Climate Funds Update, n.d.).[19]

Meeting stated goals

Climate funds counter the problem of international collective action which leads to underfunding for climate change mitigation

The close alignment of climate funds with the global public good of climate change mitigation is generally considered a key advantage, enabling them to counter the problem of international collective action which leads to underfunding. Their clear focus on achieving internationally agreed goals, such as climate change mitigation and adaptation and preserving biodiversity, is central to their potential to mobilize financial resources, particularly in the current climate of fiscal consolidation in the developed world. Along the same lines, their involvement in renewable energy technology transfer and adaptation facilitates the leveraging of private investment, which is essential to a green economy transition.

In some cases, results orientation is also a priority. The GEF Trust Fund, for example, has a stated goal of demonstrating three to four innovative low-carbon technologies in 10–15 developing countries. Similarly, the European Commission Global Energy Efficiency and Renewable Energy Fund has established specific goals, such as bringing one gigawatt of clean energy capacity to developing countries' markets. However, it is too early to assess their performance against these goals.

Stability and predictability

The ability of climate funds to deliver stable, sustainable and predictable resources will depend on their sources of finance, as different IDF mechanisms have different implications in this regard. The levy on Clean Development Mechanism transactions could, in principle, provide a relatively stable and automatic source of finance; but in practice, the trading of emission certificates as financial assets and speculative investments can generate high volatility in carbon prices. The stability of funds from emissions trading will also depend on the sustainability of the Mechanism itself. Notwithstanding the recent extension of the second commitment period of the Kyoto Protocol, this remains uncertain.

Proceeds from the auctioning of EU ETS emission permits also have the potential to provide substantial (and somewhat more predictable) funds if there is a genuine political commitment by European countries to auctioning a larger share of emission allowances (as opposed to the prevalent practice of granting them without charge) and to earmarking a significant portion of the proceeds for helping developing countries address climate change post–2013. REDD+ financing could also provide stable resources, particularly if it evolved into an emissions trading mechanism. However, its future design remains unclear, and such uncertainty could weaken the momentum of and support for this initiative. In contrast, debt-for-nature swaps entail one-off deals and therefore cannot be considered either stable or predictable sources of finance.

Currency and financial transaction taxes could provide sizeable and stable financial resources for climate change

New large-scale mechanisms such as currency and financial transaction taxes could, by contrast, provide sizeable, stable and sustained financial resources for climate change, despite their pro-cyclical nature.

---

19   The four exceptions include the initiatives set up under GEF; namely, the GEF Trust Fund (1994), the Special Climate Change Fund (2001), the Least Developed Countries Fund (2002) and the Strategic Priorities on Adaptation (2004).

As in the case of health, however, even if financing mechanisms offer stability and predictability in respect of raising funds globally, this will not necessarily translate into stability and predictability of disbursements at the country level, which is also dependent on disbursement mechanisms. In this regard, the current large discrepancies between the amounts pledged, deposited and approved and actual disbursements are a cause for concern.

The sustainability of climate finance flows also depends on the lifespan of climate funds, which is often very uncertain. The Adaptation Fund is to operate "indefinitely"—presumably as long as it commands political support—while the lifespan of the Amazon Fund and the Forest Carbon Partnership Facility are "undetermined". The GEF Trust Fund will be operational until 2014; but having operated for almost two decades and been replenished five times, it seems likely to continue beyond this date. Similarly, the Congo Basin Forest Fund will operate until 2018, with the possibility of extension. World Bank initiatives—including the Clean Technology Fund, the Strategic Climate Fund, and the Forest Investment Program—may conclude their operations should a new United Nations Framework Convention on Climate Change financial architecture (such as the Green Climate Fund) come into force (Climate Funds Update, n.d.).

Climate change is likely to stay high in the international agenda for some time to come. The long-term sustainability of international assistance for climate change hinges largely on the political commitment of funders to supporting the global public good of climate change mitigation and the development priority of adaptation. Provision of additional climate finance could involve a shift away from the conventional notion of development assistance aimed at long-term national financial self-reliance, towards a new global public goods paradigm encompassing sustained finance over the long term. While this could ensure sustained funding, it would also imply a shift of focus in the use of funds from the interests of recipient countries towards those of the international community, including the donors themselves.

A new global public-goods paradigm could lead to sustained finance for climate change over the long term

Fragmentation

Despite the potential of innovative development finance to provide new and more stable climate finance, the plethora of funds emerging in recent years risks adding to the complexity of an already highly fragmented aid architecture, within which 31 DAC donors operate 1,571 environmental partnerships, alongside 30 or more non-DAC donors and dozens of small multilateral environmental agencies (Castro and Hammond, 2009). The proliferation of financing instruments and disbursement mechanisms risks giving rise to inefficiencies, coordination failures, duplication of efforts and higher transaction costs.

A plethora of funds adds to the complexity of an already highly fragmented aid architecture

Established in 2008 to support low-carbon and climate-resilient development in developing countries, the World Bank Climate Investment Funds (CIFs) in particular have been criticized for creating parallel structures for financing climate change mitigation and adaptation outside the multilateral framework under the United Nations Framework Convention on Climate Change for ongoing climate change negotiations (Climate Funds Update, n.d.), although similar criticisms could also be levelled at bilateral climate funds.

Many of the concerns associated with the significant transaction costs and administrative burdens imposed by the presence of multiple donors with different agendas, reporting requirements and delivery mechanisms, particularly in resource-scarce countries, could be addressed in part by a Green Climate Fund if that Fund were to act as the principal multilateral financing mechanism for supporting climate action in developing countries by channelling a significant share of international climate finance. The World Bank, which is to act as the interim trustee of the Green Climate Fund for its first three years, foresees an important role for the existing Climate Investment Funds in providing concessional climate finance (over the next five years) until the Green Climate Fund becomes fully operational (World Bank Institute, 2012). Thereafter, the Climate Investment Funds may become integrated under the Green Climate Fund itself (Climate Funds Update, n.d.).

Local ownership and alignment

The disbursement of climate finance through sector-specific funds oriented towards global public good objectives raises the risk of distorting national priorities and undermining country ownership. Recognizing such concerns, the majority of climate funds are committed to ensuring that projects they fund are country-driven, and aligned with national development strategies, through inclusive consultation processes and governance structures and clear endorsement by recipient countries.

Increased provision of technical assistance, and direct access to resources (as in the case of the GEF Trust Fund), are also important to enhance countries' capacity to manage financial flows and resist intrusive conditionalities, and to enhance local ownership.

Governance implications of scaling up innovative development finance

Innovative finance would have to be scaled up considerably to fulfil resource needs

Innovative finance mechanisms have so far played a relatively minor role in quantitative terms, and have largely been based on ODA rather than on generating additional resources. They would thus need to be scaled up considerably and to change significantly in nature in order to fill the gap between feasible scenarios for ODA and resource needs, particularly for climate change mitigation and adaptation and green development paths. In principle, this could be achieved by scaling up existing mechanisms, or through the implementation of new large-scale IDF mechanisms (such as those discussed in chap. II) designed to generate a larger pool of funds which could be used more flexibly for a range of development and/or global public goods-related purposes. Either approach would raise potentially important issues of global governance.

Mobilizing private finance

Aid will have to leverage private finance to meet resource needs

It is neither realistic nor appropriate to assume that the additional resource requirements will be met entirely from external public sources: increasing the availability of domestic fiscal and private resources is also critical. The considerable volume of financing needed for climate change mitigation and adaptation, in particular, implies an important role for private as well as public finance. This suggests a hybrid approach entailing the use of aid to leverage private finance—an approach that has been adopted, inter alia, by the Global Environment Facility, Germany's International Climate Initiative, Japan's Fast Track Finance and the EU Global Energy Efficiency and Renewable Energy Fund, and is envisaged in the recently agreed structure for the Global Climate Fund.

Such efforts could usefully seek to leverage resources from new long-term institutional investors such as pension funds and sovereign wealth funds (SWFs). Sovereign wealth funds are of particular importance in light of their very considerable capital base (estimated at $3.5 trillion in assets in developing countries), very long term liabilities, and already significant green investments. Their mandate to preserve and transfer wealth to future generations arguably makes green investment particularly appropriate, to the extent that the risks associated with climate change represent a potential liability to nation States (Bolton, Guesnerie and Samama, 2010). There is also a need to reform financial market regulation, corporate governance, and rules regarding fiduciary responsibility so as to ensure that private investors face appropriate incentives to scale up the provision of climate finance (United Nations, General Assembly, 2012).

Scaling up existing mechanisms

If innovative development finance is to generate the resources required for development and global public goods, it is essential that it should generate genuinely additional resources rather than attract limited ODA from other uses. A careful balance is also required between funding for targeted global initiatives and that for aid institutions with a wider developmental remit (Isenman and Shakow, 2010). The role of aid in encouraging and supplementing national resource mobilization to meet national development goals suggests the need for a further shift of ODA towards budget support, so as to reinforce both national ownership and the accountability of Governments to their national constituencies rather than to donors.

> Innovative development finance must generate genuinely additional resources

Nonetheless, depending on the institutional and governance environment of the recipient country, earmarking of funds for particular uses may be justified in supporting developing countries' contributions to the production of global public goods with important development dimensions. Trust funds or fiscal stabilization funds could provide a useful mechanism for facilitating the alignment of donor funding for such purposes with country priorities, ensuring long-term financing, and aligning traditional ODA with innovative forms of development financing (United Nations, 2010a).

The operations and modalities of IDF disbursement mechanisms should also be designed to ensure that their disbursements at the country level, as well as their funding at the global level, are stable, sustainable and predictable. They should have sufficient flexibility to ensure national ownership and coherence with national development strategies and priorities; and they should minimize administrative burdens imposed on recipient countries with serious financial and/or human resource constraints.

> Disbursements need to be stable, predictable and sustainable, and effectively coordinated and to ensure national ownership

The achievement of these objectives could be facilitated by preventing the proliferation of disbursement channels which has been observed in the climate sector in recent years, and through efforts to pool resources from multiple sources in a small number of institutions, so as to address both the fragmentation problem and overdependency of disbursement channels on particular funding mechanisms (like that of GAVI on IFFIm).

Even if the number of disbursement channels were reduced, effective coordination mechanisms would remain essential. In the area of health, the most appropriate framework in this regard is the World Health Organization, given its constitutional mandate "to act as the directing and co-ordinating authority on international health work" (article 2 (a) of the WHO Constitution, signed on 22 July 1946). The United Nations Framework Convention on Climate Change (which was opened for signature in 1992 at the United Nations Conference on Environment and Development and has been ratified by 192 countries) is the central global coordination mechanism for climate change. The functions of such coordination mechanisms should include ensuring both that the balance of funding availability for different purposes broadly reflects the pattern of needs so as to prevent the skewing of priorities, and that their administrative and monitoring requirements are consistent so as to minimize the imposition of administrative burdens on recipients.

Support to global public goods must simultaneously strengthen national systems

While support to global public goods is needed, it is essential that such support be accompanied by complementary support to the national systems on which they depend (for example, health system support needs to accompany support to vertical programmes) so as to ensure that such systems are strengthened rather than weakened. The Health Systems Strengthening Platform, as originally conceived, provides a useful model in this regard. Sustained political commitment to disbursement mechanisms is also essential, and may be more readily attainable for fewer, larger and broader mechanisms than for the various climate funds whose lifespan is currently uncertain.

Finally, it is important that the governance frameworks of global funds should be firmly established on the basis of democratic principles of representation, accountability and transparency. Many of the existing global climate and health funds, when compared with some other international agencies, are commendable for the transparency and inclusivity of their governance. However, and particularly in the case of use-specific funds, the mechanisms through which they are created and coordinated should be guided by similar principles.

International taxes

The implementation of international taxes will likely raise intense political resistance

Implementation of a tax (for example, on financial or currency transactions or carbon emissions) in a coordinated fashion across countries, and determination of the use of the proceeds at the global level, would raise a number of potentially problematic issues. Not least among these is the issue of tax sovereignty—the unique right of the nation State to levy taxes on its citizens—which is likely to be the basis for intense political resistance on the part of some Governments.

This also raises the issue of the choice among "feasible globalizations". Rodrik (2002) argues that the nation State system, democratic politics and full economic integration are mutually incompatible, and that at most two of these three pillars can co-exist. The post–1945 system of global governance was based on the principle of subordinating international economic integration to the demands of national economic management and democratic national politics. Even if some limits on integration were preserved, the issue of international taxation versus the democratic nation State as the dominant political unit would still remain a source of tension.

Global or globally coordinated taxes would also raise the question which body should receive and allocate the resources generated. While a comparative assessment is beyond the scope of this chapter, each multilateral institution clearly has its own weaknesses in terms of coverage, representation and operational capacity (Buira, ed., 2005). The experience of health—and more particularly climate—finance suggests, however, that the establishment of new disbursement mechanisms should be avoided, and existing mechanisms consolidated as far as possible, so as to minimize the costs associated with fragmentation. It is also important that the governance of such mechanisms should be representative, accountable and transparent.

One advantage of a global or globally coordinated tax would be its potential to reduce the financial dependency of international institutions, which risks skewing their decision-making towards the interests of their funders, even where this is not institutionalized in their formal governance structures. However, such a prospect could represent a further hurdle to implementation, as it may be expected to strengthen resistance among those countries whose influence in global governance would be diminished as a result. Their opposition might be rationalized by portraying global taxation proposals as an attempt by international institutions to establish their autonomy and reduce accountability through the generation of revenues not directly controlled by member States.

> A global tax would reduce the financial dependence of international institutions on their funders

Tax cooperation

Another prominent tax-related proposal—although it does not strictly fall within the purview of innovative development finance—is international tax cooperation, which could help to bring significant volumes of untaxed financial assets into national tax jurisdictions. By strengthening national resource bases, and thereby diminishing the reliance of international institutions on the goodwill of donors, this could help to increase the financial sustainability, national ownership and coherence of development strategies.

> Tax cooperation could bring significant volumes of untaxed financial assets into national tax jurisdictions

Increased tax cooperation would require the strengthening of international tax structures, which currently allow citizens and firms to avoid and/or evade taxes or otherwise defraud national tax systems. Cooperative arrangements among sovereign jurisdictions could offer the possibility of increasing public revenues substantially in both developing and developed countries (FitzGerald, 2012).

A decade ago, the High-level Panel on Financing for Development (also known as the Zedillo Commission) proposed the creation of an international tax organization to compile and share tax information, monitor tax developments, restrain tax competition among countries to attract investment, and arbitrate country tax disputes (United Nations, General Assembly, 2001). Such an institution could be built on existing frameworks, and could be relatively limited in scale, as it would not collect taxes, but rather regulate the flows between tax jurisdictions. Any redistribution towards poorer or smaller countries that might be considered desirable would be carried out through existing institutions.

While the proposal for an international tax organization was not endorsed in the Monterrey Consensus of the International Conference on Financing for Development,[20] subsequent developments—including the global financial crisis, non-governmental organization campaigns focusing on "tax justice", and improved institutional capacities of tax authorities in developing countries—suggest a renewed interest in the establishment of an agency to carry out the Zedillo Commission's aim of establishing "a mechanism for multilateral sharing of tax information, like that already in place within the Organization for Economic Cooperation and Development (OECD), so as to curb the scope for evasion of taxes on investment income earned abroad" (United Nations, General Assembly, 2001, p. 7). Such an international tax cooperation agency could build on the work of existing OECD and United Nations bodies, with technical support from IMF (FitzGerald, 2012).

---

20 *Report of the International Conference on Financing for Development, Monterrey, Mexico, 18-22 March 2012* (United Nations publication, Sales No. E.02.II.A.7), chap I, resolution 1, annex.

Special drawing rights

An SDR allocation requires
an 85 per cent majority
in IMF

Allocations of special drawing rights could help developing countries add to their official foreign reserves, thereby reducing their need for balance-of-payments surpluses or borrowing to build those reserves, and thus freeing resources for more development-oriented purposes. However, an SDR allocation requires the support of an 85 per cent majority in the IMF, which, given the Fund's "economically weighted" voting system, allows the United States of America (or any three other G7 countries) to veto such a proposal. Historically, this has proved a major obstacle, and only three allocations have taken place (in 1970–1972, 1979–1981 and 2009). The scale of the challenge is demonstrated by the 2009 special allocation (which provided additional SDRs to countries that were not IMF members when earlier allocations had been made): while this had been agreed in 1997, it was ratified only in 2009, in the wake of the global financial crisis.

Allocations proportional to quotas constrain potential developmental benefits

The developmental benefits of SDR allocations are seriously constrained by the fact that SDRs can only be allocated in proportion to quotas, so that 58 per cent accrues to developed countries (after full implementation of the 2010 quota reform). By comparison, only 3.2 per cent accrues to low-income countries, and 2.3 per cent to least developed countries (International Monetary Fund, n.d.). However, breaking the link to quotas would require an amendment to the Fund's Articles of Agreement, which would again require an 85 per cent majority voting power (and the support of three fifths of the membership).

It has also been proposed that the share of reserve-rich countries in SDR allocations could be used to finance development and/or global public goods, for example, through the creation of "trust funds", which could provide the capital for a "Green Fund" or a development fund with other objectives (see chap. II). Developed (and potentially other reserve-rich) countries would place their unused SDRs in the trust fund as equity, and the return on investments by the trust fund could be used to service the interest payments on the drawdown of their stock of SDRs (Erten and Ocampo, 2012).

Alternatively, IMF could cooperate with the multilateral development banks in allowing some of the resources generated by an SDR allocation to be invested (by IMF itself or by countries with excess holdings) in bonds issued by multilateral development banks (ibid.). While such bonds would be offered at market interest rates, in principle they could be used for concessional lending if combined with grant funding financed, for example, by revenues from an international tax or from ODA.

Another proposal is for IMF members to lend some of their SDRs to IMF to supplement the usual quota-based resources for regular IMF conditional lending programmes, for example, by treating some unused SDRs as deposits in (or lending to) IMF (United Nations, 2009a; Ocampo, 2011). However, such an approach would be impeded by the division of IMF accounts between "general resources" and the SDR Department. Overcoming this problem would again require an amendment to the Fund's Articles of Agreement.

Conclusion

The major disbursement mechanisms through which innovative development finance for health passes (notably the GAVI Alliance and the Global Fund) have been highly successful in attracting funding, and have used such funding to achieve significant results in their respective fields. While the financial contribution of innovative financing mechanisms remains modest in the area of health, and more so in that of climate change, innovative financing has the potential to be scaled up substantially in the latter in the coming years. However, the potential of innovative financing to close the considerable gaps between ODA and financing needs in both these areas is limited, as almost all existing innovative financing is either derived from or passed through ODA budgets, thereby seriously limiting additionality. The focus of innovative development finance on global public goods may therefore also signify a shift of development financing from national needs towards global priorities, potentially at the expense of national ownership and alignment with national development strategies.

While it is relatively early to make an assessment, there are signs that certain forms of IDF are somewhat more stable and more predictable than conventional ODA, although issues such as the sustainability of the International Finance Facility for Immunization (the largest source of IDF for health) and the very low level of disbursements from the Adaptation Fund are of concern in this regard. Particularly in the area of climate change, the proliferation of funding mechanisms raises concerns in respect of the further fragmentation of a highly diffuse aid architecture.

Meeting developing countries' financing needs with regard to achieving agreed global goals, notably the Millennium Development Goals and climate change mitigation and adaptation, would thus imply both a major increase in the volume of IDF and a shift in its focus so as to ensure greater additionality. Scaling up existing mechanisms would also risk further compounding the fragmentation of the aid architecture. In principle, larger-scale IDF mechanisms such as those discussed in chapter II, represent a potentially more viable route if the political obstacles can be overcome.

Chapter V
The recipient perspective

Summary

♦ Innovative sources of financing thus far have remained very small not only in aggregate amounts, but also relative to the financing needs of recipient countries. Only in a few low-income countries have innovative mechanisms contributed a significant share even of health sector financing.

♦ Developing countries appreciate innovative financing as long as it is additional to existing official development assistance committed by traditional donors.

♦ Recipient Governments would generally prefer development financing in forms allowing greater flexibility in use, as delivery of innovative development finance through vertical global health funds is not necessarily aligned with national priorities and risks being unsupportive of strengthening national health systems.

Introduction

The previous chapters have discussed innovative development finance (IDF) primarily from the perspective of donors and the global community as a whole. At least as important, however, is the perspective of recipient countries: the key issue is development impact, which can be assessed only at the country level.

Presenting recipient perspectives is complicated both by the diversity of recipient-country experiences and by the limited availability of information. Further complications arise from the fact that IDF is often provided in combination with other sources of funding, particularly official development assistance (ODA) and, in some cases, private philanthropy, through vertical global funds. This makes it difficult to distinguish the impact of programmes funded through IDF from that of programmes funded by other sources.

Despite such complications, the present chapter aims at addressing a number of issues arising at the level of the recipient country, including the quantitative significance of innovative development financing, its direct benefits, its stability and predictability, and various aspects of its development effectiveness. Serious assessment of the effectiveness of IDF-financed climate funds from the perspective of recipient countries is impeded by the limited information available. Hence, the major part of the analysis undertaken in this chapter focuses on the various health funds, primarily the GAVI Alliance, the Global Fund to Fight AIDS, Tuberculosis and Malaria and UNITAID.

Top-down and bottom-up views of IDF

Views of innovative development finance mechanisms differ considerably between, on the one hand, donors and global policy discussions and, on the other hand, officials and other stakeholders in recipient countries. In the former context, the definition and scope of the term "innovative development finance", and whether or not a particular financial mechanism falls within this definition, may have considerable significance, for example, in establishing the parameters of decision-making processes or interpreting donors' commitments. Recipient countries, in contrast, are less concerned with the origin of funding, but rather with the overall resources they can access and use for development. For their part, global institutions such as the GAVI Alliance and the Global Fund are clearly aware of, and have a direct interest in, the nature of the mechanisms through which they receive innovative development finance; however, this is not of primary interest to recipient countries.

Most of these mechanisms operate in one of two ways. Some (notably UNITAID, the advance market commitment for pneumococcal vaccine and the Affordable Medicines Facility - malaria) entail direct co-payments to pharmaceutical companies for purchases of particular products, rather than financial transfers to countries. In such cases, the effect at the country level is a reduction in the prices of those products rather than a receipt of resources for expenditure. Proceeds from other mechanisms (notably the International Finance Facility for Immunisation (IFFIm) and Product Red) are pooled with resources from other official and private philanthropic sources, for disbursement mostly through the GAVI Alliance and the Global Fund. These disbursement channels had already existed, and most countries had already received substantial funding from them, even before the advent of innovative financing mechanisms. Since their disbursements at the country level are not generally differentiated by source of financing, the connection with innovative development financing is not apparent. The only mechanism that visibly generates resources at the national level is debt conversion involving debts which would otherwise have been serviced (see chap. III). Having been in existence for some 25 years, this may not be perceived as innovative; and it has generated significant resources (beyond what would otherwise have been provided under multilateral debt reduction initiatives) in only a handful of countries.

Financial dimensions of existing mechanisms

Assessing the significance of IDF at the country level is complicated by the fact that it is largely channelled through global funds rather than disbursed directly to countries. As a result, there are no separate data on its distribution among regions and countries. The assessment below therefore assumes that the IDF contribution to the overall financing of each vertical fund at the global level is allocated among recipient countries in proportion to the disbursements of the fund to each country. See box V.1 for an explanation of the assumptions made.

The issue of additionality in financing is not addressed in this assessment. Since almost all existing innovative development finance comes from or is channelled through aid budgets, it is likely that the following analysis considerably overstates the significance of the net increase in resources for development resulting from innovative development finance.

Box V.1

Estimating IDF disbursements

Estimation of the amount of IDF that is disbursed at the country level is complicated by the fact that such financing generally is part of a broader financing mechanism involving various sources of funding. The pooling of resources makes it difficult to distinguish which part of the resources allocated to individual countries is IDF and which part is from other sources. The country-level estimates presented in the present chapter are based on the simple assumption that all recipients of resources from the global fund receive an equal proportion of IDF contributing to the total resources of the fund.

In the case of the GAVI Alliance, disbursements to recipients are multiplied by the proportion of GAVI financing provided by IFFlm between 2006 and 2010 (42 per cent, based on GAVI Alliance (2012b)). For the Global Fund, IDF comes directly from Product Red and indirectly from the Voluntary Solidarity Contribution (via UNITAID). In this case, the contribution of UNITAID to the Global Fund (1.9 per cent) is weighted by the share of IDF in UNITAID's own financing (75 per cent). This yields a share of 1.4 per cent of IDF from these two sources in the disbursement mechanism's resources.

In the case of the Global Fund, however, two further adjustments are required for mechanisms that provide support to specific countries. The first is for Debt2Health. Since no information is available on the timing of disbursements, it is assumed that the pattern of payments of all debt conversions is the same as in the first case considered part of Debt2Health, that is, the conversion of €50 million of Indonesia's debt to Germany, agreed in July 2010. In that case, the funds generated were made available in five equal annual instalments, beginning in the year following the transaction (Global Fund to Fight AIDS, Tuberculosis and Malaria, 2008). This implies amounts between 2006 and 2010 of $20.5 million for Indonesia and $10.0 million for Pakistan. Since the Indonesia/Australia and Côte d'Ivoire/Germany transactions were initiated in 2010, it is assumed that disbursements started in 2011. The triangular Ethiopia/Egypt/Germany transaction was completed only in 2011 and hence is also not reflected in the data presented in this chapter. All resources generated by Debt2Health are counted as IDF.

The second adjustment is for the eight countries involved in the pilot programme of the Affordable Medicines Facility - malaria (AMFm): Cambodia, Ghana, Kenya, Madagascar, the Niger, Nigeria, Uganda and the United Republic of Tanzania. While AMFm does not disburse funds directly to countries, it makes co-payments on behalf of first-line buyers in each country for the purchase of artemisinin-based combination therapies, and these payments are included as part of IDF. However, up to the end of 2010, co-payments were made only in respect of four countries, for a total of $4 million.[a]

In the case of disbursements originating from UNITAID, co-payments on behalf of first-line users in each country (as recorded up to the end of 2010) were obtained from UNITAID. The co-payments were weighted by the proportion of UNITAID income from innovative sources (75 per cent, financed by the solidarity levy on airline tickets and Norway's carbon dioxide emissions tax).

In addition to these channels for IDF in the health sector, two climate change funds also qualify as being financed in part by IDF: the Adaptation Fund, and Germany's International Climate Initiative. However, no data are available for the country allocation of their disbursements.

Source: UN/DESA.

a Information provided by the Global Fund to Fight AIDS, Tuberculosis and Malaria.

Macroeconomic and sectoral significance

Figure V.1 compares the size of ODA and IDF combined with flows of migrants' remittances and foreign direct investment (FDI)[1]. As might be expected, the balance among these three flows varies very widely across developing countries, with FDI predominating

IDF flows are insignificant relative to FDI and remittances

---

1   It should of course be noted that these flows differ considerably in their nature and purpose. While ODA and IDF are directed towards public purposes, FDI is productive investment for commercial purposes, and migrants' remittances are private transfers from migrants to their families and others in their home countries, generally for consumption purposes.

Figure V.1

IDF relative to other sources of external finance of developing countries by region, 2006-2010

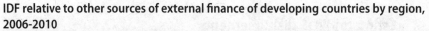

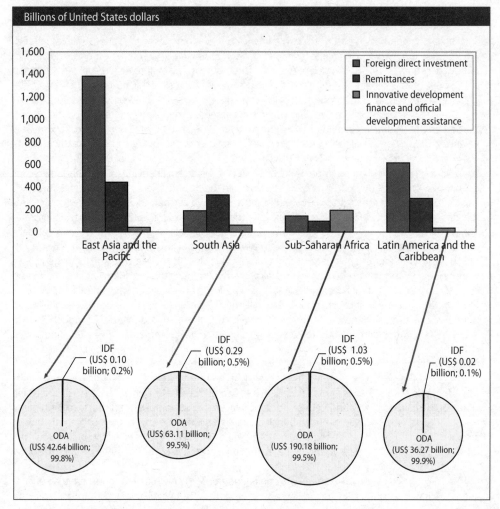

Sources: GAVI Alliance (http://www.gavialliance.org/results/disbursements/); Global Fund to Fight AIDS, Tuberculosis and Malaria (http://portfolio.theglobalfund.org/en/DataDownloads/Index); UNITAID; and World Development Indicators online database (available from http://databank.worldbank.org/ddp/home.do).

in East Asia and the Pacific and in Latin America and the Caribbean, and remittances predominating in South Asia. Only in sub-Saharan Africa is the combination of ODA and innovative development finance comparable in scale with these other flows, being one third greater than FDI and approximately double the level of migrants' remittances.

However, the scale of innovative development finance is extremely small relative to ODA in all regions presented, ranging between 0.3 and 0.5 per cent in the two Asian regions and sub-Saharan Africa, and being still lower (0.07 per cent) in Latin America and the Caribbean.

In all regions shown in table V.1, IDF is also very small relative to other relevant macroeconomic aggregates, such as gross domestic product (GDP), public expenditure and net national savings. The highest ratios are found in sub-Saharan Africa; but even here, region-wide, IDF is equivalent to only 0.8 per cent of net national savings, 0.1 per cent of Government expenditure and 0.02 per cent of GDP. In South Asia, the respective ratios are 0.02 per cent, 0.01 per cent and 0.003 per cent, and they are even smaller in East Asia and the Pacific and Latin America and the Caribbean.

IDF flows are insignificant macroeconomically...

Table V.1

IDF for global health funds compared with ODA, Government expenditure, national savings and gross domestic product, selected regions, 2006-2010[a]

Region/country	Global health funds		Health IDF as a percentage of:			
	Total (millions of US dollars)	IDF component (millions of US dollars)	ODA	Total Government expenditure	Net national savings	GDP
East Asia and the Pacific	1,495	104	0.2564	0.0025	0.0014	0.0004
(excluding China)	1,046	95	0.2746	0.0092	0.0116	0.0015
South Asia	1,562	286	0.4527	0.0138	0.0200	0.0031
(excluding India)	877	229	0.4338	0.0393	0.1018	0.0086
Sub-Saharan Africa	7,923	1,028	0.5475	0.0978	0.7718	0.0219
(excluding South Africa)	7,751	1,025	0.5604	0.1491	0.9002	0.0318
Latin America and the Caribbean	719	25	0.0694	0.0004	0.0019	0.0001
Total	11,699	1,442	0.4409	0.0110	0.0138	0.0024

Sources: GAVI Alliance (http://www.gavialliance.org/results/disbursements/); Global Fund to Fight AIDS, Tuberculosis and Malaria (http://portfolio.theglobalfund.org/en/DataDownloads/Index); UNITAID; and World Development Indicators online database (available from http://databank.worldbank.org/ddp/home.do).

a Cumulative.

While IDF may have very limited significance at a macroeconomic level, its overwhelming concentration to date in the health sector means that it is of somewhat greater significance for the sector (figure V.2). As yet, however, its contribution remains modest even relative to total health expenditure. In most low-income sub-Saharan countries, IDF disbursements are between about 1 and 3 per cent of total health expenditure. It is higher in only one country: the Gambia, at 4.5 per cent. Outside this region, the ratio reaches 1 per cent in only one country (Afghanistan) and exceeds 0.5 per cent in three others (Bangladesh, Cambodia and Pakistan).

... but also small relative to total expenditure on health, too

Additionality

The primary concern of recipient countries in relation to innovative development finance is that it should be additional to ODA, and to donor commitments to provide 0.7 per cent of their national income in aid. This was the main recurrent theme of developing-country interventions in relation to innovative development finance at the fifth High-level Dialogue on Financing for Development, held on 7 and 8 December 2011,[2] and a major preoccupation of respondents to a survey of country offices conducted by the United Nations Development Programme (UNDP) in 2011 (Hurley, 2012).

This may be indicative of concerns that existing mechanisms are in practice substituting for ODA, rather than increasing the envelope of resources for development. As discussed in chapter III, most existing IDF mechanisms are either funded from or channelled through ODA budgets, seriously limiting additionality at the global level.

Developing countries are concerned that IDF is not additional to ODA

---

2 Written statements submitted to the fifth High-level Dialogue are available from http://www.un.org/esa/ffd/hld/HLD2011/plenary_statements.htm#ga79p.

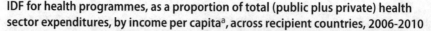

Figure V.2

IDF for health programmes, as a proportion of total (public plus private) health sector expenditures, by income per capita[a], across recipient countries, 2006-2010

Sources: GAVI Alliance (http://www. gavialliance.org/results/disbursements/); Global Fund to Fight AIDS, Tuberculosis and Malaria (http://portfolio.theglobalfund.org/en/DataDownloads/Index); UNITAID; Population Division, UN/DESA; and World Development Indicators online database (available from http://databank.worldbank.org/ddp/home.do).

a IDF for health as a percentage of total (public plus private) health expenditures (average for 2006-2010) and income per capita in current United States dollars (2010).

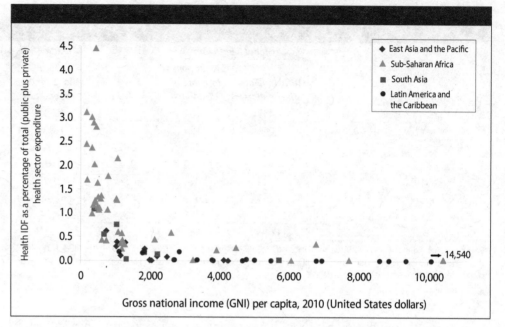

The recent development of innovative development finance and its very limited scale to date mean that it is not possible to make any meaningful assessment of its additionality to ODA receipts at the country level. Even to the extent that innovative development finance provides resources additional to the ODA which would otherwise have gone to the recipient country, the very limited degree of additionality at the global level (see chap. III) clearly implies that this comes at the expense of such assistance to other countries.

The question of additionality also arises at the level of individual projects. Concerns have been raised in some recipient countries that programmes supported by the Global Fund and the GAVI Alliance are in practice substituting for pre-existing donor-supported programmes, for example, in Benin (Hurley, 2012) and Bangladesh, where some

Such concerns can only be increased by the considerable fiscal pressures now felt by most donor countries as a result of the current financial crisis, and the major shortfall of aid disbursements compared to donor commitments made at the time of the 2005 World Summit held in September 2005. Even before the financial crisis, an assessment by the Organization for Economic Cooperation and Development (OECD) Development Assistance Committee (DAC) projected that country programmable aid would increase by only $20 billion between 2004 and 2010, compared with a commitment of $50 billion (Organization for Economic Cooperation and Development, Development Assistance Committee, 2008). While country programmable aid had increased relatively strongly in 2008–2009, partly closing the gap, it fell in real terms in 2010 and 2011, and is projected to remain only marginally above its 2009 peak even in 2015. Even in 2015, country programmable aid is projected to be only $25 billion above the 2004 level at 2011 prices, compared with a commitment to increase it by $50 billion at 2004 prices by 2010 (Organization for Economic Cooperation and Development, Development Assistance Committee, 2012).

policymakers consider that the GAVI and Global Fund programmes effectively substituted for a successful pre-existing United Nations Children's Fund (UNICEF) vaccination programme and a multi-donor Health and Population Sector programme (Sobhan, 2012).

Predictability

A secondary attraction of innovative development finance from a recipient perspective— beyond the generation of additional funding for development—is its potential to generate more stable and predictable funding than is the case for ODA. As noted in chapter IV, while existing innovative financing mechanisms appear to provide a reasonable level of stability in funding at the global level, this does not necessarily translate into stability and predictability of disbursements at the level of recipient countries, which depend on the policies, practices and performance of the disbursement mechanism.

IDF disbursements are not more stable than ODA

Again, assessing this issue is seriously complicated by the pooling of resources from innovative development with funding from other official and private philanthropic sources, and by its recent advent, which means that stability can be assessed only over a relatively short period. At most, a very preliminary assessment can be made, on the basis of flows from the major disbursement mechanisms for innovative financing to date, namely, the GAVI Alliance and the Global Fund.

Overall, both the Global Fund and, especially, the GAVI Alliance disbursements appear to have been somewhat less stable than total ODA, as measured through the coefficient of variation in annual flows (figure V.3).[3]

The importance of stability varies considerably across countries. Focusing on those countries where the GAVI Alliance and the Global Fund have provided the greatest share of health expenditure, Global Fund disbursements appear to follow a relatively smooth trajectory, while those of the GAVI Alliance are visibly more erratic (figures V.4 and V.5).

These results need to be considered with some caution, however. Apart from the very short periods analysed, the much greater number of projects financed by ODA (in total) in each country than that for the GAVI Alliance or the Global Fund means that fluctuations in disbursements for individual projects may be expected to offset each other to a greater extent. This is likely to bias the results substantially towards showing greater volatility for disbursements from IDF mechanisms. Conversely, it should be noted that, given the period covered by this analysis, the effects of the suspension of the Global Fund's eleventh funding window is not covered. This will obviously increase the volatility of Global Fund disbursements.

It is also important to consider the reasons for fluctuations in disbursements by the GAVI Alliance and the Global Fund, particularly because the vertical nature of the projects that they support limits wider impacts. In some cases, no disbursements may occur in a particular year because of the planned schedule of disbursements, or because underspending (for example, due to project delays) results in a situation where the unspent balances available from past disbursements are sufficient to cover planned expenditures. Similarly, support to one-time expenditure (for example, for establishing a stockpile of

---

    3   The coefficient of variation is defined as the standard deviation divided by the mean of annual flows for the period analysed. The results in figure V.3 should be viewed with the necessary caution. The number of observations is small and, since IDF disbursements begin from near zero at the beginning of the period, this overstates actual volatility of the GAVI Alliance and Global Fund disbursements vis-à-vis ODA. Nonetheless, the results may be seen as indicative of visible volatility in disbursements, as also confirmed by figures V.4 and V.5 below.

Figure V.3

Volatility in disbursements from the Global Fund and the GAVI Alliance as compared with volatility of total ODA, across recipient countries, 2001-2010

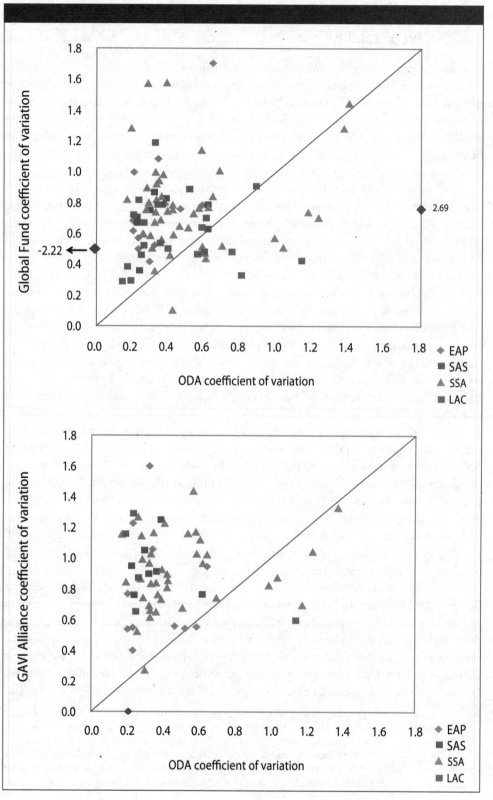

Sources: GAVI Alliance (http://www. gavialliance.org/results/disbursements/); Global Fund to Fight AIDS, Tuberculosis and Malaria (http://portfolio. theglobalfund.org/en/DataDownloads/Index); and World Development Indicators online database (available from http://databank. worldbank.org/ddp/home.do).

Abbreviations: EAP, East Asia and the Pacific; LAC, Latin America and the Caribbean; SAS, South Asia; SSA, sub-Saharan Africa.

Figure V.4

Global Fund disbursements per capita for six countries with the highest ratio of disbursements to total (public plus private) health expenditure, 2003-2010

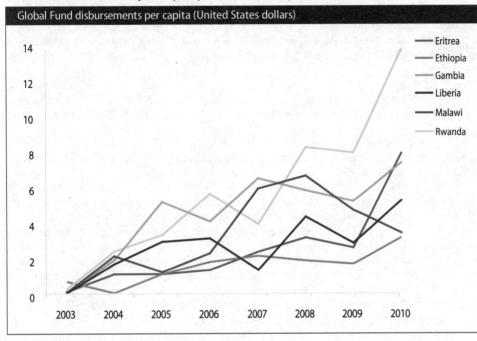

Sources: Global Fund to Fight AIDS, Tuberculosis and Malaria (http://portfolio. theglobalfund.org/en/ DataDownloads/Index); and World Development Indicators online database (available from http://databank. worldbank.org/ddp/home.do).

Figure V.5

GAVI Alliance disbursements per capita for six countries with the highest ratio of disbursements to total (public plus private) health expenditure, 2001-2010

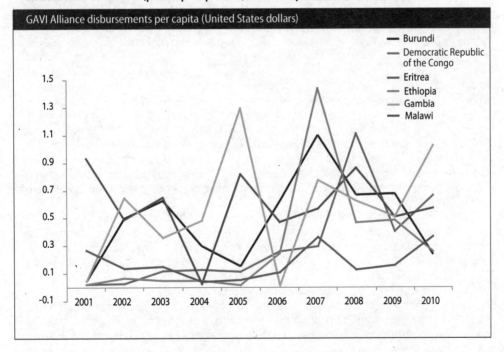

Sources: GAVI Alliance (http:// www. gavialliance.org/results/ disbursements/); and World Development Indicators online database (available from http://databank. worldbank.org/ddp/home.do).

Box V.2

Problems in assessing health impacts of global funds

Despite widely quoted figures attesting to the health benefits of global vertical funds such as the Global Fund to Fight AIDS, Tuberculosis and Malaria and the GAVI Alliance, assessing their impacts is much more complex than it may seem at first sight. The data on which such estimates are based are often much less reliable than they appear, owing to limited health information systems (and health systems more generally) in many developing countries. Causes of death are often not routinely recorded and diagnosis of diseases is inevitably constrained in countries where a large proportion of the population have limited or no access to health services. As a result, morbidity and mortality indicators often rely on indirect estimation methods. A recent study found, for instance, that global mortality from malaria appears to be nearly double that indicated by previous estimates. Among adults, the number of deaths caused by malaria was found to be eight times higher than previously thought (Murray and others, 2012).

While recording the delivery of certain interventions, such as vaccinations, should be more straightforward, here, estimates, too, are susceptible to considerable margins of error and potential bias. The GAVI Alliance, for example, uses coverage estimates from WHO and UNICEF as a basis for its estimates of the number of lives saved. However, the WHO and UNICEF data rely on reporting by entities administering vaccinations and, in some cases, on self-reporting by parents on past vaccinations of their children, collated by national health systems. Even baseline data on the size of relevant age cohorts of the populations may be unreliable (Das and Dasgupta, 2000). In addition, there are concerns of biases towards over-reporting so as to secure or retain donor funding (Onta, Sabroe and Hanson, 1998; Brugha, Starling and Walt, 2002). The basis for such concerns is strengthened by marked inconsistencies between the official estimates used by WHO and UNICEF and those based on actual surveys, and considerable overestimation of rates of increase in vaccination coverage in countries receiving immunization system strengthening support from the GAVI Alliance (Lim and others, 2009). A WHO-sponsored audit of immunization monitoring systems found considerable over-reporting in 9 out of 23 countries, moderate over-reporting in 7, and no cases of significant under-reporting (Ronveaux and others, 2005).

Two other potentially serious problems may affect the evaluation of the impact of health programmes. First, it is often difficult to identify to what extent changes in health outcome variables are directly related to specific programmes or interventions and to what extent those changes involve other determinants (such as nutritional, behavioural and environmental influences on health, as well as other health services and interventions). This problem hampers assessment of the impact of the GAVI Alliance and the Global Fund, in sub-Saharan Africa in particular. While 60 per cent or more of disbursements from these mechanisms went to the region, their provision coincided with a major favourable turnaround in key determinants of health. For example, the proportion of the population below the $1.25 per capita poverty line in the region fell by 10.4 percentage points between 1999 and 2008, compared with an increase of 6.4 percentage points over the previous 18 years (World Bank, n.d.a); and per capita public expenditure on health (excluding South Africa) increased by 150 per cent in real purchasing power parity terms, from $18.50 to $45.60, between 2002 and 2009. Even if the entire increase in external support for health in this period contributed to public expenditure, this would account for only one third of the increase (UN/DESA estimates, based on data from World Bank, n.d.b). These developments might be expected to have considerable, but not readily quantifiable, benefits in all areas of health, regardless of the operations of the GAVI Alliance and the Global Fund.

Second, the possibility exists that an intervention with health benefits may also have unanticipated negative consequences, which may not even be recognized in subsequent assessments. These may include direct effects on health outcomes, as well as potential impacts of vertical programmes on health systems and other health interventions (as discussed below). Such health effects may be felt only after long and very uncertain time lags. For example, reducing the exposure of children to malaria (e.g., by promoting the use of insecticide-treated bed nets) may prevent them from acquiring resistance to the disease, which is a major factor limiting future mortality from malaria among older children and adults (Doolan, Dobaño and Baird, 2009). In these circumstances, the observed reduction in child (or even total) mortality from malaria during the course of a project may substantially overstate its long-term benefits. (This may be one possible explanation for the apparently serious underestimation of adult mortality from malaria described above.)

Source: UN/DESA.

vaccines or pharmaceuticals) may result in a spike in disbursements. In such cases, the associated volatility in disbursements will have no adverse effects.

Where fluctuations are a result of non-disbursement due to underperformance at the project level, there may be some justification for a reduction or suspension of payments, but this is likely to cause some disruption to the project. Given the nature of the activities supported by the GAVI Alliance and (particularly) the Global Fund, and their legitimate focus on projects that would not otherwise be financed, such disruption may have serious ethical and humanitarian implications. For example, cessation of funding for a project supplying antiretroviral therapy to people living with HIV/AIDS without there being the potential for funding from other sources would mean depriving beneficiaries of a clinically necessary treatment. In the case of treatment for malaria and tuberculosis, non-completion of treatment may also have potentially serious wider health impacts including increased drug resistance.

Effects on health outcomes

Despite the limited significance of IDF mechanisms in financial terms, what ultimately matters is the impact that the programmes they fund have on health outcomes. To date, it is possible to assess such impacts only for the programmes supported by the GAVI Alliance and the Global Fund.[4]

In some respects, the focus of these programmes on particular diseases and interventions (the Global Fund on AIDS, Tuberculosis and Malaria, UNITAID on medications for these three diseases, and GAVI on immunization), and on measurable outcome indicators, eases such impact assessment. The Global Fund and the GAVI Alliance, in particular, frequently highlight estimates of the health benefits of their operations, often quantified in millions of lives saved, as a central part of their promotional activities. In practice, however, there are a number of serious problems associated with assessing programme effectiveness on this basis (see box V.2).

Existing IDF mechanisms are focused on specific disease control programmes

The GAVI Alliance

Figure V.6 summarizes progress in immunization achieved up to 2010, as presented by the GAVI Alliance (2011a). According to this summary, immunization coverage for diphtheria, pertussis and tetanus (DPT3) has reached 79 per cent in GAVI-supported countries, and more than 5 million deaths had been prevented with GAVI-funded vaccines (figure V.6). Country-level information shows that rates of vaccination and immunization (as gauged by the DPT3 coverage rate) are high in East Asia and Latin America. Several countries of South Asia (such as Bangladesh) have also achieved high rates. By comparison, rates in sub-Saharan Africa remain low (World Bank, n.d.b).

An assessment by the World Health Organization (WHO) found that GAVI Alliance support to vaccine programmes up to the end of 2008 had averted 3.4 million deaths from pertussis (whooping cough), *Haemophilus influenzae type B* (Hib) disease and hepatitis B, this figure being expected to increase to about 4 million by the end of 2009. Despite the inevitably wide margin of error, this evaluation points to a very significant achievement in terms of health outcomes (CEPA, 2010).

In comparing the rate of country adoption of vaccines before and after the inception of the GAVI Alliance in 2001, the second evaluation of the GAVI Alliance,

The GAVI Alliance has helped increase immunization rates

---

4   UNITAID is not considered here, as the independent review process remains at a very early stage.

Figure V.6
Progress in immunization rates in GAVI Alliance-supported countries, 2000-2011

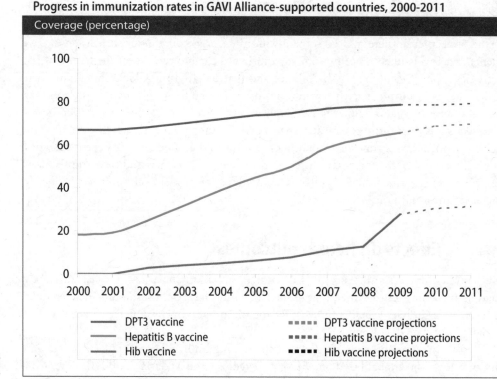

Source: GAVI Alliance
(2011a), p.4.

conducted by Cambridge Economic Policy Associates, found that 48-52 additional countries had adopted a Hib-containing vaccine, 23-34 additional countries had adopted a hepatitis B-containing vaccine, and 2-6 additional countries had adopted yellow fever vaccination than if the previous trend had continued. Particularly in the first two cases, the resulting increases in coverage rates were impressive: from 7 to 83 per cent, and from 29 to 79 per cent, respectively. Yellow fever coverage also increased substantially, from 46 to 86 per cent. While the GAVI Alliance had increased the demand for pneumococcal vaccine and supported the introduction of rotavirus vaccine in some Latin American countries, it was too early to assess whether the adoption of these vaccines was accelerated (CEPA, 2010).

These figures again need to be interpreted with caution. While the official data incorporated in the WHO and UNICEF data set (as used by the GAVI Alliance) showed an increase in DPT3 vaccination coverage in countries receiving GAVI Alliance support of 13.9 million children up to 2006, survey data in the same countries indicated a figure little more than half this level (7.4 million) in the same period (Lim and others, 2009). Nonetheless, even when allowing for over-reporting on this scale, the magnitude of the reported increases in coverage points to substantial health benefits.

The Global Fund

The Global Fund has had
success in controlling and
treating AIDS, tuberculosis
and malaria

The five-year evaluation of the Global Fund, completed in 2009, found that it had been highly successful in mobilizing resources for HIV/AIDS, tuberculosis and malaria, contributing to increases in service availability and coverage, and a reduction in the disease burden (Global Fund Technical Evaluation Reference Group, 2009b).

Table V.2 shows the progress made on the indicators adopted by the Global Fund to assess country performance, in the five countries in each region with the highest for each disease since the Global Fund's establishment in 2002. The results appear to be very positive overall, though by no means universally so. Performance against the Global Fund's key performance indicators has been strongest for HIV/AIDS in sub-Saharan Africa, all of the five largest recipients therein (in per capita terms) having achieved "demonstrated impact" on all three indicators (reduced HIV incidence, reduced HIV deaths, and adequate progress towards achieving universal access to antiretroviral therapy by 2015), except for Rwanda, where the incidence of HIV/AIDS remained constant. Rates of reduction of HIV deaths in the region were very rapid, ranging from 10 to 30 per cent per year. Major recipients of funding for malaria in South Asia also performed very well, all achieving "demonstrated impact" on the available indicators (progress towards meeting 2015 targets for reduction of malaria case rates and death rates), except for Bangladesh, which achieved "consolidated progress towards impact".

In the case of tuberculosis, in contrast, major recipients in sub-Saharan Africa had the weakest performance. All four countries for which data are available recorded "no progress" on at least one indicator. Performance on tuberculosis was also very weak in Latin America and the Caribbean, although this was primarily driven by lack of progress across all indicators in Suriname, including a very rapid increase (7.5 per cent per year) in tuberculosis incidence. Lack of progress in malaria in Timor-Leste (by far the largest recipient in per capita terms in East Asia and the Pacific) and Haiti similarly contrasts with more favourable performances elsewhere in their respective regions.

Despite the Global Fund's positive direct health impacts, the five-year evaluation also contained important caveats about other aspects of its performance. In particular, it identified health system weaknesses as a critical constraint on the Global Fund's performance, highlighting the need for considerable strengthening of health systems in most developing countries if any further significant expansion of services was to be achieved. It also found that, with no narrowing of gaps between disadvantaged groups and the remainder of the population, and few mechanisms to monitor equity, more action was needed to achieve a more equitable distribution of resources. The performance-based funding system was also found to be complex and burdensome, excessively focused on project inputs and outputs rather than on development outcomes, and critically limited by inadequate in-country capacities.

Vertical funds and health systems

As discussed in chapters III and IV, the narrow focus of IDF and disbursement mechanisms on specific diseases (the Global Fund) and interventions (the GAVI Alliance, the Affordable Medicines Facility - malaria, advance market commitments) of particular priority for donors has been critical to their ability to attract funding. There is also little doubt that they have had a major positive impact on health in their respective areas: the uncertainties highlighted above relate only to the magnitude of this impact and the widely publicized figures of lives saved.

However, for recipient countries, particularly those with weak and under-resourced health systems and serious human resource constraints, such disease- and intervention-specific support can be problematic, and can have potentially important effects on the other dimensions of the health system. Many of the issues are illustrated by the experiences of Mozambique with the Global Fund (box V.3).

The operation of vertical health funds has created problems

Table V.2

Indicators of impact in the top recipient countries of support from the Global Fund to Fight AIDS, Tuberculosis and Malaria in selected recipient countries

Country	Percentage of households owning an insecticide-treated net, 2009 (annual change (%), 2005-2009)	Percentage achieved of 2009 interim target (to reduce malaria case rate by 75% from 2000-2015)	Percentage achieved of 2009 interim target (to reduce malaria death rate by 75% from 2000-2015)	Per capita disbursements for malaria-related programmes (US dollars)	Tuberculosis case detection rate, all forms (%), 2009 (annual change (%), 2005-2009)	Tuberculosis treatment success rate (%), 2008 (annual change (%), 2004-2008)	Percentage achieved of 2009 interim tuberculosis target (to halve TB mortality rate, from 1990-2015)	Annual change in tuberculosis incidence, 2005-2009 (%)	Per capita disbursements for tuberculosis-related programmes (US dollars)	Percentage achieved of 2009 interim HIV target (to provide universal access to antiretroviral therapy by 2015)	Annual change in HIV deaths, 2005-2009 (%)	Annual change in HIV incidence, 2005-2009 (%)	Per capita disbursements for HIV/AIDS-related programmes (US dollars)
East Asia and the Pacific													
Cambodia	:	66.0	95.1	6.21	60 (0)	95 (1.0)	100.0	-1.1	1.68	100.0	-17.0	0.0	10.99
Timor-Leste	:	2.9	8.8	10.51	85 (0)	85 (0)	:	0.0	4.08	:	:	:	9.36
Lao People's Democratic Republic	:	100.0	100.0	7.09	69 (0)	93 (1.8)	100.0	0.6	2.36	100.0	0.0	:	4.64
Mongolia					75 (0)	87 (0)	100.0	0.0	4.93		-1.2	:	5.66
Thailand										100.0	8.0	-9.7	3.19
Philippines	:	100.0	100.0	0.69	56 (0)	88 (0)	63.0	-1.8	0.87				
Myanmar	:	26.0	35.0	0.55									
South Asia													
Bhutan	:	100.0	100.0	5.47	102 (0)	91 (0)	100.0	-4.2	2.62	:	-1.7	:	3.12
Nepal	:	100.0	100.0	0.71	73 (0)	89 (0.5)	100.0	0.0	0.74	25.0	-2.9	-5.7	1.05
Bangladesh	:	79.0	78.0	0.26	45 (4.3)	91 (0)	75.0	0.0	0.60	29.0	-1.4	0.0	0.43
Maldives										7.5	-1.4	:	11.70
India										56.0	-5.2	-7.7	0.49
Sri Lanka		100.0	100.0	1.25	72 (0)	85 (0)	60.0	0.0	0.52				
Pakistan					63 (13.2)	90 (2.8)	100.0	0.0	0.38				
Afghanistan	:	100.0	100.0	1.12									
Sub-Saharan Africa													
Rwanda	58 (0)	71.0	100.0	13.65	19 (0)	87 (2.8)	0.0	-2.6	4.52	100.0	-30.0	0.0	32.76
Swaziland										100.0	-12.0	-7.0	105.33
Namibia					75 (0)	82 (4.6)	0.0	-2.6	6.99	100.0	-15.0	-19.8	58.22
Lesotho					94 (0)	73 (0)	45.0	-0.2	5.25	100.0	-10.0	-4.1	41.60

Table V.2 (cont'd)

Country	Percentage of households owning an insecticide-treated net, 2009 (annual change (%), 2005-2009)	Percentage achieved of 2009 interim target (to reduce malaria case rate by 75% from 2000-2015)	Percentage achieved of 2009 interim target (to reduce malaria death rate by 75% from 2000-2015)	Per capita disbursements for malaria-related programmes (US dollars)	Tuberculosis case detection rate, all forms (%), 2009 (annual change (%), 2005-2009)	Tuberculosis treatment success rate (%), 2008 (annual change (%), 2004-2008)	Percentage achieved of 2009 interim tuberculosis target (to halve TB mortality rate, from 1990-2015)	Annual change in tuberculosis incidence, 2005-2009 (%)	Per capita disbursements for tuberculosis-related programmes (US dollars)	Percentage achieved of 2009 interim HIV target (to provide universal access to antiretroviral therapy by 2015)	Annual change in HIV deaths, 2005-2009 (%)	Annual change in HIV incidence, 2005-2009 (%)	Per capita disbursements for HIV/AIDS-related programmes (US dollars)
Zambia										100.0	-13.0	-8.5	26.71
Gambia	49 (0)	32.0	100.0	24.44	47 (0)	84 (0)	0.0	2.0	6.14				
Republic of South Sudan									5.36				
Sao Tome and Principe	64 (0)	43.0	100.0	44.82									
Equatorial Guinea	47 (75)	56.0	100.0	32.85									
Gabon	66 (68)	81.0	100.0	11.65									
Latin America and the Caribbean													
Guyana		97.0	85.0	5.44	90 (0)	69 (0)	100.0	-0.7	3.86	100.0	0.0	..	35.16
Suriname	..	100.0	100.0	14.40	25 (-)	59 (-)	0.0	7.5	3.32	89.0	0.0	-1.0	16.68
Haiti	..	0.0	0.0	3.13	..	..	100.0	-3.4	1.82	90.0	-13.0	-4.9	16.34
Jamaica										99.0	-20.0	-7.2	24.68
Belize										86.0	-2.1	-2.1	12.94
Peru					96 (0)	82 (0)	100.0	-5.4	2.20				
Paraguay					78 (0)	81 (0)	0.0	0.0	1.40				
Nicaragua	..	100.0	100.0	2.12									
Honduras	..	100.0	37.0	1.52									

Demonstrated impact | Consolidated progress towards impact | Limited progress | No progress | Not applicable

Sources: Global Fund to Fight AIDS, Tuberculosis and Malaria (2011b); Global Fund to Fight AIDS, Tuberculosis and Malaria (http://portfolio.theglobalfund.org/en/DataDownloads/Index) and Population Division, UN/DESA.

Box V.3

The Global Fund in Mozambique

The Global Fund plays a prominent role in Mozambique's health sector. Since the Fund's inception, it has disbursed $243 million, ranking second in size only to the United States of America as a major donor of health aid in recent years. It has had a strong impact in all three of its priority areas, making a key contribution to the country's large-scale antiretroviral therapy programme, which reaches 250,000 people living with AIDS; detecting and treating 60,000 tuberculosis cases; and distributing almost 4 million bed nets (Global Fund to Fight AIDS, Tuberculosis and Malaria, 2012).

This contribution has to be seen within a context of severe underinvestment in the health sector and heavy dependence on foreign aid. Mozambique's health infrastructure is still hampered by destruction from war, particularly in rural areas. It has one of the lowest densities of health workers worldwide, with only 0.03 doctors and 0.21 nurses per 1,000 inhabitants (World Health Organization, 2009b). In 2010, almost half of the national health budget was externally financed. Such levels of aid dependency give rise to important challenges for the national health system and with respect to priority-setting by national authorities and for sustainability of health interventions.

In order to strengthen the national health system, donors have contributed sector-specific budget support through PROSAUDE, a common fund for health, since 2003. The Global Fund initially supported the sector-wide approach, and Mozambique became the first country to integrate Global Fund grants into a common on-budget funding arrangement (Koenig and Goodwin, 2011). Only a few years later, however, they were taken off-budget again, at the request of the national ministry of health, as it had proved too difficult to harmonize procedures for Global Fund grants with the pooled funding arrangement. Application procedures and reporting requirements tied up significant resources, and the ministry was constrained in policy implementation by delays in disbursement. In 2007, for example, the Global Fund had disbursed only 54 per cent of promised funds, all in the final four weeks of the year (Informal Governance Group and Alliance 2015, 2010). Eventually, a separate, external unit in the ministry of health had to be set up to deal with the administrative requirements of Global Fund grants (KPMG Mozambique, 2010).

The Global Fund is not alone in its struggle to harmonize procedures and to reduce the transaction costs of aid. Pooled funding continues to represent only a small share of total aid to health. In 2009, the common fund received $80 million, while vertical funding, including project aid, amounted to $376 million (ibid.). Despite the commitment by donors to follow a sector-wide approach, aid to health thus remains fragmented and largely off-budget. However, the Global Fund does participate in the International Health Partnership Country Compact, which allows donors that operate outside the common fund (also including the GAVI Alliance and USAID) to align their actions. The Country Compact is seen by many stakeholders as a useful process, and has, for example, validated and facilitated funding for a joint human resource strategy (Koenig and Goodwin, 2011).

The disproportionate role of donor funding in Mozambique's health budget also means that the spending priorities of donors are strongly reflected in overall health expenditure. The national Government's highest priority is to increase equity in access to and quality of health services, in particular primary health care. While donors support this process, they put a much greater emphasis on HIV/AIDS. Between 2006 and 2008, more than half of total health aid was directed towards the fight against HIV/AIDS, compared with only 7 per cent for basic health infrastructure and 4 per cent for basic health care (Koenig and Goodwin; 2011). The Global Fund dedicated almost 70 per cent of its total funding to HIV/AIDS. However, there is evidence of increasing integration of HIV/AIDS programmes with other health services, increasing access to treatment in rural areas and strengthening health service infrastructure (Pfeiffer and others, 2010). The Global Fund has also financed new health worker training in Mozambique, albeit on a relatively small scale (Oomman, Bernstein and Rosenzweig, 2008).

Heavy dependence on external funding renders Mozambique's health system extremely vulnerable to reductions in aid inflows. Cutbacks in international funding for the fight against HIV/AIDS—as evidenced not only in the cancellation of the Global Fund's eleventh funding round, but also in the planned reductions to the United States initiative on AIDS relief—could have a devastating impact on the country's treatment programme. As a result, shortages of antiretroviral medication are anticipated by the end of 2012. Current funding for tuberculosis—provided almost entirely by the Global Fund—is scheduled to end in mid-2013, and there are no immediate prospects for alternative funding (Médicins sans Frontières, 2011; 2012).

Source: UN/DESA.

While it should be emphasized the GAVI Alliance and the Global Fund represent only a relatively small part of this problem, it is nonetheless important to take these issues into account, not only in their operations but in any future scaling up of innovative development finance for health, and in other sectors.

Vertical versus horizontal approaches to health system support

The issue of vertical versus horizontal approaches as it relates to external support to health services has given rise to a long-running debate—one that dates back nearly 50 years in the academic and policy literature, when it was already described as "a matter of growing concern during the last two decades". Even then, disease-specific "mass campaigns" were considered a "temporary expedient", which should be complementary to health systems development, with "progressive convergence and ultimate merging of the two approaches" (Gonzales, 1965). Around the same time, tuberculosis expert Halfdan T. Mahler (subsequently Director General of WHO, a post he occupied for 15 years) wrote that "all communicable disease campaigns have overwhelmingly demonstrated that only through falling back on strong basic health services in developing countries is it possible to achieve a consolidation of these campaigns" (Mahler, 1966).

However, a review of subsequent developments in this field over the following 40 years found a conspicuous lack of progress, either in substance or in the state of knowledge and research on the issue (Mills, 2005). As noted in chapter IV and illustrated in figure IV.1, a rapid expansion of vertical programmes has been the major driving force behind increasing international assistance to health in recent years. By 2009, some 60 per cent of all ODA allocations to the health sector were destined to programmes oriented towards specific infectious disease control, and nearly 40 per cent was allocated to HIV/AIDS programmes alone.

Both the GAVI Alliance and the Global Fund operate on the basis of the vertical approach. A review of 31 empirical studies of vertical global HIV programmes between 2002 and 2007 (of which 27 included the Global Fund and 24 focused on it exclusively) suggests that the vertical approach continued to give rise to a number of potentially serious problems. Among the problems identified were distraction of Governments from coordinated efforts to strengthen health systems, distortion of national priorities and adverse effects on donor harmonization, potentially undermining the coherence of health policies (Biesma and others, 2009).

> Disputes regarding the suitability of the vertical approach have a long history

Health system fragmentation

Vertical programmes give rise to potentially serious issues of fragmentation in health systems. A multiplicity of separate, coexisting disease-specific programmes, often focusing on the same diseases, creates problems of coordination and coherence, raising issues of duplication and overlapping mandates. In this respect, the Global Fund and the GAVI Alliance have the potential to play a positive role, to the extent that they act as channels of funding from other donors and multilateral development banks. However, this potential has not been fulfilled, especially in the case of the Global Fund, thereby raising the risk that they will simply add to the fragmentation of development assistance delivery. This problem is compounded by the proliferation of non-governmental and non-profit private providers of health services. While such providers may help to fill the gaps left by

> Evidence indicates that vertical funds have aggravated fragmentation of aid

inadequate and under-resourced public health services, they also contribute considerably to problems of coordination. This phenomenon is particularly conspicuous in the area of HIV/AIDS, where there were an estimated 60,000 AIDS-related non-governmental organizations globally in 2007 (Garrett, 2007). Non-governmental organizations often have limited capacity and weak accountability, an issue that has given rise to concerns, for example, in Benin, Ethiopia, Malawi, South Africa and Uganda. In Angola, the effort to involve multiple stakeholders in the programmes of global health funds even led to the channelling of funds for health through several different ministries rather than through the health ministry alone (Biesma and others, 2009). The Global Fund, in particular, arguably adds to such problems, as it provides much of its financing to non-governmental organizations.

Administrative burdens and capacity

Global funds' modus operandi creates an administrative burden for recipient countries

Many low-income countries have limited administrative capacity, reflecting a combination of limited financial and human resources and often weak governance systems. The multiplicity of coexisting, often overlapping vertical programmes not only results in duplication in planning and in financial and programme management systems, and increased complexity in financial management arising from multiple funding channels, each with its own monitoring and evaluation system, but also creates problems in terms of integrating funds into coordinated national plans (Biesma and others, 2009). The different fiscal-year cycles of the various funds and programmes, together with uncertainty over disbursement amounts in some cases, make it difficult for recipient countries to integrate their resources into their national budgets. In the cases of the Global Fund and the GAVI Alliance, the absence in recipient countries of any direct physical presence of these global funds may represent a further complication.

The much greater complexity of coordination processes in fragmented systems also gives rise to substantial additional time costs. Donor missions alone can represent a major drain on human resources: in 2005, Mozambique had 120 projects funded by 20 donors in the health sector, and received 59 missions (Martins, 2006). The opportunity cost of the time of senior officials and specialists in seriously resource-constrained countries may be considerable, giving rise to significant adverse effects on policymaking and policy implementation and on the effectiveness of administrative systems.

At the same time, the burden on resource-constrained administrative systems of complex and time-consuming systems of application, monitoring and reporting may be a significant obstacle or disincentive to accessing funds. As noted above, the five-year assessment of the Global Fund highlighted the problems arising from the administrative burden associated with its performance-based funding system.

The "challenge fund" nature of the Global Fund's project selection process, which implies projects must compete for a limited pool of funding, with only half of all proposals being accepted for that funding (Isenman and Shakow, 2010), is also problematic in this regard. Not only does it create a risk that funding allocations will be biased towards those countries with the greatest administrative capacity (and which are therefore best able to put together proposals of a quality and in a form that will favour their acceptance), but the likelihood that any given project will be rejected gives rise to a high risk that the time and effort put into preparing the proposal will be wasted. This may generate a significant disincentive for resource-constrained countries to even seek funding.

Domestic brain drain

In countries with serious shortages of health professionals (including least developed and most other low-income and sub-Saharan African countries), fragmentation and verticalization of health systems and the prioritization of particular diseases also generate potentially serious problems through the diversion of human resources. Shifts of health professionals occur on several levels: from general health services to disease-specific programmes, from programmes focused on underfunded diseases to those favoured by donors (notably HIV/AIDS) and from the public sector to the non-governmental (and donor) sector.

In Ethiopia, activities supported by the Global Fund have led to the movement of health workers from the public sector to the private sector, non-governmental organizations, and bilateral organizations, owing to the prospect of higher salaries and compensation (Banteyerga and others, 2005; Banteyerga, Kidanu and Stillman, 2006). Studies of Global Fund programmes in Zambia and the regions of Europe and Eurasia reported proactive recruitment of qualified staff through the offer of higher salaries and other incentives (Donoghue and others, 2005; Drew and Purvis, 2006). In Benin, workers in the existing public sector received no financial compensation for Global Fund-related additional workloads while those recruited with Global Fund resources received higher salaries (Smith and others, 2005).

Global funds' parallel implementation mechanism acts to draw away skilled personnel

Health system strengthening

Increasing awareness of the issues discussed above—in terms of the implications for their own operations as well as for health in beneficiary countries—has led both the GAVI Alliance and the Global Fund to shift in some way towards providing broader support to health systems. From its inception, the Global Fund provided some funding for health systems strengthening within disease-specific projects. It introduced a separate health systems strengthening window for round 5 of grant applications in 2005, although this was dropped for round 6 in 2006, and has not been reintroduced. The GAVI Alliance introduced a separate health systems strengthening support window in 2006, with the aim of addressing broader health system bottlenecks, so as to improve immunization coverage and maternal and child health outcomes. The establishment (with the World Bank and WHO) of the Health Systems Funding Platform in 2009 was driven by similar considerations (Schäferhoff, Schrade, and Yamey, 2011).

Global funds have introduced health systems strengthening components to counteract fragmentation…

Support for health systems strengthening from the GAVI Alliance remains relatively modest, amounting to some 13.5 per cent of its disbursements, while support from the Global Fund is substantially greater (Schäferhoff, Schrade, and Yamey, 2011). As shown in figure V.7, however, there is very wide variation among countries, with much higher shares in many low-income countries in sub-Saharan Africa and in South-East Asia.

In both the Global Fund and the GAVI Alliance, support to health systems strengthening is also closely tied to their respective mandates. In the case of the Global Fund, it has been possible to seek support for health systems strengthening (except in 2005–2006) as part of HIV/AIDS, tuberculosis or malaria projects.

This disease-specific focus sets serious limits to the potential benefits of the health systems strengthening dimensions of the programmes supported by the Global Fund and the GAVI Alliance, as it skews the support towards the particular activities supported by the funder. For example, health systems strengthening may support in-service training for health professionals in disease-specific or immunization-related activities, but

Figure V.7

Share of health system strengthening of total GAVI Alliance disbursements against 2010 GNI per capita, across recipient countries, 2006-2010

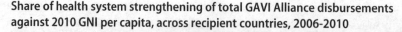
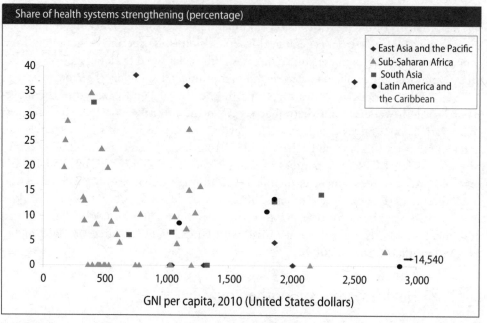

Sources: GAVI Alliance (http://www.gavialliance.org/results/disbursements/); Population Division, UN/DESA; and World Development Indicators online database (available from http://databank.worldbank.org/ddp/home.do).

contribute only to a very limited extent to the training of new health professionals outside these fields, so as to help relieve often acute national shortages. Of 45 health systems strengthening projects supported by the GAVI Alliance, 99 per cent financed in-service training, but only 29 per cent supported pre-service training; further, 69 per cent provided training for managers, compared with figures of 24 per cent for medical personnel and 43 per cent for nurses (Vujicic and others, 2012).

Preliminary assessments show that country proposals for GAVI Alliance health systems strengthening were well aligned with country priorities and contributed to harmonization of immunization goals with health systems strengthening efforts, although the required analytical exercises and coordination of multiple stakeholders gave rise to significant transaction costs (Galichet and others, 2010). The independent evaluation of the GAVI Alliance broadly confirmed these results, finding that recipient countries valued activities in the area of health systems strengthening because of the greater transparency, flexibility and predictability provided by the separate funding window compared with similar support from other funders. However, the amounts of funding were comparatively small and transaction costs high (CEPA, 2010).

... however, they are often neither sufficient nor adequate

As originally conceived, the Health Systems Funding Platform had the potential to contribute significantly to resolving both the tensions between vertical programmes and horizontal systems and the fragmentation of health systems. It would simultaneously have provided the additional funding needed to establish functional health systems, thereby also strengthening health service provision outside donor-defined disease-specific enclaves, and greatly improved donor coordination within the health sector, reducing administrative burdens.

As noted in chapter IV, however, while some progress has been made, some considerable distance between ambitions and their achievement remains to be covered: few additional resources have been generated and engagement by other donors has been limited. It is likely that further progress on both health systems strengthening and the Health Systems Funding Platform will continue to be limited by the reluctance of some board members of the GAVI Alliance and the Global Fund to move beyond a very narrow interpretation of their respective mandates (Hill and others, 2011). This is likely to remain an important constraint on further progress towards improving the effects of GAVI Alliance and Global Fund programmes on health systems.

This, coupled with the limited success of the Health Systems Funding Platform in attracting additional funding for health systems or engaging other funders, means that reconciling vertical funds' objectives with sector- and economy-wide agendas of developing countries remains problematic (Glassman and Savedoff, 2011; Schäferhoff, Schrade and Yamey, 2011).

Ownership and priorities

As noted in chapter IV, the concentration of external funding for health in disease- and intervention-specific mechanisms whose scope and mandates are determined at the global level, primarily by donor preferences, gives rise to a risk of skewing health systems away from national priorities. This in turn gives rise in turn to a tension between this approach and the principles of ownership, alignment and harmonization as criteria of aid and development effectiveness, as established by the Paris Declaration on Aid Effectiveness,[5] the Accra Agenda for Action[6] and the Busan Partnership for Effective Development Cooperation (Group of Twenty, 2011b), agreed at the Fourth High-level Forum on Aid Effectiveness, held in Busan, Republic of Korea, from 29 November to 1 December 2011.

As serious as HIV/AIDS, tuberculosis, malaria are, and notwithstanding the great potential health benefits of immunization, these challenges represent only part of the health needs of developing countries. A key long-term priority in any developing country is the establishment of an effective health system, accessible to the whole population, and providing quality interventions for all of their health needs. The channelling of most of the external support for health into programmes targeted at these particular areas, with much more limited support for health systems and other aspects of health— and still less budgetary support that can be directed according to priorities established by the Government itself—inevitably skews health systems towards externally determined priorities. To the extent that vertical programmes have adverse side effects on health systems as a whole, unfunded areas of health may not merely fail to benefit from the operations of vertical funds but may be negatively affected by them.

The Global Fund has attempted to deal with the issue of ownership by establishing multi-stakeholder Country Coordination Mechanisms in recipient countries, designed to develop and submit project proposals and ensure consistency with national development and health programmes. This has undoubtedly had some benefits, particularly in comparison with the less participatory approaches of many other donors.

Global funds' priorities often do not coincide with recipient countries' national priorities

---

5   Available from http://www.oecd.org/documents/18/0,3746,en_2649_3236398_35401554_1_1_1_1,00.html#Paris.

6   Available from http://siteresources.worldbank.org/ACCRAEXT/Resources/4700790-1217425866038/AAA-4-SEPTEMBER-FINAL-16h00.pdf.

However, it has also led to duplication of efforts of national bodies in planning, notably for HIV/AIDS, for example, in Angola, the Democratic Republic of the Congo, Malawi, Uganda and the United Republic of Tanzania. In some countries, such as Mozambique and Uganda, Country Coordination Mechanisms proved too large and unwieldy, with inadequate communication among participating agencies and lack of trust between public sector and non-governmental agencies (Biesma and others, 2009).

Lessons for the future

The success of global funds is clouded by unintended problems they have created

While focusing on specific diseases and interventions has proved to be an effective means of harnessing donor resources for health, this comes at a price in terms of the effects on health systems. Much of the attraction to donors is that interventions can be delivered without reliance on often weak, fractured, under-resourced and sometimes dysfunctional health systems, allowing visible results to be achieved more quickly and effectively than through the much slower process of health system strengthening. They are, in this sense, a temporary expedient, and were recognized as such as early as the 1960s.

However, channelling funding through vertical programmes may itself perpetuate the failure of health systems—a problem highlighted by continued reliance of the donor community on the same temporary expedient for more than 50 years. Were more resources devoted to the development of effective health systems over this period, rather than the support of disease-specific vertical programmes, the need for institutions such as the GAVI Alliance and the Global Fund today would be much more limited. At the very least, their task would be considerably easier.

It should be emphasized that the GAVI Alliance and the Global Fund represent a relatively small part of a much larger picture—and in many respects perform considerably better than many bilateral donors. They have also learned from their experiences, and have shown some flexibility in responding to the problems they have encountered, although their ability to do so has been constrained by their particular mandates and their decision-making processes.

In the present context, however, the significance of this issue extends far beyond these two particular institutions. If innovative development financing for health is scaled up substantially and provides genuinely additional resources, translating that funding into health benefits will require it to extend beyond HIV/AIDS, tuberculosis, malaria and vaccination into other areas of health. However, if it does so based on the model of the GAVI Alliance and the Global Fund, by creating further new vertical programmes in parallel with existing bilateral and multilateral vertical programmes, such financing will further compound the problems highlighted above.

Ideally, those additional resources should be channelled towards supporting the development of effective and accessible health systems, although experience to date suggests that donors will resist such an approach. Should this not be possible—because, for example, donors are willing to support programmes only for specific aspects of health—it would be much more beneficial to broaden the mandates of existing institutions rather than create additional institutions focused on other specific diseases.

As innovative financing mechanisms are developed, and resources begin to be disbursed on a significant scale, in other areas—notably climate change adaptation and mitigation—similar issues may be expected to arise. Here, too, it is important to learn the lessons of the health sector over the last half-century.

Other sources of development finance

As discussed at the beginning of this chapter, the primary interest of developing countries is not in whether a particular source of financing can, or cannot, be considered "innovative", but rather in the scale and development potential of the resources it provides. As originally conceived—as a source of substantial sums additional to ODA, which would be stable and predictable over time, and could be used flexibly by developing countries in accordance with their own development priorities—innovative development finance could provide considerable benefits from this perspective.

However, the innovative mechanisms that have been realized to date have failed to live up to these expectations. While they have been successful in achieving specific objectives, they have been very limited in scale and restricted in their use to donor-approved programmes within narrowly defined areas; further, the mechanisms through which they are disbursed are potentially problematic in resource-constrained countries. These represent serious constraints on the usefulness of innovative mechanisms, in their current form, as sources of financing for development. Moreover, the prospects for realizing mechanisms that would better fulfil the original aspirations of innovative development finance in the near future are seriously limited by political obstacles and the current framework of global governance.

If the resources generated by financial mechanisms were to be increased substantially, this would also require much greater attention to other issues, which are now of limited significance because of the very limited scale of innovative financing. With flows of innovative development financing at their current very low levels, volatility is of significance only at the sectoral or project level, and potential macroeconomic effects, for example, on international competitiveness ("Dutch disease") are negligible. A scaling up of innovative development financing of any kind to the levels required to fill the financing gaps discussed in chapter III would require much more careful consideration of such issues, as well as more proactive development of administrative and absorptive capacity, particularly in many low-income countries.

In practice, increasing innovative development financing to this extent seems at best a remote prospect. This, coupled with the relatively weak prospects for ODA in the light of fiscal pressures in most donor countries, notwithstanding donor commitments, will require developing countries to rely primarily on other sources of financing for their development needs in the foreseeable future.

In an ideal world, such financing—public and private—would be generated domestically; and for many emerging market economies, this is now a realistic prospect. For most low-income countries, however, despite better external conditions and much improved economic performance (at least prior to the current financial crisis), domestic financing can be expected to cover no more than a limited part of financial needs in the foreseeable future. Other external financial flows will therefore be increasingly important.

As shown in figure V.1, flows of FDI and migrants' remittances are already much greater than ODA in most developing regions. There has also been a dramatic increase in South-South financial cooperation in recent years, most notably (but by no means exclusively) from China. While comprehensive and systematic data are not available, China's aid to African countries alone between 2002 and 2009 has been estimated at $87 billion (Noman, 2012). Such estimates suggest that South-South cooperation is already at a much greater scale than can be expected for innovative development finance for many years to come, and is becoming significant in scale relative to traditional ODA.

IDF has so far not met expectations with regard to size and impact

While the use of funds from South-South cooperation, as of resources from ODA, is largely driven by conditions of the providing development partner, the less considerable gap between the economic and political power of donors and recipients, the commonality of their developing-country status, and in some cases their geographical proximity and sociocultural ties, make the dynamics of the provider-recipient relationship substantially different. Together with greater similarities in stages of development and in, for example, climate and epidemiology, these factors may also allow South-South cooperation to better reflect the needs of the recipient country.

In the absence of much greater and faster progress than has been achieved to date in developing innovative financing mechanisms that allow countries to meet their own needs in accordance with their own priorities, it thus seems likely that the attention of developing countries may shift further from innovative development finance towards other financial flows in the coming years, including South-South cooperation and promoting diaspora support for social projects. Funding on the necessary scale, however, is only part of what would be required if the full benefits were to be reaped. Essential as well would be effective management of the resources generated, regardless of source, through appropriate macroeconomic policies and development strategies.

Conclusion

IDF has had a limited and mixed effect so far

The financial contribution of innovative development financing has thus far been extremely limited, not only relative to other financial flows to developing countries and in macroeconomic terms, but even to expenditure in the health sector, where such flows have to date been overwhelmingly concentrated.

Nonetheless, the primary mechanisms for disbursement of these funds, the GAVI Alliance and the Global Fund to Fight AIDS, Tuberculosis and Malaria, have undoubtedly contributed to the achievement of major health improvements in their respective areas (notwithstanding a greater degree of uncertainty than is generally acknowledged regarding the scale of their impact). The International Finance Facility for Immunisation allowed the impact of the GAVI Alliance to be achieved some years sooner than might otherwise have been the case; and other innovative financing sources have made a modest contribution to the impact of the Global Fund. Such impacts can be expected to increase in the coming years, as new mechanisms currently at the pilot stage (notably advance market commitments and the Affordable Medicines Facility - malaria) come to fruition; and funding from climate funds supported by innovative sources of financing should soon become significant.

The future of IDF depends on an increase in size and a change in its utilization pattern

In the current system of global economic governance, establishing any form of innovative development finance in practice requires active support from developed-country Governments. To date, such support has been forthcoming only for mechanisms targeted towards specific challenges that are high in donors' agendas: HIV/AIDS, tuberculosis, malaria, vaccination, and climate change mitigation and adaptation. However, particularly in the health sector, such narrow targeting gives rise to potentially significant negative effects on health systems; and this limits developing countries' ability to meet their own needs and priorities in the future, increasing their dependency on external support, as well as impeding the operation and effectiveness of the vertical funds themselves.

Realizing the potential of innovative development finance mechanisms of the type developed to date will entail not only greatly increasing the scale of such financing but also reorienting it towards the needs and priorities of recipients rather than those of donors, and sector-wide priorities rather than uses for very specific subsector programmes designated by funding agencies. Much greater potential benefits would be realizable through the establishment of larger-scale mechanisms which allow greater flexibility in the use of the resources generated, such as those discussed in chapter II, provided that these resource flows were managed well, through appropriate macroeconomic and development policies.

Bibliography

Adugna, Abebe (2009). How much of official development assistance is earmarked? CFP Working Paper, No. 2. Washington, D.C.: World Bank, Concessional Finance and Global Partnerships.

Agence Française de Développement (n.d.). C2Ds: Debt Reduction-Development Contracts. Available from http://www.afd.fr/lang/en/home/outils-de-financement-du-developpement/C2D (accessed 2 May 2012).

Anand, P.B. (2002). *Financing the Provision of Global Public Goods. WIDER Discussion Paper*, No. 2002/110. Helsinki: United Nations University/World Institute for Development Economics Research. November.

Aryeetey, Ernest (2005). A development-oriented allocation of the Special Drawing Rights. In *New Sources of Development Finance*, A.B. Atkinson, ed. UN-WIDER Studies in Development Economics. New York: Oxford University Press. Pp. 90-109.

Atkinson, A.B. (2005). Over-arching issues. In *New Sources of Development Finance*, A.B. Atkinson, ed. New York: Oxford University Press.

_____, ed. (2005). *New Sources of Development Finance*. New York: Oxford University Press.

Atun, Rifat, and others (2010). Interactions between critical health system functions and HIV/AIDS, tuberculosis, and malaria programmes. *Health Policy and Planning*, vol. 25, Supplement 1, pp. i1-i3.

Baba, Chikako, and Annamaria Kokenye (2011). Effectiveness of capital controls in selected emerging markets in the 2000s. IMF Working Paper, No. WP/11/281 (December). Washington, D.C.: International Monetary Fund.

Baca-Campodónico, Jorge, Luiz de Mello and Andrei Kirilenko (2006). The rates and revenues of bank transaction taxes. OECD Economics Department Working Paper, No. 494. ECO/WKP(2006)22. Paris: Organization for Economic Cooperation and Development.

Bank for International Settlements (2011). *High-frequency Trading in the Foreign Exchange Market*. Report submitted by a Study Group established by the Markets Committee. Basel, Switzerland. September.

Banteyerga, H., A. Kidanu and K. Stillman (2006). The systemwide effects of the Global Fund in Ethiopia: final study report. Bethesda, Maryland: The Partners for Health Reform*plus* Project, Abt Associates Inc. September.

Banteyerga, H., and others (2005). The system-wide effects of the Global Fund in Ethiopia: baseline study report. Bethesda, Maryland: The Partners for Health Reform*plus* Project, Abt Associates Inc. October.

Barder, Owen, and Ethan Yeh (2006). The costs and benefits of front-loading and predictability of immunization. Center for Global Development Working Paper, No. 80. Washington, D.C.: Center for Global Development. February. Available from SSRN: http://ssrn.com/abstract=984043; or from http://dx.doi.org/10.2139/ssrn.984043.

Biesma, Regien G., and others (2009). The effects of global health initiatives on country health systems: a review of the evidence from HIV/AIDS control. *Health Policy and Planning*, vol. 24, No. 4, pp. 239-252.

Binger, Albert (2003). Global public goods and potential mechanisms for financing availability. Background paper prepared for the fifth session of the Committee for Development Policy, New York, 7-11 April 2003.

Birdsall, Nancy, and Benjamin Leo (2011). Find me the money: financing climate and other global public goods. CGD Working Paper, No. 248 (April). Washington, D.C.: Centre for Global Development.

Bolton, Patrick, Roger Guesnerie and Frederic Samama (2010). Towards an international green fund. Mimeo. October.

Boughton, James (2001). *Silent Revolution: The International Monetary Fund, 1979-1989*. Washington, D.C.: International Monetary Fund.

Bredenkamp, Hugh, and Catherine Pattillo (2010). Financing the response to climate change. IMF Staff Position Note, No. SPN10/06. Washington, D.C.: International Monetary Fund. 25 March.

Brugha, R., M. Starling and G. Walt (2002). GAVI, the first steps: lessons for the Global Fund. *Lancet*, vol. 359, pp. 435-438.

Buchner, Barbara, and others (2011). The landscape of climate finance. CPI report. Venice, Italy: Climate Policy Initiative. 27 October.

Buckley, Ross P. (2011a). French exchanges. In *Debt-for-Development Exchanges: History and New Applications*, Ross P. Buckley, ed. Cambridge, United Kingdom: Cambridge University Press.

_____ (2011b). German exchanges. In *Debt-for-Development Exchanges: History and New Applications*, Ross P. Buckley, ed. Cambridge, United Kingdom: Cambridge University Press.

_____ (2011c). Other debt-for-development exchanges. In *Debt-for-Development Exchanges: History and New Applications*, Ross P. Buckley, ed. Cambridge, United Kingdom: Cambridge University Press.

_____, ed. (2011). *Debt-for-Development Exchanges: History and New Applications*. Cambridge, United Kingdom: Cambridge University Press.

Buckley, Ross P., and Steven Freeland (2011). Debt-for-nature exchanges. In *Debt-for-Development Exchanges: History and New Applications*, Ross P. Buckley, ed. Cambridge, United Kingdom: Cambridge University Press.

Buira, Ariel, ed. (2005). *The IMF and the World Bank at Sixty*. G24 Research Programme. London: Anthem Press.

Bulíř, Ales, and A. Javier Hamann (2003). Aid volatility: an empirical assessment. *IMF Staff Papers*, vol. 50, No. 1. Washington, D.C.: International Monetary Fund.

Burcky, Urs (2011). Trends in in-country aid fragmentation and donor proliferation: an analysis of changes in aid-allocation patterns between 2005 and 2009. Report on behalf of the OECD Task Team on Division of Labour and Complementarity. 10 June.

Caribbean Catastrophe Risk Insurance Facility (2010). A guide to understanding CCRIF: a collection of questions and answers. Grand Cayman, Cayman Islands. March.

_____ (2011a). CCRIF: a natural catastrophe risk insurance mechanism for the Caribbean—a collection of papers, articles and expert notes, vol. 2. Grand Cayman, Cayman Islands. November.

_____ (2011b). A snapshot of the economics of climate adaptation study in the Caribbean. Grand Cayman, Cayman Islands. November.

_____ (2011c). Quarterly report: September-November 2011. Cayman Islands. Available from http://www.ccrif.org/sites/default/files/publications/CCRIF_Quarterly_Report_Sept_Nov_2011.pdf.

Cassimon, Danny, Robrecht Renard and Karel Verbeke (2008). Assessing debt-to-health swaps: a case study on the Global Fund Debt2Health Conversion Scheme. *Tropical Medicine and International Health*, vol. 13, No. 9 (September), pp. 1188-1195.

Castro, Rocio, and Brian Hammond (2009). The architecture of aid for the environment: a ten year statistical perspective. CFP Working Paper, No. 3. Washington, D.C.: World Bank, Concessional Finance and Global Partnerships. October.

CEPA (2010). GAVI second evaluation report. 13 September. Available from http://www.gavialliance.org/library/gavi-documents/evaluations/second-gavi-evaluation-2006-2010/.

Cernuschi, Tania, and others (2011). Advance market commitment for pneumococcal vaccines: putting theory into practice. *Bulletin of the World Health Organization* (online), vol. 89, No. 12, pp. 913-918.

Chee, Grace, and others (2007). Evaluation of the first five years of GAVI Immunization Services Support funding. Bethesda, Maryland: Abt Associates. September.

Chicago Political Economy Group (2010). Taxing Wall Street to revive Main Street. CPEG fact sheet. Chicago, Illinois: University of Illinois at Chicago. 20 June. Available from http://www.nijwj.org/uploads/FTTFactSheet-Final.docx.

Claessens, Stijn, Michael Keen and Ceyla Pazarbasioglu, eds. (2010). Financial sector taxation: the IMF's report to the G20 and background material. Washington, D.C.: International Monetary Fund. September.

Climate Funds Update (n.d.). Available from http://www.climatefundsupdate.org/listing. (accessed 30 March 2012).

Coelho, Isaias (2009). Taxing bank transactions: the experience in Latin America and elsewhere. Paper presented at the International Tax Dialogue Global Conference "Financial Institutions and Instruments: Tax Challenges and Solutions", Beijing, 26-28 October 2009.

Collier, Paul, and David Dollar (2001). Can the world cut poverty in half? how policy reform and effective aid can meet international development goals. *World Development*, vol. 29, No. 11 (November), pp. 1787-1802.

Das R.K., and P. Dasgupta (2000). Child health and immunisation: a macro perspective. *Economic and Political Weekly*, vol. 15, No. 8/9, pp. 645-655.

Department for International Development (2009). Advance market commitments for low-carbon development: an economic assessment. Final report. London: DFID. March. Available from http://www.vivideconomics.com/docs/Vivid%20Econ%20AMCs.pdf.

_____ (2010a). A potential role for an AMC in supporting dish/Stirling concentrating solar power. Case study annex. London: DFID. March. Available from http://www.vivideconomics.com/uploads/reports/low-carbon-amcs/Micro_CSP_case_study.pdf (accessed 9 April 2012).

_____ (2010b). A potential role for AMCs in promoting green mini-grids in Tanzania. Case study annex. GVEP International. March. Available from http://www.vivideconomics.com/uploads/reports/low-carbon-amcs/Tanzania_case_study.pdf (accessed 9 April 2012).

Dervis, Kemal, and Sarah Puritz Milsom (2011). Development aid and global public goods: the example of climate protection. In *Catalyzing Development: A New Vision for Aid*, Homi Kharas, Koji Makino and Woojin Jung, eds. Washington, D.C.: The Brookings Institution.

Desai, Monica, and others (2010). Critical interactions between Global Fund-supported programmes and health systems: a case study in Indonesia. *Health Policy and Planning*, vol. 25, pp. i43-i47.

Desai, Raj, and Homi Kharas (2010). The determinants of aid volatility. Paper presented at the International Studies Association (ISA) Annual Convention, on the theme "Theory vs. Policy? Connecting Scholars and Practitioners" held in New Orleans, Louisiana from 17 to 20 February 2010.

Dodd, Rebecca, and Christopher Lane (2010). Improving the long-term sustainability of health aid: are Global Health Partnerships leading the way? *Health Policy and Planning*, vol. 25, No. 5, pp. 363-371. Available from http://heapol.oxfordjournals.org/content/25/5/363.full.pdf+html.

Donoghue, M., and others (2005). Global Fund tracking study: Zambia country report. London: London School of Hygiene and Tropical Medicine; and Lusaka: Institute of Economic and Social Research. January.

Doolan, Denise L., Carlota Dobaño and J. Kevin Baird (2009). Acquired immunity to malaria. *Clinical Microbiology Reviews*, vol. 22, No. 1, pp. 13-36.

Drew, R., and G. Purvis (2006). Strengthening health systems to improve HIV/AIDS programs in the Europe and Eurasia region using Global Fund resources. Produced for review by the United States Agency for International Development and prepared by the authors on behalf of Social & Scientific Systems, under the Synergy Project. Washington, D.C.: USAID, Bureau for Global Health, Office of HIV/AIDS. January.

Elliot, Kimberly (2010). Pulling agricultural innovation and market together. Center for Global Development Working Paper, No. 215. June. Washington, D.C.: Center for Global Development.

Erten, Bilge, and José Antonio Ocampo (2012). SDRs as an innovative source of financing. Background paper prepared for *World Economic and Social Survey 2012*.

European Commission (2011). Proposal for a Council Directive on a common system of financial transaction tax and amending Directive 2008/7/EC. Brussels. 28 September. COM(2011) 594 final; 2011/0261 (CNS).

Evidence to Policy Initiative (2011). The Health Systems Funding Platform: a primer. E2Pi policy brief.

Figueroa, Michael (2008). Rainforest-for-carbon-credits save UluMasen forest from conversion into palm oil plantation. East Asia and Pacific on the rise. 5 March. Available from http://blogs.worldbank.org/eastasiapacific/node/2795.

FitzGerald, Valpy (2012). International tax cooperation and innovative development finance. Background paper prepared for *World Economic and Social Survey 2012*.

Frankman, Myron J. (1996). International taxation: the trajectory of an idea from Lorimer to Brandt. *World Development*, vol. 24, No. 5 (May), pp. 807-820.

Galichet, B., and others (2010). Linking programmes and systems: lessons from the GAVI Health Systems Strengthening window. *Tropical Medicine and International Health*, vol. 15, No. 2 (February), pp. 208-215.

Garrett, Laurie (2007). The challenge of global health. *Foreign Affairs*, vol. 86, No. 1 (January/February), pp. 14-17.

Gates, Bill (2011). Innovation with impact: financing 21st century development. A report by Bill Gates to G20 leaders, Cannes Summit, November 2011. The Gates Notes. Available from http://www.thegatesnotes.com/Topics/Development/G20-Report-Innovation-with-Impact.

GAVI Alliance (2011a). GAVI Alliance progress report 2010. Geneva. Available from http://www.gavialliance.org/library/publications/gavi-progress-reports/.

_____ (2011b). Donor contributions and proceeds to GAVI 2000-2030 as at 30 June 2011. Available from http://www.gavialliance.org/library/gavi-documents/funding/donor-contributions-and-proceeds-to-gavi-2000-2030-(30-june-2011)/.

_____ (2012a). Pneumococcal vaccine support. Geneva. Available from http://www.gavialliance.org/support/nvs/pneumococcal/.

_____ (2012b). Donor contributions and proceeds to GAVI 2000-2031 as of 31 January 2012. Available from http://www.gavialliance.org/funding/donor-contributions-pledges/ (accessed 12 April 2012).

_____ (2012c). GAVI Alliance: cash received 2000-2011 as of 31 December 2011. Available from http://www.gavialliance.org/funding/donor-contributions-pledges/.

GAVI Alliance Secretariat (2011). Advance market commitment for pneumococcal vaccines. Annual report: 1 April 2010-31 March 2011. Geneva.

GAVI Alliance and World Bank (2012). IFFIm: International Finance Facility for Immunisation. From the IFFIm library. IFFIm_website_investor_presentation_(Jan_24_2012)FINAL-2. Available from http://www.iffim.org (accessed 21 March 2012).

German Watch (2011). An innovative approach: the German use of ETS revenues for national and international climate financing. Briefing note. Berlin. November. Available from http://www.germanwatch.org/klima/clifin-ets11.pdf.

Girishankar, Navin (2009). Innovating development finance: from financing sources to financial solutions. CFP Working Paper Series, No. 1. Washington, D.C.: World Bank, Concessional Finance and Global Partnerships Vice Presidency. June.

Glassman, Amanda, and William Savedoff (2011). The Health Systems Funding Platform: resolving tensions between the aid and development effectiveness agendas. CGD Working Paper, No. 258. Washington, D.C.: Center for Global Development. Available from http://www.cgdev.org/content/publications/detail/1425300.

Global Environment Facility (2010). System for Transparent Allocation of Resources (STAR). Available from http://www.thegef.org/gef/sites/thegef.org/files/publication/GEF_STAR_A4_april11_CRA.pdf.

Global Fund Technical Evaluation Reference Group (2009a). *The Impact of Collective Efforts on the Reduction of the Disease Burden of AIDS, Tuberculosis, and Malaria*: Final Report—*Global Fund Five-Year Evaluation: Study Area 3*. Geneva. May.

_____ (2009b). *Technical Evaluation Reference Group Summary Paper on the Synthesis Report of the Five-Year Evaluation of the Global Fund*. Geneva. April.

Global Fund to Fight AIDS, Tuberculosis and Malaria (n.d.a). Private sector: (RED). Available from http://www.theglobalfund.org/en/privatesector/red/ (accessed 16 April 2012).

_____ (n.d.b). The Global Fund to Fight AIDS, Tuberculosis and Malaria: pledges. Available from http://www.theglobalfund.org/documents/core/financial/Core_PledgesContributions_List_en/ (accessed 16 April 2012).

_____ (2008). Start of Debt2Health in Indonesia. 1 June. Available from http://www.theglobalfund.org/en/innovativefinancing/Announcements/Start_of_Debt2Health_in_Indonesia/.

_____ (2011a). *The Global Fund Annual Report 2010*. Geneva. May.

_____ (2011b). *Making a Difference: Global Fund Results Report 2011*. Geneva.

_____ (2012). Mozambique: regional grant portfolio. Available from http://portfolio.theglobalfund.org/en/Country/Index/MOZ.

Gonzales, C.L. (1965). Mass campaigns and general health services. Public Health Papers, No. 29. Geneva: World Health Organization. General conclusions reprinted in *Bulletin of the World Health Organization*, vol. 83, No. 4 (April 2005), pp. 317-319.

Gottschalk, Ricardo (2012). Innovative development finance: the Latin American experience. Background paper prepared for *World Economic and Social Survey 2012*.

Griffith-Jones, Stephany, and Krishnan Sharma (2006). GDP-indexed bonds: making it happen. DESA Working Paper No. 21. New York: Department of Economic and Social Affairs of the United Nations Secretariat. April. ST/ESA/2006/DWP/21.

Griffith-Jones, Stephany, and Avinash Persaud (2012a). Why critics are wrong about a financial-transaction tax. European Voice.com. 12 March. Available from http://www.europeanvoice.com/article/2012/march/why-critics-are-wrong-about-a-financial-transaction-tax/73843.aspx.

_____ (2012b). Financial transaction taxes. IPD Network Paper. New York: Initiative for Policy Dialogue, Columbia University. 8 February.

Group of Twenty (2011a). Cannes Summit final declaration: building our common future—renewed collective action for the benefit of all. 4 November. Available from http://www.g20-g8.com.

_____ (2011b). Busan Partnership for Effective Development Cooperation, agreed at the Fourth High-level Forum on Aid Effectiveness, 29 November - 1 December 2011, Busan, Republic of Korea. Available from http://www.aideffectiveness.org/busanhlf4/images/stories/hlf4/ OUTCOME_DOCUMENT_-_FINAL_EN.pdf.

Group of Twenty-four (1979). Outline for a Programme of Action on International Monetary Reform. Prepared by the Intergovernmental Group of Twenty-four on International Monetary Affairs and adopted by the Group of 77 at its ministerial meeting held in Belgrade on 29 September 1979. A/C.2/34/13.

Hanvoravongchai, Piya, Busaba Warakamin and Richard Coker (2010). Critical interactions between Global Fund-supported programmes and health systems: a case study in Thailand. *Health Policy and Planning*, vol. 25, pp. i53-i57.

Hardon, Anita, and Stuart Blume (2005). Shifts in global immunisation goals (1984-2004): unfinished agendas and mixed results. *Social Science Medicine*, vol. 60, No. 2 (January), pp. 345-356.

Haq, Mahbub ul, Inge Kaul and Isabelle Grunberg, eds. (1996). *The Tobin Tax: Coping with Financial Volatility*. New York: Oxford University Press.

Health Action International (2012). Retail prices of ACTs co-paid by the AMFm and other antimalarial medicines: Ghana, Kenya, Madagascar, Nigeria, Tanzania and Uganda. Report of price tracking surveys. January.

Herman, Barry (2011). Contribution to *Recovery with a Human Face*. UNICEF e-discussion. Available from https://sites.google.com/site/recoverywithahumanfacenetwork/home. 3 May. Accessed 19 March 2012.

_____, José Antonio Ocampo and Shari Spiegel (2009). The case for a new international reform effort. In *Dealing Better with Developing Country Debt*, Barry Herman, José Antonio Ocampo and Shari Spiegel, eds. New York: Oxford University Press.

Hill, Peter, and others (2011). The Health System Funding Platform: is this where we thought we were going? *Globalization and Health*, vol. 7, No. 16, pp. 1-10.

Hurley, Gail (2012). Some country perspectives on innovative sources of development finance. Background paper prepared for *World Economic and Social Survey 2012*.

I-8 Group/Leading Innovative Financing for Equity (L.I.F.E.) (2009). Innovative financing for development. Available from http://www.un.org/esa/ffd/documents/ InnovativeFinForDev.pdf.

Independent Commission on International Development Issues (1980). *North-South: A Program for Survival*. Cambridge, Massachusetts: The MIT Press; and London: Pan Books.

Informal Governance Group and Alliance 2015 (2010). Aid and budget transparency in Mozambique: constraints for civil society, the parliament and the government. Available from http://www.trocaire.org/sites/trocaire/files/pdfs/ policy/Aid_Budget_Transparency_in_Moz.pdf.

Institute of Medicine of the National Academies (2004). *Saving Lives, Buying Time: Economics of Malaria Drugs in an Age of Resistance*, Kenneth J. Arrow, Claire B. Panosian and Hellen Gelband, eds. Washington, D.C.: National Academies Press.

Inter-American Development Bank (2010). Ten years of innovation in remittances: lessons learned and models for the future. Independent review of the Multilateral Investment Fund Remittance Portfolio: Multilateral Investment Fund projects, research and dissemination activities from 2000-2009. Washington, D.C. January.

Intergovernmental Panel on Climate Change (2008). Climate Change 2007: Synthesis Report. Contribution of Working Groups I, II and III to the Fourth Assessment Report of the Intergovernmental Panel on Climate Change. Geneva. Summary for policymakers.

International Development Association (2007). Aid architecture: an overview of the main trends in official development assistance flows. Washington, D.C. February.

International Energy Agency (2008). *Energy Technology Perspective 2008: Scenarios and Strategies to 2050*. Paris.

International Monetary Fund (n.d.). Quota and voting shares before and after implementation of reforms agreed in 2008 and 2010 (in percentage shares of total IMF quota). Available from http://www.imf.org/external/np/sec/pr/2011/pdfs/quota_tbl.pdf.

_____ (2008). *World Economic Outlook: Housing and the Business Cycle—April 2008*. Washington, D.C.

_____ (2009). *Balance of Payments and International Investment Position Manual (BPM6)*, 6th Ed. Washington, D.C.

_____ (2011). Enhancing international monetary stability: a role for the SDR? Paper prepared by the Strategy, Policy, and Review Department in collaboration with the Finance, Legal, Monetary and Capital Markets Departments, and in consultation with the Research and Area Departments. Washington, D.C. 7 January.

Isenman, Paul, and Alexander Shakow (2010). *Donor Schizophrenia and Aid Effectiveness: The Role of Global Funds. IDS Practice Paper* 5. Brighton, United Kingdom: Institute of Development Studies, University of Sussex. April.

Isenman, Paul, Cecilie Wathne and Geraldine Baudienille (2010). Global funds: allocation strategies and aid effectiveness. Final report. London: Overseas Development Institute. 14 July.

Kaul, Inge, and Pedro Conceição (2006). Why revisit public finance today? In *The New Public Finance: Responding to Global Challenges*, Inge Kaul and Pedro Conceição, eds. New York: Oxford University Press.

Kaul, Inge, Isabelle Grunberg and Mark Stern (1999). *Global Public Goods: International Cooperation in the 21st Century*. Oxford: Oxford University Press.

Keen, Michael, and Jon Strand (2007). Indirect taxes on international aviation. *Fiscal Studies,* vol. 28, No. 1 (March), pp. 1-41.

Ketkar, Suhas (2012). Aid securitization: beyond IFFIm. Background paper prepared for *World Economic and Social Survey 2012*. 15 January.

Kharas, Homi (2008). Measuring the Cost of Aid Volatility. *Wolfensohn Center for Development Working Paper*, No. 3. Washington, D.C.: The Brookings Institution.

Knack, Stephen, and Aminur Rahman (2004). Donor fragmentation and bureaucratic quality in aid recipients. World Bank Policy Research Working Paper, No. 3186. Washington, D.C.: World Bank.

Koeberle, Stefan, Zoran Stavreski and Jan Walliser, eds. (2006). *Budget Support as More Effective Aid? Recent Experiences and Emerging Lessons*. Washington, D.C.: World Bank.

Koenig, Sybille, and Frazer Goodwin (2011). Health spending in Mozambique: the impact of current aid structures and aid effectiveness. Report produced by the German Foundation for World Population (DSW) for Health. Available from http://www.euroresources.org/fileadmin/user_upload/AfGH_Policy_Briefs/PolicyBriefing4_Mozambique.pdf.

KPMG Mozambique (2010). Final report: Paris Declaration evaluation phase 2—Mozambique. July. Available from http://www.oecd.org/dataoecd/61/0/47083538.pdf.

Kremer, Michael (2000). Creating markets for new vaccines: part I-rationale. Harvard University, The Brookings Institution and NBER. 24 May. Available from http://www.economics.harvard.edu/faculty/kremer/files/vaccine1.pdf.

Landau, J.P. (2004). Groupe de travail sur les nouvelles contributions financières internationales: rapport à Monsieur Jacques Chirac, le Président de la République. Paris: Government of France.

Leading Group on Innovative Financing for Development (2010). Globalizing solidarity: the case for financial levies. Report of the Committee of Experts to the Taskforce on International Financial Transactions and Development. Paris: French Ministry of Foreign and European Affairs, Permanent Leading Group Secretariat.

_____ (2011a). Innovative Financing for Development: promoting and scaling up their mobilization to support development. Presentation for Round Table 3, Fifth High-level Dialogue on Financing for Development, New York, 7 and 8 December.

_____ (2011b). How can we implement today a multilateral and multi-jurisdictional tax on financial transactions? International Expert Report. October.

_____ (2012). Peer review of existing innovative financings for development. Permanent Secretariat. Available from http://www.leadinggroup.org/IMG/pdf/Mapping_FIDENG-3.pdf (accessed 22 March 2012).

Lim, Stephen S., and others (2009). Tracking progress towards universal childhood immunisation and the impact of global initiatives: a systematic analysis of three-dose diphtheria, tetanus, and pertussis immunisation coverage. *Lancet*, vol. 372, No. 9655, pp. 2031-2047.

Littrell, Megan, and others (2011). Monitoring fever treatment behavior and equitable access to effective medicines in the context of initiatives to improve ACT access: baseline results and implications for programming in six African countries. *Malaria Journal*, 10:327, pp.1-14.

Machlup, Fritz (1964). *International Payments, Debts, and Gold*. New York: Charles Scribner's Sons.

Mahler (1966). The tuberculosis programme in the developing countries, *Bulletin of the International Union against Tuberculosis and Lung Disease*, vol. 37, pp. 77-82.

Markandya, Anil, Vladimir Ponczek and Soonhwa Yi (2010). What are the links between aid volatility and growth? World Bank Policy Research Working Paper, No. 5201. Washington, D.C.: World Bank.

Martins, P. (2006). Health sector partners' performance report (ACA V). Paper prepared for the Swiss Agency for Development and Cooperation (SDC) in Mozambique.

Matheson, Thornton (2010). Taxing financial transactions: issues and evidence. In Financial sector taxation: the IMF's report to the G20 and background material, Stijn Claessens, Michael Keen and Ceyla Pazarbasioglu, eds. Washington, D.C.: International Monetary Fund. Pp. 144-187.

Matowe, Lloyd, and Olusoji Adeyi (2010). The quest for universal access to effective malaria treatment: how can the AMFm contribute? Commentary. *Malaria Journal*, 9:274.

McAuliffe, Elizabeth Winslow (2006). The state-sponsored lottery: a failure of policy and ethics. *Public Integrity*, vol. 8, No. 4 (fall), pp. 367-379.

McKinsey & Company (2009). Pathways to a low-carbon economy: version 2 of the global greenhouse gas abatement cost curve.

Médicins sans Frontières (2011). Reversing HIV/AIDS? How advances are being held back by funding shortages. MSF briefing note. December.

_____ (2012). Losing ground: how Global Fund shortages and PEPFAR cuts are jeopardising the fight against HIV and TB. MSF issue brief. 21 March.

Millennium Foundation (n.d.a). The Voluntary Solidarity Contribution. The Millennium Foundation's Flagship Project. Available from http://www.internationalhealthpartnership.net/CMS_files/documents/voluntary_solidarity_contribution_EN.pdf (accessed 21 March 2012).

_____ (n.d.b). Who we are: MASSIVEGOOD. Available from http://www.millenium-foundation.org/wordpress/?page_id=16.

Mills, Anne (2005). Mass campaigns versus general health services: what have we learnt in 40 years about vertical versus horizontal approaches? *Bulletin of the World Health Organization*, vol. 83, No. 4 (April), pp. 315-316.

Moody's Investors Service (2011). International Finance Facility for Immunisation (IFFIm). Credit analysis. 21 December. Available from http://www.iffim.org/bonds/rating-reports/ (accessed 17 April 2012).

Murray, Christopher J.L., and others (2012). Global malaria mortality between 1980 and 2010: a systematic analysis. *Lancet*, vol. 379, No. 9814 (4-10 February), pp. 413-431.

Nakhooda, Smita, Alice Caravani and Liane Schalatek (2011). REDD-plus finance. Climate Finance Fundamentals brief 5. Climate Funds Update. London: Overseas Development Institute; and Washington, D.C.: Heinrich Böll Stiftung North America. November.

Nakhooda, Smita, and Liane Schalatek (2012). The Green Climate Fund: ready, set, go? Available from http://www.climatefundsupdate.org/news/green-climate-fund-ready-set-go.

Nakhooda, Smita, and others (2011). Adaptation finance. Climate Finance Fundamentals brief 3. Climate Funds Update. London: Overseas Development Institute; and Washington, D.C.: Heinrich Böll Stiftung North America. November.

Ndikumana, Leonce, and James K. Boyce (2011). *Africa's Odious Debts: How Foreign Loans and Capital Flight Bled a Continent*. London: Zed Books.

Nell, Edward, Willi Semler and Armon Rezai (2009). Economic growth and climate change: cap and trade or emission tax? SCEPA Working Paper, No. 2009-4. New York: Schwartz Center for Economic Policy Analysis, The New School for Social Research. February.

Noman, Akbar (2012). Innovative development financing in Africa. Background paper prepared for *World Economic and Social Survey 2012*.

Nugent, Rachel A., and Andrea B. Feigl (2010). Where have all the donors gone? scarce donor funding for non-communicable diseases. CGD Working Paper, No. 228. Washington, D.C.: Center for Global Development. November.

Ocampo, José Antonio (2011). *Reforming the International Monetary System*. *WIDER Annual Lecture* 14. Helsinki: UNU World Institute for Development Economics Research.

_____, and Stephany Griffith-Jones (2011). Innovative sources of financing. New York: Columbia University, Initiative for Policy Dialogue.

Onta, S.R., S. Sabroe and E.H. Hanson (1998). The quality of immunization data from routine primary healthcare reports. *Health Policy and Planning*, vol. 13, No. 2, pp. 131-139.

Oomman, Nandini, Michael Bernstein, and Steven Rosenzweig (2008). *Seizing the Opportunity on AIDS and Health Systems*. Washington, D.C.: Center for Global Development.

Ooms, Gorik, and others (2011). Global health: what it has been so far, what it should be, and what it could become. Studies in Health Services Organisation and Policy Working Paper, No. 2. Antwerp, Belgium: Department of Public Health, Institute of Tropical Medicine.

Organization for Economic Cooperation and Development (1997). *Model Double Taxation Convention on Income and Capital*. Paris.

_____ (2011a). Mapping of some important innovative finance for development mechanisms. Note circulated to members of the Working Party on Statistics, Development Cooperation Directorate, Development Assistance Committee. Paris. DCD/DAC/STAT/RD(2011)1/RD1.

_____ (2011b). Progress and challenges in aid effectiveness: what can we learn from the health sector? Final report of the OECD Working Party on Aid Effectiveness Task Team on Health as a Tracer Sector. 24 June.

_____ (2011c). Creditor Reporting System. StatExtracts. Available from http://stats.oecd.org/Index.aspx?datasetcode=CRS1.

_____ (2011d). First-ever comprehensive data on aid for climate change adaptation. Available from http://www.oecd.org/dataoecd/54/43/49187939.pdf.

_____, Development Assistance Committee (2008). Report of 2008 survey of aid allocation policies and indicative forward spending plans. May.

_____ (2012). Outlook on aid: survey on donors' forward spending plans 2012-2015. Available from http://www.oecd.org/dataoecd/45/25/50056866.pdf.

Pearson, Mark, and others (2011). Evaluation of the International Finance Facility for Immunisation (IFFIm). Available from http://www.gavialliance.org/library/documents/gavi-documents/evaluations/iffim-evaluation--full-report/. London: HLSP. June.

Pfeiffer, James, and others (2010). Integration of HIV/AIDS services into African primary health care: lessons learned for health system strengthening in Mozambique—a case study. *Journal of the International AIDS Society*, vol. 13, No. 3.

Piva, Paolo, and Rebecca Dodd (2009). Where did all the aid go? an in-depth analysis of increased health aid flows over the past 10 years. *Bulletin of the World Health Organization*, vol. 87, No. 12 (December), pp. 930-939.

Pontifical Council for Justice and Peace (2011). Towards reforming the international financial and monetary systems in the context of global public authority. Vatican City.

Radelet, Steven, and Ruth Levine (2008). Can we build a better mousetrap? three new institutions designed to improve aid effectiveness. In *Reinventing Foreign Aid*, William Easterly, ed. Cambridge, Massachusetts: The MIT Press.

Rappuoli, Rino, Henry Miller and Stanley Falkow (2002). The intangible value of vaccination. *Science*, vol. 297, No. 5583, pp. 937-939.

Reisen, Helmut, Marcelo Soto and Thomas Weithöner (2008). Financing global and regional public goods through ODA? In *Development Finance in the Global Economy*, Tony Addison and George Mavrotas, eds. Basingstoke, United Kingdom: Palgrave Macmillan. Pp. 124-150.

Richard, Fabienne, and others (2011). Sub-Saharan Africa and the health MDGs: the need to move beyond the "quick impact" model. *Reproductive Health Matters*, vol. 19, No. 38, pp. 42-45.

Richards, Michael (1999). *Internalising the Externalities of Tropical Forestry: A Review of Innovative Financing and Incentive Mechanisms*. European Union Tropical Forestry Paper, No. 1. London: Overseas Development Institute. January.

Rodrik, Dani (2002). Feasible globalizations. *NBER Working Paper*, No. 9129. Cambridge, Massachusetts: National Bureau of Economic Research.

Ronveaux, O., and others (2005). The immunization data quality audit: verifying the quality and consistency of immunization monitoring systems. *Bulletin of the World Health Organization*, vol. 83, No. 7, pp. 503-510.

Sabot, Oliver, and others (2011). A path to an optimal future for the Affordable Medicines Facility – malaria. *Health Policy and Planning*, vol. 26, No. 6, pp. 441-444. E-publication: 27 September 2011.

Sagasti, Francisco, and Keith Bezanson (2001). *Financing and Providing Global Public Goods: Expectations and Prospects*. Stockholm: Department for International Development Cooperation, Ministry for Foreign Affairs.

Sandor, Elisabeth, Simon Scott and Julia Benn (2009). Innovative financing to fund development, progress and prospects. DCD Issues Brief. Paris: Organization for Economic Cooperation and Development, Development Cooperation Directorate. November.

Schalatek, Liane, Smita Nakhooda and Neil Bird (2012). The Green Climate Fund. Climate Finance Fundamentals brief 11. Climate Funds Update. London: Overseas Development Institute; and Washington, D.C.: Heinrich Böll Stiftung North America. February.

Schäferhoff, Marco, and Gavin Yamey (2011). Estimating benchmarks of success in the Affordable Medicines Facility - malaria (AMFm) phase 1. San Francisco, California: Evidence-to-Policy initiative. 14 January.

Schäferhoff, Marco, Christina Schrade and Gavin Yamey (2011). The Health Systems Funding Platform: a primer. E2Pi (Evidence to Policy Initiative) policy brief. San Francisco, California: Global Health Sciences, University of California, San Francisco. Available from http://globalhealthsciences.ucsf.edu/sites/default/files/content/ghg/e2pi-health-systems-funding-platform-primer.pdf.

Schmidt, Rodney, and Aniket Bhushan (2011). The currency transactions tax: feasibility, revenue estimates and potential uses of revenue. Human Development Research Paper, No. 2011/09. New York: United Nations Development Programme. November.

Seers, Dudley (1964). International aid: the next steps. *Journal of Modern African Studies*, vol. 2, No. 4 (December), pp. 471-489.

Sengupta, Arjun (1987). The allocation of Special Drawing Rights linked to the reserve needs of countries. In United Nations Conference on Trade and Development, *International Monetary and Financial Issues for the Developing Countries*. Sales No. E.87.II.D.3. Pp. 311-328.

Sheikh, Pervaze A. (2010). Debt-for-nature initiatives and the Tropical Forest Conservation Act: status and implementation. Congressional Research Service report for Congress. Washington, D.C. 30 March.

Smith, O., and others (2005). Benin: system-wide effects of the Global Fund—interim findings. Bethesda, Maryland: The Partners for Health Reform*plus* Project, Abt Associates Inc. July.

Smith, Richard, and others (2003). *Global Public Goods for Health: Health Economics and Public Health Perspectives*. Oxford: Oxford University Press.

Snyder, Christopher M., Wills Begor and Ernst R. Berndt (2011). Economic perspectives on the advance market commitment for pneumococcal vaccines. *Health Affairs*, vol. 30, No. 8, pp.1508-1517.

Sobhan, Rehman (2012). Absorbing innovative financial flows: looking at Asia. Background paper prepared for *World Economic and Social Survey 2012*.

Soros, George (2002). *George Soros on Globalization*. New York: Public Affairs.

Spicer, Neil, and others (2010). National and subnational HIV/AIDS coordination: are global health initiatives closing the gap between intent and practice? *Global Health*, vol. 6, No. 3, pp. 1-16.

Spiegel, Shari (2008). Macroeconomic and growth policies. National Development Strategies Policy Note. New York: Department of Economic and Social Affairs of the United Nations Secretariat.

Standard and Poor's Ratings Services (2012). International Finance Facility for Immunisation downgraded to 'AA+'; outlook negative. 17 January. Available from http://www.iffim.org/library/documents/ratings-reports/ (accessed 17 April 2012).

Stern, Nicholas (2007). *The Economics of Climate Change: The Stern Review*. Cambridge, United Kingdom: Cambridge University Press.

Stiglitz, Joseph E. (1998). IFIs and the provision of international public goods. *Cahiers Papers*, vol. 3, No. 2, pp. 116-134. Luxembourg: European Investment Bank.

_____ (2000). *Economics of the Public Sector*, 3rd ed. New York: W.W. Norton & Co.

_____, and others (2011). A modest proposal for the G20. Statement issued following a meeting held in Beijing, co-organized by the Initiative for Policy Dialogue, Columbia University , New York, and the School of Finance at Central University of Finance and Economics Beijing. Available from http://policydialogue.org/files/publications/Beijing_Statement.pdf. Accessed 18 March 2012.

Taskforce on Innovative International Financing for Health Systems (2009). Constraints to scaling up and costs. Working Group 1 report. Available from www.internationalhealthpartnership.net/en/taskforce/taskforce-reports.

This is Africa (2012). Going long on diaspora bonds. 5 March. Available from http://www.thisisafricaonline.com/news/fullstory.php/aid/393/Going_long_on_diapora_bonds.html?current_page=2.

Tobin, James (1978). A proposal for international monetary reform. *The Eastern Economic Journal*, vol. 4, Nos. 3-4 (July/October), pp. 153-159.

Treves, Tulio (2008). United Nations Convention on the Law of the Sea. United Nations Audiovisual Library of International Law. Available from http://untreaty.un.org/cod/avl/pdf/ha/uncls/uncls_e.pdf.

Unger, Jean-Pierre, Pierre de Paepe and Andrew Green (2003). A code of best practice for disease-control programmes to avoid damaging health care services in developing countries. *International Journal of Health Planning and Management*, vol. 18, Supplement No. 1 (October-December), pp. 27-39.

UNITAID (2011). UNITAID in 2011. Available from http://www.unitaid.eu/images/NewWeb/documents/UNITAID_in_2011/UNITAID_in_2001_EN_June13.pdf. Accessed 4 March 2012.

United Nations (1992). *Report of the United Nations Conference on Environment and Development, Rio de Janeiro, 3-14 June 1992, vol. I, Resolutions Adopted by the Conference*. Sales No. E.93.I.8 and corrigendum. Resolution 1, annex I: Rio Declaration on Environment and Development.

_____ (2002). *Report of the International Conference on Financing for Development, Monterrey, Mexico, 18-22 March 2002*. Sales No. E.02.II.A.7. Chapter I, resolution 1, annex.

_____ (2008). *World Economic and Social Survey 2008: Overcoming Economic Insecurity*. Sales No. E.08.II.C.1.

_____ (2009a). Report of the Commission of Experts of the President of the United Nations General Assembly on Reforms of the International Monetary and Financial System. 21 September. Available from http://www.un.org/ga/econcrisissummit/docs/FinalReport_CoE.pdf.

_____ (2009b). *World Economic and Social Survey 2009: Promoting Development, Saving the Planet*. Sales No. E.09.II.C.1.

_____ (2010a). *World Economic and Social Survey 2010: Retooling Global Development*. Sales No. E.10.II.C.1.

_____ (2010b). Report of the Secretary-General's High-Level Advisory Group on Climate Change Financing. 5 November. Available from http://www.un.org/wcm/webdav/site/climatechange/shared/Documents/AGF_reports/AGF%20Report.pdf .

_____ (2011a). *World Economic and Social Survey 2011: The Great Green Technological Transformation*. Sales No. E.11.II.C.1.

_____ (2011b). *MDG Gap Task Force Report 2011: The Global Partnership for Development—Time to Deliver*. Sales No. E.11.I.11.

_____, Economic and Social Council (1970). Report of the Committee for Development Planning on its sixth session (5-15 January 1970). *Official Records of the Economic and Social Council, Forty-ninth Session, Supplement No. 7*. E/4776.

_____ (1996). Document prepared by the Secretariat on new and innovative ideas for generating funds. E/1996/CRP.1.

_____ (2009). Report of the United Nations Forum on Forests on the special session of the ninth session. E/2009/118.

_____ (2011). Report of the United Nations Forum on Forests on the ninth session (1 May 2009 and 24 January to 4 February 2011), *Official Records of the Economic and Social Council, 2011, Supplement No. 22*. E/2011/42.

_____, Commission on Sustainable Development (1996). Report of the Secretary-General on financial resources and mechanisms for sustainable development: overview of current issues and developments; and on financial resources and mechanisms. 22 February. E/CN.17/1996/4 and Add.1.

United Nations, General Assembly (2001). Letter dated 25 June 2001 from the Secretary-General to the President of the General Assembly, transmitting the report of the High-level Panel on Financing for Development. 26 June. A/55/1000.

_____ (2004). Identical letters dated 20 September 2004 from the Permanent Representatives of Brazil, Chile, France and Spain, to the United Nations addressed to the Secretary-General and the President of the General Assembly, transmitting the report of the Technical Group on Innovative Financing Mechanisms entitled, "Action against hunger and poverty". Annex. 1 October. A/59/398.

_____ (2009). Progress report of the Secretary-General on innovative sources of development finance. A/64/189 and Corr.1.

_____ (2011). Report of the Secretary-General on innovative mechanisms of financing for development. 1 September. A/66/334.

_____ (2012). Note by the Secretary-General on resilient people, resilient planet: a future worth choosing. 1 March. A/66/700. Available from http://www.un.org/ga/search/view_doc.asp?symbol=A/66/700&Lang=E.

United Nations Conference on Trade and Development (2009). Enhancing the role of domestic financial resources in Africa's development: a policy handbook. Geneva. UNCTAD/ALDC/AFRICA/2009/1.

_____ (2010). *World Investment Report 2010: Investing in a Low-Carbon Economy.* Sales No. E.10.II.D.2.

United Nations Development Programme (2003). *Providing Global Public Goods: Managing Globalization*, Inge Kaul and others, eds. New York: Oxford University Press.

_____ (2007). *Human Development Report 2007/2008: Fighting Climate Change— Human Solidarity in a Divided World.* Basingstoke, United Kingdom: Palgrave Macmillan.

_____ (2012). Innovative financing for development: a new model for development finance? Discussion paper. New York.

United Nations Educational, Scientific and Cultural Organization (2011). Debt swaps and debt conversion development bonds for education. Final report for UNESCO Advisory Panel of Experts on Debt Swaps and Innovative Approaches to Education Financing. August. ED-11/EFA/ME/5 Rev.

United Nations Environment Programme (2011). Towards a green economy: pathways to sustainable development and poverty eradication—a synthesis for policy makers. Nairobi.

United Nations Framework Convention on Climate Change (2007). *Investment and Financial Flows to Address Climate Change.* Bonn. Available from http://unfccc.int/resource/docs/publications/financial_flows.pdf.

_____ (2010). Report of the Conference of the Parties on its sixteenth session, held in Cancun from 29 November to 10 December 2010: addendum Part two: action taken by the Conference of the Parties at its sixteenth session. FCCC/CP/2010/7/Add.1. Decision 1/CP.16, entitled "The Cancun Agreements: outcome of the work of the Ad Hoc Working Group on Long-term Cooperative Action under the Convention".

United States Treasury (2010). Report to Congress on the use of Special Drawing Rights by IMF member countries. August. Available from http://www.treasury.gov/about/organizational-structure/offices/International-affairs/Documents/Report%20to%20Congress%20on%20SDR%20Use%20--%20August%202010.pdf.

Vargas Hill, Ruth (2005). Assessing rhetoric and reality in the predictability of aid. Human Development Report Office occasional paper 2005/25. New York: United Nations Development Programme.

Vujicic, Marko, and others (2012). An analysis of GAVI, the Global Fund and World Bank support for human resources for health in developing countries. *Health Policy and Planning* (13 February), pp. 1–9. Available from http://heapol.oxfordjournals.org/content/early/2012/02/13/heapol.czs012.abstract?sid=63404f6e-16b7-4024-a510-ce371a75c980.

World Bank (n.d.a). PovCalNet database. Available from http://iresearch.worldbank.org/PovcalNet/index.htm?1 (accessed 26 April 2012).

_____ (n.d.b). World Development Indicators database. Available from http://databank.worldbank.org/ddp/home.do?Step=12&id=4&CNO=2 (accessed 27 April 2012).

_____ (2008). Global program funds at country level: what have we learned? Prepared by the Global Programs and Partnership Group, Concessional Finance and Global Partnerships Vice Presidency. Washington, D.C.

_____ (2010a). Innovative finance for development solutions: initiatives of the World Bank Group. Washington, D.C.: World Bank. Available from http://siteresources.worldbank.org/CFPEXT/Resources/IF-for-Development-Solutions.pdf.

_____ (2010b). 10 years of experience in carbon finance: insights from working with the Kyoto mechanisms. Washington, D.C.

_____ (2010c). *World Development Report 2010: Development and Climate Change.* Washington, D.C.

_____ (2011). Agricultural Pull Mechanism (AGPM) Initiative: Overview. Washington, D.C. November. Available from http://siteresources.worldbank.org/CFPEXT/Resources/AGPM_OVERVIEW_dec2011.pdf.

_____, and others (2011). Mobilizing climate finance: a paper prepared at the request of the G20 Finance Ministers. 6 October.

World Bank Institute (2012). Climate change signals from Durban. Available from http://wbi.worldbank.org/wbi/stories/climate-change-signals-durban. 26 January.

World Commission on Environment and Development (1987). *Our Common Future* Oxford: Oxford University Press.

World Health Organization (2008). *The Global Burden of Disease: 2004 Update.* Geneva.

_____ (2009a). *World Malaria Report 2009.* Geneva.

_____ (2009b). *WHO Country Cooperation Strategy 2009-2013: Mozambique.* Brazzaville: WHO Regional Office for Africa.

_____ (2010). UNITAID annual report 2010. Geneva: UNITAID Secretariat.

_____, Maximizing Positive Synergies Collaborative Group (2009). An assessment of interactions between global health initiatives and country health systems. *Lancet*, vol. 373, No. 9681 (20 June), pp. 2137-2169.

Yuvraj, Joshi (2009). Can Red lattes beat AIDS in Africa? *The Guardian*, 1 December. Available from http://www.guardian.co.uk/commentisfree/2009/dec/01/project-red-starbucks-campaign (accessed 27 March 2012).

United Nations publication
Sales No. E.12.II.C.1
ISBN 978-92-1-109165-6
eISBN 978-92-1-055511-1